Fruma Zachs is Associate Professor and Chair of the Department of Middle East History at the University of Haifa, Israel. She is the author of *The Making of a Syrian Identity: Intellectuals and Merchants in Nineteenth–Century Beirut* and co-editor of *Ottoman Reform and Muslim Regeneration* (I.B.Tauris).

Sharon Halevi is a Senior Lecturer and Chair of the Women's and Gender Studies Program at the University of Haifa, Israel. She is the editor of *The Other Daughters of the Revolution* and author of *Revolutionary Selves* (forthcoming).

GENDERING CULTURE IN GREATER SYRIA

Intellectuals and Ideology in the
Late Ottoman Period

FRUMA ZACHS AND SHARON HALEVI

I.B. TAURIS

LONDON · NEW YORK

Published in 2015 by I.B.Tauris & Co Ltd
6 Salem Road, London W2 4BU
175 Fifth Avenue, New York NY 10010
www.ibtauris.com

Distributed in the United States and Canada
Exclusively by Palgrave Macmillan
175 Fifth Avenue, New York NY 10010

Library of Middle East History 51

ISBN: 978 1 78076 936 3
eISBN: 978 0 85773 672 7

A full CIP record for this book is available from the British Library
A full CIP record is available from the Library of Congress

Library of Congress Catalog Card Number: available

Typeset in Garamond Three by OKS Prepress Services, Chennai, India
Printed and bound by CPI Group (UK) Ltd, Croydon, CR0 4YY

For my parents, Rachel and Pesach Schreier
— Fruma

For my parents, Sylvia and Samuel Ezekiel
— Sharon

CONTENTS

LIST OF ILLUSTRATIONS

NOTE ON TRANSLITERATION

When transliterating from Arabic, we follow the system used in the *International Journal of Middle East Studies*. Diacritical marks are omitted, but the *ayn* (') and *hamza* (') are retained. We do not transliterate place names, but leave them as they are commonly rendered. Arabic first and last names are transliterated, but most foreign-language proper names are not, even if they deviate from the system of transliteration. For clarity's sake we sometimes translate the titles of articles from the Arabic press into English.

ACKNOWLEDGMENTS

It is always a pleasure to thank those who have supported and encouraged our work. We would particularly like to thank Amer Karkabi and Manhal Zreik, from the Periodicals Department of the University of Haifa Library, for their invaluable assistance in finding and pointing out items of particular interest and answering our questions. Our colleagues Butrus Abu-Manneh, Ami Ayalon, Basilius Bawardi, Yuval Ben-Bassat, Orna Blumen, Amalia Levanoni, Vardit Rispler-Haim, Holly Schissler, Reuven Snir, Mechal Sobel, Ibrahim Taha, and several anonymous readers read earlier versions of this work and raised several issues we had not fully considered; we could not have hoped for a better group of commentators.

We also wish to thank the Van Leer Jerusalem Institute for generously funding and hosting our two-year research group, "The Novel as a New Framework for Thinking about the Middle East in the Modern Period," and, of course, its members who joined us in this endeavor to retrace the impact of the fictional on the factual. The Research Authority of the University of Haifa generously contributed to the funding of this research. Esther Singer deserves special thanks for her careful editing of the book. We would also like to express our appreciation to Maria Marsh and Azmina Siddique from I.B.Tauris Publishers who oversaw the project and who responded to our needs and concerns quickly and efficiently.

Finally, we would like to thank our families, who tolerated our endless discussions on this book even in the midst of social and family occasions.

PREFACE

Our love for reading led each of us to our academic field and this study. Books, and novels in particular, held a special place for us when we were growing up and probably shaped us in ways we have yet to recognize. Though we both became academic historians, as undergraduates our other fields of study were Arabic literature and English literature, respectively. Thus, when over a casual cup of coffee we began discussing our shared literary passions and our interest in early Arabic and early English and American novels, we began to realize how profoundly such fictions shaped and were shaped by the historical realities surrounding them, reflecting open concerns as well as hidden desires and dreams. As the literary products of the early Arab *Nahda* have attracted scant scholarly consideration, we decided to devote our attention to it. Even though at the outset we were acquainted mainly with leading novels of the *Nahda*, as we came to comprehend the vast intellectual enterprise that was the *Nahda* movement, we were continually amazed by its wealth of literary richness. It is this delight and amazement that we wish to share with our readers.

Writing a book together is never an easy project. We debated and interrupted each other, took turns at the keyboard, laughed together, at times were frustrated when a paragraph didn't work out satisfactorily, but almost every sentence in this book was written together. Writing together requires considerable discipline, both on the personal and the professional level. Writing together enables more perspectives and voices to enter the work, it provides both a framework and incentive for completing the project, and has an inbuilt support system. We found that this enabled us to be more creative in our approach to our subject matter and in our writing, and we learned a great deal from each other. It also requires the co-authors to consider how to deal with differences in opinion when they arise; we found that even this can be very productive, as we had to go home and explicitly put down in words the reasons for our disagreement and were forced to come back the next day and convince (or be convinced by) the other. We believe that this process only sharpened our argument or required us to explain it in detail to the reader. We hope that our work will encourage others to embark on collaborative projects and recognize both the personal and (inter)disciplinary value of such projects.

INTRODUCTION

In 1849 Butrus al-Bustani (1819–1883), a leading Beiruti author, publisher and intellectual, delivered a lecture entitled *A Lecture on the Education of Women* (*Khitab fi Ta'lim al-Nisa'*)[1] in the framework of the Syrian Society for the Acquisition of Sciences (*al-Jam'iyya al-Suriyya li-Iktisab al-'Ulum wal-Funun*) a cultural society catering to Arab intellectuals and American missionaries that was active from 1847 to 1852. In the course of the lecture he argued:

How many women in this region (*biladina*) know how to read? And how many schools in *Barr al-Sham* were founded to educate them? Is it not true that the denial of their degradation and their lack of religious and secular knowledge is equivalent to denying the sun's existence at midday? Don't men refuse to mention them, or if they do, they add "you are most praised" or "may your mention never be coupled with hers" or other sayings, as if they were talking about an animal or an unclean, disgusting thing? Are they [women] honored or respected? Are they [women] not engaged in the same tasks as the women of barbarian nations? What are these women most interested in? Is it not cosmetics, clothes and tattoos? Do we not hear voices of rejection of such things from all sides? What do they know about raising children, housekeeping (*tartib al-buyut*) or attending to the sick? How many superstitions do they believe in, despite the fact that they are prohibited in religious texts?

Haven't books, journals (*kazitat*) and travelogues been filled with descriptions of their situation? Does anybody who has the slightest knowledge of the situation of children and parents not know more than I do and often grumble about this burden, calling for the situation to be remedied? These examples are probably enough in this context and I will not explore them any further to avoid boring you since what I would mention is common knowledge. It is the expert's duty to look more deeply into what has not been mentioned. Even though I beg men to restore women's situation and rescue them from the depths of degeneration, I intend, through this lecture, to awaken (*inhad*) women themselves to learn so as to gain in dignity.[2]

When criticizing men's attitudes toward women, al-Bustani wrote:

It is surprising to see that many members of this generation, even in civilized places, have neglected this sex (*jins*), are unwilling to elevate it from its uncivilised (*mutawahhisha*) state to one appropriate to an individual who has the same mental capacities, and [they] can help them remedy the conditions of the people (*jumhur*) and the region (*bilad*).[3]

How can we convince him that teaching her is akin to placing an antidote in deteriorating patient's mouth or pouring oil and wine on a serious mortal wound?[4]

Al-Bustani also explained that an educated woman should know her place in society. Hence, she should be educated and refomed but not in a way that challenges the traditional patriarchal gender order. He wrote:

I say to the civilized woman (*al-mar'a al-mutamaddina*) that being a very useful and important member of the group should not lead her to narcissism and arrogance or compel her to talk down to her husband even if she was more knowledgeable because minor issues should not annul the essentials. A woman's place in comparison to a man's is known and she should not cross the line or circumvent it under any circumstances.[5]

In this lecture, al-Bustani portrayed women as the building blocks in a civilizing process, who should be instructed to become fully-fledged members of a civilized society. He believed, as did other intellectuals of his generation, that the transformation from a barbaric society to a civilized (*mutamaddin*) one begins with the education of women. This lecture was intended to raise consciousness of the condition of Arab women, whom he termed "the deprived sex" (*al-jins al-miskin*), and to assert their right to an education. Strikingly, his call to educate women was made ten years before his defense of the Arab culture and language. In 1859 in his *Khutba fi Adab al-'Arab*, a speech before the cultural association, the Syrian Scientific Society (*al-Jam'iyya al-'Ilmiyya al-Suriyya*; founded in Beirut, 1858), Butrus al-Bustani appealed to all those "who have the will and desire to awaken (*inhad*) the Arab race from its deteriorated state (*halatuha al-saqita*)" to gird their loins and act. Reminding his listeners of the glorious Arab past in days gone by, he contended that "an age of darkness had engulfed" the Arab world since the end of the fourteenth century. Al-Bustani asked his readers:

> Where are the poets? Where are the physicians? Where are the orators? Where are the schools? Where are the libraries? Where are the philosophers? Where are the engineers? Where are the historians? Where are the astronomers? Where are those science books? Where are the learned scholars? ... Where is the magnificence of Aleppo? Where are the [architectural] embellishments of Alexandria? Where are the beauty of Andalusia and the glory of Damascus?

Bemoaning this decline, al-Bustani called upon his listeners to rise to a new intellectual challenge, to take up and revive long neglected cultural and scientific endeavors, to restore the glory of Arab culture and remedy the current situation:

> Arise! Awake [and] hark! . . . For here is Culture knocking from all directions upon your doors, begging to be let in . . . Set aside your sectarianism and your feuds, and your personal desires, and reach out your hand to shake hers [Culture's] in greeting; open the door to an old friend, who has returned to visit after a long absence [in foreign lands]. Receive her well and joyfully so that she will fill your land with peace and glory.[6]

Al-Bustani's call to arms was eagerly taken up by scores of Arab intellectuals, journalists, novelists and their middle-class compatriots in Greater Syria (as well as in Egypt), and together they embarked upon one of the more fascinating cultural endeavors of the time, which they themselves termed the *Nahda* (awakening). They saw themselves as "the generation of light and knowledge" and believed they were on the brink of "a new era" (*al-'asr al-jadid*); an era in which the East would regain its former prominence and hopefully would even outpace the West.[7] This self-styling and harkening back to a mythic "golden age" of cultural and intellectual activity emphasizes these intellectuals' desire to portray their movement as an attempt to reestablish a continuity with the past and not as a rejection of the past, or an attempt to break away from it.

The *Nahda*, which played a major role in shaping modern Arab culture, worldviews and self-perceptions, commenced in the first half of the nineteenth century and lasted until after World War I.[8] A key component involved the encounter of Arab culture and values with those of the modern world and their reconciliation. The exposure to modern ideas, culture, and technology inspired great admiration, but with it came a growing understanding of the need to preserve the Arab heritage. The *Nahda* period had two partially overlapping facets: the cultural facet, which included a resurgence of linguistic, literary and journalistic activity, began in the first half of the nineteenth century and persisted well into the early twentieth century; and the political facet, which focused on issues of political identity and nationhood evolved in the latter half of the nineteenth century, especially in its closing decades, as a response to indirect and direct colonialism.[9]

The *Nahda* occurred concomitantly with two major developments in the Arab world: the Ottoman *Tanzimat* reforms (1839–1876) and the growing economic and cultural encounter with Europe.[10] The *Tanzimat* reforms, inspired by Westernizing reformers, came in response to the need to strengthen the power of the Ottoman Empire in the face of European territorial expansion and cultural encroachments. Thus, the Ottomans introduced reforms pertaining to the status of the non-Muslim minorities; for example, in 1855 they abolished the poll tax (*jizya*), which had been imposed on non-Muslims, and in 1856, with the publication of the *Hatt-ı Hümayun*, they granted equal civil rights to non-Muslims.[11] Scholars such as Ehud Toledano and Jens Hanssen have also shown that this reformist impulse percolated into the Empire's Arab provinces and that varying combinations of Ottoman and local elites developed shared class traits and proto-national identities.[12] Just as significantly, these reforms and socio-political changes helped to instigate a decades' long Arab intellectual debate on modernity.[13] The Arab intellectual engagement with modernity was not the exclusive purview of Arab secularists; rather men and women of all faiths and degrees of religiosity were involved, including leading Muslim modernist thinkers such as Yusuf al-Asir (1815–89) of Beirut, Muhammad 'Abduh (1849–1905) of Cairo, Shaykh Husayn al-Jisr (1865–1935), Rashid Rida (1845–1909) of Tripoli, and Tahir al-Jaza'iri (1851–1920) of Damascus,[14] as well as Jewish intellectuals such as Ya'qub Sanu' (1839–1912) of Cairo, Shim'un Muyal (1866–1915) and his wife Istir Azhari Muyal (Esther Azhari Moyal) (1873–1948) of Beirut and Jaffa.[15]

Historian Deniz Kandiyoti has argued that it was within this particular Ottoman and Arab historical juncture that "the 'woman question' became part of the ideological terrain" upon which concerns about the social order and national identity were articulated and debated. Historian Hisham Sharabi cautioned scholars to bear in mind the particular nature of this historical juncture. Sharabi conceded that during the *Nahda* the patriarchal structures within Arab society were challenged and a provisional foundation was formed upon which women and men could renegotiate their relationships within and outside the family; as a result women seized the opportunity to re-maneuver their power and positions in society. However, Sharabi contended that the *Nahda* was ultimately a failure in that the patriarchal structures within Arab society were not displaced or truly modernized; rather they were strengthened and/or maintained in deformed, "modernized" forms. This "neopatriarchy," as he termed it, was neither *modern* nor *traditional* but rather a hybrid that served to contain change.[16] Our book attends precisely to this juncture and its lasting impact in one Arab region, Greater Syria. As scant attention has been given to this early period and its relationship with questions of gender, culture, modernization and social order in the histories of the Arab provinces in the Ottoman Empire, we believe it is necessary to re-examine it before returning to reassess its highly debated success or failure in modernizing Arab society.

The experiences and expressions of modernities outside "the West" have been a source of contention in the historiography of modernity, as recent scholarship has more than adequately demonstrated. Not only were there numerous paths leading to modernity, but the "Western" form of modernity was only one among many. In this study we explore how one particular strand of modernity, modern gender, was articulated, performed and renegotiated in Greater Syria during the second half of the nineteenth century and the first two decades of the twentieth. We follow the research agenda set by Timothy Mitchell, who argued that: "The modern occurs only by performing the difference between the modern and the non-modern, the West and the non-West, each performance opening the possibility of what is figured as non-modern contaminating the modern, displacing it, or disrupting its authority."[17] We explore what ideas concerning modern gender roles emerged in nineteenth-century Greater Syria. How were they incorporated into daily lives, consumer patterns and cultural activities? Were these modern ideas concerning gender classed? How were modern gender subjectivities molded and articulated in fictional and non-fictional texts?

Our goal in this book is to rethink all of this cultural activity in Greater Syria from an interdisciplinary gendered perspective, in order to provide a new vantage point when reassessing the *Nahda*'s social aspects and cultural impact. The political and economic facets of the *Nahda* period have received the bulk of historians' attention; far less has been devoted to the crucial intersection of social history, the cultural products of the *Nahda* and the changing ideologies of gender. We argue that by drawing the gendered contours of the *Nahda* we can provide a new framework for rethinking the dynamics of cultural and social change in this period. We also expand the prevailing view of the *Nahda* and re-conceptualize its lasting impact on discourses of gender and nation, which became more prominent during the last decades of the nineteenth century and continues to be of great lay and academic interest to this day. By uncovering the roots of the gender discourse in the *Nahda* and historicizing men's and women's activities in this period, we further the project of analyzing both the cultural and historical contexts that construct a given society at a particular point in time. Hence, this book formulates a novel interpretation of the cumulative impact of the *Nahda*. It is our hope that this interpretation will engender a fundamental historiographical revision in the understanding of this period and push well beyond the current boundaries of the study of the socio-cultural phenomenon of the *Nahda* and of gender in modern Arab history.

We set out to re-envision this early period and the debate concerning gender (women and men alike) by examining the cultural texts of the *Nahda* including novels, novellas, short stories, newspaper and periodical literature (including transcribed public lectures, scientific articles, household advice columns, and advertisements), supplemented by biographies, memoirs, and selected personal correspondence. Our intention is to re-examine these cultural texts to delineate the evolution of the discourse on gender and to learn about women's and men's "real-life" activities as writers, readers and participants in philanthropic and cultural societies, salons, and educational enterprises. In so doing, we re-emphasize the *Nahda*'s position as an innovative, deeply influential, and significant socio-cultural and political movement in its own right, rather than a preamble for events yet to come.

Greater Syria

Nineteenth-century Greater Syria, namely the three Ottoman provinces (*vilayets*) of Aleppo, Sidon and Damascus, was a heterogeneous and multi-cultural society that would evolve into the late-twentieth-century nation states of Syria, Lebanon, Jordan and Israel/the Palestinian Authority.[18] Although Greater Syria encompassed numerous ethnic groups and religious sects, the dominant cultural tone was set by a group of Arab-Muslim and Arab-Christian intellectuals who lived mainly in the urban centers of Damascus,[19] Aleppo,[20] Tripoli,[21] Beirut and Mount Lebanon. Historian Philip Khoury showed that by the turn of the twentieth century "a fairly stable local upper class emerged in the Syrian towns." This class was made up of "the major status groups that provided urban leadership in Syria" which had coalesced into "a single elite with a similar economic base."[22]

Although all the urban areas of Greater Syria underwent rapid social and economic changes during the second half of the nineteenth century, historians have noted that the effects of these changes were uneven. Rashid Khalidi pointed out that "while the great cities of the interior, notably Damascus and Aleppo, still retained their preeminence in a variety of ways, it is clear that both economic and demographic growth were faster along the coast," with the city of Beirut taking a leading role. Beirut in the latter half of the nineteenth century was the economic and cultural hub of Greater Syria. In 1915, the population of Beirut was estimated to be around 175,000 (compared to 250,000 in Damascus and 200,000 in Aleppo).[23] Christians of various denominations made up the majority of Beirut's population, followed by Muslims and Druze. It should be emphasized that while the middle class in Beirut was mainly Christian, it evolved within a Muslim majority. On matters of culture it was the Christian Arabs who had the dominant voice in local newspapers,[24] but as we show, the ideas found in the press were an amalgam of the points of view of Christian and Muslim Arab thinkers.

The city of Beirut and its burgeoning foreign trade attracted growing numbers of merchants and entrepreneurs from the periphery. It was during this period that the middle classes rose to ascendancy, accumulating increasing wealth and marrying among themselves.[25] The exigencies of trade and contact with foreigners necessitated the expansion of the traditional educational systems; missionaries (including American missionaries of various Protestant denominations) set up a network of schools (and later colleges) for boys and girls. Members of the bourgeoisie gradually (and cautiously) adopted Western ideas, styles and tastes; the city's architecture took on a European appearance; and members of the wealthier classes (both Christian and Muslim) took up a more modern lifestyle, moving to the suburbs, and consuming newly imported European and Ottoman fashions, goods and cultural products.[26] The middle class residents of Beirut also developed a rich cultural and social life, establishing salons and cultural societies,[27] a theater, as well as newspapers and periodicals. They also began reading novels, first those translated from European languages and then original Arabic novels written from the mid-nineteenth century onwards.

On Gender and Genre

The debates concerning modern gender roles (for men and women) found on pages of the mid- to late nineteenth-century Arab press are expressions of an increasingly modern understanding of gender and simultaneously the producers of a particular form of a modern Arab gender schema.[28] The earliest texts concerning women, their characteristics and their roles in modern life, written by both men and women writers and published in the first years of *Hadiqat al-Akhbar* (the first privately published journal), use the term *jins* (previously employed to denote "kind" or "species") to refer to "sex." Terms such as *jins al-nisa'* (the female sex), *al-jins al-karim* (the reputable sex), *al-jins al-latif* (the fair sex), *al-jins al-zarif al-latif* (the gentle and fair sex), and *al-jins al-nashit wal-latif* (the industrious and fair sex) abound, as does the occasional pairing of *al-jins al-da'if* (the weak sex) with *al-jins al-qawiyy* (the strong sex) or *al-jins al-nisa'i* with *jins al-rijal* (the sex of men).[29] In Butrus al-Bustani's 1870 dictionary, *Muhit al-Muhit* (*Ocean of Oceans*), the word *jins* does not appear under a separate entry. However, under the entry for "*janasat*" there appears a discussion of the various colloquial uses of *jins*. Al-Bustani wrote that the word was used to denote species (of animals) and races (of humans).[30] He also provided the following example under sub-category of *al-jinsiyya*: "... as they say the man (*rajul*) is preferable (*afdal*) to the woman (*mar'a*), or this sex (*jins*) is preferable to the other."[31] This terminology suggests that a modern understanding of gender, one in which men and women were viewed as complementary opposites, was already found in intellectual circles in Greater Syria and by the late 1850s it had begun to appear in the periodical press.

The Arabic novels, newspapers, and periodical literature written and published in the mid-nineteenth and early twentieth centuries have received significant attention in recent years,[32] and several historians have indeed turned their attention to the discourse on gender.[33] With important exceptions,[34] however, historians have studied the press and the novels mainly in connection to a political, international or patriotic/national, discourse and not necessarily as part of the *Nahda*. In contrast, literary scholars studying these texts, especially the novels, often view them as a preliminary stage in the development of twentieth-century Arabic prose literature.[35] We focus on the press and the novels both because it was in this period that narrative prose writing (both fictional or factual) came into prominence and acquired a significantly wider readership, and because we view them as an integral cultural product of this renaissance and as a major site for the renegotiation of gender.

In her influential study *Sensational Designs: The Cultural Work of American Fiction*, Jane Tompkins argued that "novels and stories should be studied not because they manage to escape the limitations of their particular time and place, but because they offer powerful examples of the way a culture thinks about itself, articulating and proposing solutions for the problems that shape a particular historical moment." A similar view informs the work of Nancy Armstrong, who studied the eighteenth- and nineteenth-century American cultural texts that went into the creation of a new "feminine ideal" (e.g. conduct manuals, women's magazines, and domestic fiction); Armstrong contended that these texts reveal "a culture in the process of rethinking at the most basic level the dominant [...] rules for sexual exchange."[36]

Here as well, we view novels and newspapers, the literary texts, both fictional and factual, not merely as an art form but also as cultural artifacts that offer powerful examples of how a culture "thinks" at a particular historical moment, and how it works through the issues that eventually come to shape it. Hence, we approach these texts as tools that enable us to reconstruct the gendered contours of the *Nahda* and re-evaluate the socio-political significance of this cultural renaissance for modern Arab history. While similar approaches have been adopted by several leading new cultural historians,[37] relatively few scholars of the modern Middle East have integrated this approach into the study of the culture and history of the Middle East. Two notable historians who have imported these methods are Afsaneh Najmabadi, who read (visual and written) Iranian texts of the same period to demonstrate how the "hetero-normalization" of love was central to a number of political and cultural transformations that signify Iranian modernity, and Dror Ze'evi, who described how certain cultural texts, most notably the Ottoman shadow theater (*Karagöz*), depict sexuality in the Ottoman Empire.[38]

Nevertheless, at least until the closing decade of the nineteenth century all these literary genres "resided" under the same roof: the periodical (whether a newspaper or a journal). Readers perusing the newspaper or journal could easily move from a scientific essay on Darwin's theories to a medical discussion on the detrimental effects of the corset to a bio-historical piece on a *jahiliyya* poet or Queen Zenobia, then to a serialized novel, followed by the translation of new Ottoman edicts, and end with a brief glance at a list of newly arrived foreign goods at a local store. Thus in the overall context within which nineteenth-century Arabic works of literature appeared, there was an assortment of literary forms, genres and authorial voices, and varieties of Arabic ranging from classical or literary Arabic (*fusha*), a mixture of classical Arabic and its colloquial form (*wusta*), to the popular or colloquial form (*'amiyya*).

This mixture of forms, genres and styles greatly appealed to both the male and female readers who read and subscribed to these periodicals in ever- growing numbers. The journalists themselves reported (perhaps somewhat self-servingly) on the growing and avid reading audience and described readers' social and emotional responses to the entire range of materials published in the newspapers expressed at private social gatherings and in personal correspondence. Indeed, it was our initial desire to reflect more accurately the reading experience of the *Nahda* readers that propelled us to examine all the material in the periodical press. As we immersed ourselves in the study of these texts, we began to realize the extent to which they interacted with each other. Scholars studying the texts of the nineteenth-century periodical press have noted this polyvocality of the genre and authorial voice, as well as the unique order individual readers constructed when reading each journal issue. Some scholars warn against the danger of "focusing too narrowly on what we retrospectively define as the literary element of the nineteenth-century periodical." Others insist that the study of the periodical and the materials within it should be interdisciplinary, as "it not only challenges the boundaries between hitherto separately constituted fields of knowledge, but also challenges the internal hierarchies and sub-divisions within discrete academic disciplines."[39] Hence, when examining these texts we adopted a mixed reflective and constructive approach that views the texts as a mirror of culture and society and as a means of constructing opinion and identity. In order to enable the expression of these multiple voices and genres embedded in the texts, we deliberately chose slightly varied theoretical approaches in each of the chapters, at times reading the same texts through a different lens and with a different goal in mind. This approach also enables the reader to read this work in a modular fashion, and focus on issues and texts of particular interest.

We offer the reader an interdisciplinary journey through the cultural and intellectual riches of the *Nahda* period. In Chapter 1, we consider the early years of the debate on women and their rights (1858–1900), as it played out in six of the leading journals and newspapers of the period: *Hadiqat al-Akhbar, al-Jinan, al-Muqtataf, Thamarat al-Funun, Lisan al-Hal* and *al-Hilal*. We demonstrate that this dialogue was conducted both within each newspaper, and across newspapers and their readers, and confirm the existence of a lively and active community of discourse which debated gender issues, considered their implications and suggested new courses of action. We also establish that the debate on women's issues permeated well into the middle classes. Both men and women were conversant with its terms and it involved not just the leading intellectuals but a broad cross-section of readers; in addition, it was not limited solely to Beirut but seeped into the peripheral areas of Greater Syria.

In Chapter 2, we examine one early novel, Salim al-Bustani's *Asma* (1873), which appeared in serial form in *al-Jinan*. We believe that this social novel holds a special place in the history and sociology of the Arab novel, as it formed the blueprint for the plots and themes of the novels that followed. After discussing al-Bustani's contribution to the development of the Arabic novel as a genre, we examine the plot and illustrate how al-Bustani undertook the consideration of serious contemporary social issues, especially the formation of the contemporary Arab family.

In Chapter 3, we trace the emergence of one thread of the discourse on modern Arab masculinity and consider its unique use of the pre-Islamic concept of *muru'a* (manly virtue) by analyzing a selection of novels, novellas and non-fictional essays written by the three leading novelists of the period, Salim al-Bustani, Nu'man 'Abduh al-Qasatli, and Jurji Zaydan. By juxtaposing these fictional texts we reveal a complex generational gender discourse in which masculinity and femininity were reworked. We demonstrate that a re-visioning of masculinity and the role of the "new man" lay at the heart of their literary project. It was both embedded as a subtext within the discourse of femininity and the "new woman," and stood on its own.

We point out the nuances in the novelists' views on masculinity and its form and function in a modern Arab society, which were mostly absent or obscured in non-fictional texts. We also attend to the ways Arab men themselves responded to the twin challenges of modernization and feminism.

In Chapter 4, we turn our focus to the early years of the discourse of domesticity as it appeared in the late nineteenth-century Arab press (novels, articles, domestic advice columns and advertisements). We first take a look at the ideal woman promoted in the early lectures of the cultural societies; then we turn to her image as it appeared in two of the early social novels; last, we engage in a thematic examination of the prescriptive domestic advice columns and articles, which appeared in the journals of the period. We find that the domestic discourse, as it first emerged in Greater Syria, was first and foremost the product of a complex negotiation and interweaving of Arab notions concerning management of the well-ordered household (*tadbir al-manzil*) and "Western" or Enlightenment notions of progress and technology, new bodily disciplines and middle-class femininity fostered by the rise of global consumer culture.

In Chapter 5, we bring together many of the themes we dealt with in the earlier chapters. We begin with a study of the ways the late *Nahda* women novelists (such as Zaynab Fawwaz, Labiba Hashim and Farida 'Atiyya) pushed the social and political boundaries of the novel. We argue that these writers used their novels as a space in which to formulate questions and critique existing social, cultural, economic, legal, and political practices including, but not solely limited to, women. We then focus on several women who emerged both as activists and political writers during this period. We argue that the gradual progression of the literary project from a discussion of social (even familial) issues to political critique was intertwined with a similar shift of focus in women's social and political activity. Last, we devote our attention to a fin-de-siècle debate around the right of women to work and their political rights.

In Chapter 6, we examine the fictional texts of a group of late *Nahda* novelists (Alice al-Bustani, Niqula Haddad, and Jubran Khalil Jubran), who questioned the prevailing societal and sexual norms by drawing their readers into an intimacy with the fictional characters and perhaps even sought to challenge the conceptions of the status-quo regarding marriage and sexuality through their readers' emotional responses and self-reflection. All these authors offer their readers a reconsideration of their society's prevailing social structure through a re-vision of gender relations, in particular within marriage. We contend that by providing a discursive space, a "rehearsal space," in which to voice and share "outlaw emotions" these authors may have laid the foundation for a subculture opposing the prevailing gender norms. Unfortunately, the lifespan of this discursive space was brief, as from the outbreak of World War I onward there was a marked decline in literary production in Greater Syria, and "for women the decline was, in fact, a complete hiatus."[40]

CHAPTER 1

FROM *DIFA' AL-NISA'* TO *MAS'ALAT AL-NISA'* IN GREATER SYRIA: READERS AND WRITERS DEBATE WOMEN AND THEIR RIGHTS, 1858–1900

In July 1858 *Hadiqat al-Akhbar* (*The Garden of News*) published the following anecdote, entitled "The New Telegraph":

> If you want to transmit information quickly from one place to another, you should tell it to a woman and you will see that within a short time the message will pass from one place to another faster than the blink of an eye.[1]

Hadiqat al-Akhbar, edited and published (bi-weekly) by Khalil al-Khuri (1836–1907), was the first journal privately published in Beirut. The publication was quite successful early on, and within the first three months acquired 400 subscribers, and spanning over 50 years (1858–1911) some 3,000 issues were published. The journal content varied; it focused heavily on regional news, especially commercial and economic news from Beirut, but also carried news and commentary on foreign events, official Ottoman announcements, advertisements and reviews of new books, serialized original novels, as well as excerpts and translations of short stories and novels. Occasionally it also printed witticisms, epigrams, and humorous anecdotes such as the one above; the journal's women readers, however, failed to see the humor.[2]

"We expected pleasant perfumes from the flowers of this garden (*hadiqa*) but today we smelled offensive and insulting odors"; began the letter of an unnamed group of women from Tripoli addressed to the women of Beirut in which they protested about this anecdote.[3] The irate women of Tripoli were not only angered by its underlying misogyny, but were upset that their Beiruti counterparts did not rise up in defense of their sex. In their circulated letter they were not only furious at al-Khuri, who printed this item depicting all women as foolish, flighty, and indiscreet, but claimed that if women did not counter it they would in effect be conceding its truth: "What was printed is a common and ill-mannered accusation which cannot be accepted by the press, you have insulted our honor and we demand satisfaction."[4] The ensuing public outcry (or at least the female one) was evidently quite considerable, and al-Khuri felt duty-bound to reprint this letter in the following issue and make amends to his female readers. This brief exchange is the earliest known example in the Arabic press of a debate (known in Europe as the "*querelle des femmes*") in which women opposed men's unfavorable views of them and emphasized the cultural, rather than just the biological, aspect of gender.[5]

From the mid-nineteenth century onward these arguments in "defense of women" (*Difa' al-Nisa'*) would soon escalate into a full-fledged debate on the "question of women" (*Mas'alat al-Nisa'*). Throughout Greater Syria, in public lectures, letters, newspaper articles, journal essays and/or prose fiction, men and women heatedly discussed the role of the "modern woman," her contributions to her family and society, the education she should receive and even her political rights. The "woman question" was a core issue in the Arab–Western cultural encounter and renegotiation during the *Nahda* period; yet while it extended to both these facets of the *Nahda*, its early years have not attracted much scholarly attention.

In this chapter we present a threefold argument, chronological, geographical, and sociocultural, in order to demonstrate that interest in the "woman question" and the lively and at times charged debate that it stimulated began in Greater Syria in the early *Nahda* period and persisted throughout, drawing into its orbit leading intellectuals as well as members of the general public and permeating even into the peripheral areas of Greater Syria. We do so by examining the public reflection of this debate in the early *Nahda* press, mainly the privately published Beirut journals and newspapers.[6]

Concomitant with the growing interest in women's history, several studies over the past 20 years have considered various aspects of Arab women's lives, the debate on women's political rights, and the significant roles of gender in national discourse and national movements in the late nineteenth and early twentieth centuries.[7] While scholars are aware of the ongoing debate throughout the first half of the nineteenth century concerning women, their rights and roles, and its importance in shaping the parameters and terms of later discussions, the majority have focused on the turn-of-the-century and on Egypt as a case study.[8] Dagmar Glass' and Fruma Zachs's studies are focused on more general intellectual and cultural developments, whereas Marilyn Booth's exhaustive analysis of women's life-writing in the period does not deal primarily with the evolving public debate between readers and writers.[9] The relative inattention to the early phases of this debate, especially in Greater Syria, has led at least one scholar to state unequivocally that "before the 1890s [...] we have no record of women making any public speeches or demanding a greater role for women within society."[10]

To re-envision this early period and the debate concerning women, we examine the years between 1858 and 1900. During these years, early thinkers (both male and female) and their readers first turned their attention to an array of gender issues and re-cast the relationships between men and women as an intrinsic part of their overall scheme of social and political regeneration. The early stage of the debate on women and their rights, which culminated in Qasim Amin's *Tahrir al-Mar'a* (*Liberation of Woman*, 1898) and *al-Mar'a al-Jadida* (*The New Woman*, 1900), evolved throughout the nineteenth century in spurts and bursts, and women played an important role in framing it. This does not deny the importance of Qasim Amin and his oeuvres but rather broadens the unequivocal claim by earlier scholars that without Qasim Amin, "The nineteenth century might have ended without the issue of women's emancipation becoming a public concern."[11]

From a geographical perspective, we emphasize that these issues first came to the fore in Greater Syria. Many of the pioneers of Arab journalism hailed from this region and they dominated the field until the early twentieth century. Greater Syria, and in particular Beirut, its economic and cultural center, was a hub of growing intellectual ferment in the latter half of the nineteenth century, as seen in the growing numbers of bookstores and printing presses, literary salons and scientific societies.[12] Only following the repressive measures of the Hamidian regime (1876–1908) was the debate relocated to Egypt, where exiled Syrian intellectuals, writers and journalists were joined by their Egyptian counterparts.

In this chapter we sketch the sociocultural contours of the dialogue on women developing between the writers and readers of newspapers, and point out its major themes and sources of influence; we emphasize the modes and directions of the diffusion of ideas. The diffusion of ideas is an interactive process: as ideas percolate through a society they are constantly renegotiated and rearticulated. Dominick LaCapra argued that ideas are created not solely by individual authors but also by "communities of discourse," made up of authors, readers, commentators, and critics who over time discuss, revise, and expand on ideas.[13] Our study clearly demonstrates that this dialogue was carried out both within each newspaper, and between the newspapers and their readers, establishing that a lively and active community of discourse debated gender issues, considered their implications and suggested new courses of action. The debate on women's issues permeated well into the middle classes; both men and women were conversant with its terms, and it did not only involve the leading intellectuals but a broad cross-section of readers. It was not limited solely to Beirut but seeped into the peripheral areas of Greater Syria. The impact of this dialogue reverberated for years after, as issues of these periodicals continued to be read long after their publication. Readers were known to have saved the bound annual volumes, making them part of their library collections. They referred to them and lent them out to friends for perusal and entertainment.[14]

Our argument in this chapter is based on an analysis of six leading journals and newspapers of the period between 1858 and 1900: *Hadiqat al-Akhbar* (Beirut: 1858–68, 1881–8), *al-Jinan* (Beirut: 1870–86), *al-Muqtataf* (Beirut: 1876–84; Cairo: 1885–1900), *Thamarat al-Funun* (Beirut: 1875–1900), *Lisan al-Hal* (Beirut: 1877–1900) and *al-Hilal* (Cairo: 1892–1900).[15] It focuses mainly on articles, editorials, regular columns, "op-ed items," and letters to the editor that provide a broad outline of the debate on women and highlight certain critical junctures.[16] It provides a more complete sense of the richness, coherence and continuity of the debate that developed during the early *Nahda* period in Greater Syria and continued later in Egypt well into the twentieth century. We unfold this chapter in chronological order to demonstrate how arguments were articulated and reformulated. We close by considering the ramifications of the debate on women, demonstrate that the *Nahda* was a socio-cultural phenomenon, not just a cultural and literary one, and highlight the importance of the study of the place of women in modern Arab societies.

"To Demand Satisfaction for Insulting Our Honor": The Early Years of the Debate on Women

The furious exchange between the women readers of *Hadiqat al-Akhbar* and its editor, Khalil al-Khuri, raises a host of questions: who were the women of Tripoli who wrote the letter and who were the women of Beirut to whom they addressed their letter? Were they members of an organized society (literary or other) or a group of women who met to discuss the journal? How large was *Hadiqat al-Akhbar*'s female readership? Were the women among its subscribers or did they come across it in the privacy of their homes? Although the precise identification of the journal's readership and the two women's societies eludes us, it is known that several such societies were active in this period. For example, in 1847 *Akhawat al-Mahabba*, a women's charitable society, built a school, a hospital, and a sanitarium as well as a hostel for wayward girls. In 1853, a Maronite women's society was founded in Bikfayya and in 1857 a women's charitable society, *Sayyidat al-Mahabba*, was established in Beirut, as was a Jesuit-backed women's educational society in Zahle.[17] Early women graduates of the missionary schools such as Rahil ('Ata) al-Bustani (1823–94) and the daughters of prominent families who were educated privately at home, such as author Angelina Nawfal (d. 1865; mother of the leading *Nahda* intellectual Niqula Nawfal), were avid readers of a variety of texts. It is more than likely that women such as these were among the readers of the early journals and newspapers.[18]

The interest in women and their education was shared by men's cultural societies, which held several debates pertaining to them. For example, in January 1849, Butrus al-Bustani (founder of *al-Jinan* and father of author Salim al-Bustani) who had a keen interest in women's issues and had long supported the cause of women's education, addressed a meeting of the Syrian Society for the Acquisition of Sciences (*al-Jam'iyya al-Suriyya li-Iktisab al-'Ulum wal-Funun*) concerning this issue. The society, which included leading members of the Beiruti intelligentsia such as Mikha'il Mishaqa (1800–88), Nasif al-Yaziji (1800–71) and al-Bustani, often discussed matters pertaining to the progress of Arab society, and the members' wives often participated in these cultural events and educational activities.[19] In al-Bustani's lecture *On the Education of Woman*, he advocated providing women with a broad and solid education to enable them to fulfill their marital, maternal, and domestic duties for the benefit of their family, society and nation.[20] Another author associated with al-Bustani's group, As'ad Ya'qub al-Khayyat (b. 1811), also argued in favor of the liberation of women (*tahrir al-mar'a*) and stressed the need for their education in his 1847 travelogue *Sawt min-Lubnan* (*Voice from Lebanon*).[21] These two examples suggest that such ideas were circulating in Beiruti society for several years (at the very least) before being expressed publically in speeches and the media.

Evidently by 1858 the segment of female readership was significant enough for al-Khuri to address their very overt challenge and to disown authorship of the anecdote, claiming that he only reprinted it from an English newspaper. Al-Khuri acknowledged that considerable pressure was exerted on the editorial staff regarding this item and may have felt the need to set the record straight. He therefore published the letter from the women of Tripoli.[22] Al-Khuri, who was committed to the cause of female education, recognized the importance of his female readers in later issues and many of his editorial choices were taken with them in mind. For example he published translations of the works of popular French authors that dealt with women and works written by women. These included novels by Fanny Reybaud (1802–70), such as *Mademoiselle de Malepeire* (1855), which recounts the sensationalist tale of a young bourgeois woman disinherited by her family after her marriage to a farmer who she eventually murders, and Gabrielle Anne Cisterne de Courtiras, Vicomtesse de Saint-Mars ("Countess Dash," 1804–72), a member of Alexandre Dumas *fils'* circle and the author of several best-selling historical romances and works concerning women such as *Le livre des femmes* (1864), a witty guide to marriage. Al-Khuri also published pieces written by journalist Jean-Baptiste Alphonse Karr (later editor of *Le Figaro*; 1808–90).[23] A year later when he was tempted to publish lengthy excerpts from Karr's *Les femmes* (1853), which contained disparaging comments about women, al-Khuri refrained from doing so, explicitly citing his fear of his female readers' adverse reactions.[24]

These examples suggest that al-Khuri intuitively sensed that issues concerning women and marriage were of growing importance to his readers. In fact, the main theme of al-Khuri's novella, *Way. . .Idhan Lastu bi Ifranji (Alas. . .I Am Not a Foreigner*; 1859–61), the earliest known attempt at writing modern Arabic fiction, was marriage. The protagonist, an Aleppo merchant affecting Western manners, wants to marry off his young educated daughter to an imposter posing as a foreigner, although she and her mother believe she should marry her Arab suitor. The story anticipated a theme which would eventually come to dominate Salim al-Bustani's (1846–1884) social novels (serialized in the press) two decades later. Like many other Arab writers and intellectuals of the *Nahda* period, al-Khuri and al-Bustani insisted on distinguishing between modernization and Westernization. The modernization of Arab society was not to be a mere imitation of the West, but one in which certain (selected) ideas and institutions from the West would be used as a tool to advance their society. Al-Khuri's (and al-Bustani's) choice to work out this socio-political issue on gendered bodies clearly suggests that the status of women both within marriage and in other areas was a core issue requiring intense social consideration, and that both men and women were invested in this project, even at this early stage.

In the years that followed, exchanges such as the one between al-Khuri and his readers, especially the female readers, did not recur; this lull may have been a byproduct of the civil war (1860–1) in Damascus and Mount Lebanon but when the first issues of *al-Jinan* appeared a decade later, a lively exchange between writers and readers on the woman question re-emerged. *Al-Jinan*, the first pan-Arabic publication, was founded by Butrus al-Bustani and circulated throughout Greater Syria, Iraq, and Egypt. American missionary Henry Harris Jessup estimated that the local circulation was about 1,500; it even reached subscribers in the various European capitals. It published local and international news and commentary, articles, and original novels in Arabic as well as translations of French, Italian and English fiction.[25] From its inception women and their lives become an issue for consideration and debate, and several women, including some of the more influential figures of the time such as Idlid (Adelaide) al-Bustani and Maryana Fathallah Marrash (1838–1919; the sister of Fransis Marrash)[26] published their writings in the journal under their own name. Much of the original Arabic fiction serialized in *al-Jinan* had female protagonists and discussed marriage, female education and the social role of women. The first issue included a two-part novella by Idlid al-Bustani (*Henry and Amelia*),[27] as well as Jibra'il Sadqah's article "On the Rights of Women," in which he argued for the mental and physical equality of men and women. Sadqah viewed the two genders as complementary, likening them to different parts of the body: "Is it possible to argue that the hand is more important than the mouth?"[28] Both the authors and *al-Jinan*'s co-editor, Salim al-Bustani, were aware of the periodical's large female readership and often addressed it directly. Salim al-Bustani openly acknowledged its influence on his editorial decisions: "If we were not sure that these novels would be read by a lot (*kathirat*) of women we would not publish them in so many issues."[29]

In an 1871 article, Wastin Masarra of Alexandria, whose husband "permitted" her to read the journal, described the enormous impact reading articles and stories written by women had on her.[30] She was particularly impressed by an earlier article by the Aleppo-based author and poet Maryana Fathallah Marrash entitled "The Beauty Spots of the Garden." Educated at home and in missionary schools, Maryana Marrash was fluent in Arabic, French and English, well-traveled, and is known to have hosted an influential literary salon in her home during this period. In an elegant (almost poetic), richly textured article published in 1870, Marrash set out to defend her sex from the slurs of poets who, in her opinion, at times characterized women as cowardly and avaricious. Marrash challenged their claims, and noted that it was women's inferior social position that inhibited them from cultivating nobler qualities. Rather than blindly imitate male qualities, she suggested that women should develop some of their own, such as high moral standards and knowledge.[31]

Inspired by Marrash's example to expound her own views on female education, Masarra called upon women readers to insist on their right to enter "the gardens of culture and knowledge (*al-'ulum al-Adabiyya*)" as well as the sciences, despite possible male discouragement. This knowledge, she contended, would enable them to improve men, better raise their children, and thereby gain men's respect and love. Masarra's explicit appeal to her female readers is of significance; many of the writers, and all of the women writers, displayed their awareness of their growing female readership and directly appealed to them, alternately cajoling, reasoning, and berating them to take a more active stance concerning their life choices, whether in education (their own and their children's), marriage, or family life.

It is useful to compare the views of Maryana Marrash and Wastin Masarra with those of the poet Fransis Marrash (1837–73),[32] who did indeed speak out in favor of women's education, but expressed a wariness bordering on anxiousness in his writing on the subject. In the first of two articles entitled "Woman between Barbarity and Civilization," he argued that the best way to lead woman to civilization was to educate her, for "the woman is the sole source from which springs human life; she is the source of education, morals and manners."[33] In his second article, "On Female Education," Marrash elaborated further on the kind of knowledge a woman should be exposed to; she should be taught reading, writing, arithmetic, geography, grammar and the domestic arts. As he believed that man was created before woman, just as "the source is created before that which is derived from it," she was therefore intended to be his helpmeet; he argued accordingly that woman's education should focus on "that which is helpful to man." Echoing Rousseau, Marrash claimed that "there is no need for woman to delve into the sciences" as it will entail not only losing her femininity, but she may "even position herself above man."[34] Farida Shakkur, writing two years later, embraced a female education program similar to the one put forth by Marrash, stressing that "our weakness (*da'funa*) is ignorance, which causes men to belittle us." Contrary to Marrash, she stressed her belief that men and women possess equal intellectual abilities, and insisted that women could contribute to the general progress of human society as well as to the welfare of their families. Shakkur explicitly noted her reluctance to enter into this debate on female education but was emboldened to do so by the thought that such an example would encourage young women to express their views as well. Given her acknowledgement of *al-Jinan*'s large female readership, this comment suggests that the women who weighed in on this early debate were well aware of their function as role models for a future generation of women writers.[35]

Later male intellectuals, such as Salim al-Bustani, Salim Kassab and Wadi' al-Khuri, were less wary than Fransis Marrash and proposed an additional role to their female readers, suggesting that their education and involvement in that of their children and the running of their households would prove of great service to the nation, "who expects them to do so and will reward their endeavors."[36] In an address to the graduates of an American missionary school for girls (published later in *al-Jinan*), Kassab argued that both sexes, whom he viewed as complementary, had a role to play in human society.[37] He believed that the status of women reflected the state of the homeland (*watan*) and their advancement would be of benefit to the country (*maslahat al-bilad*).[38] Since he viewed the family as the most important "link" (*al-halaqa*) in the "chain" (*silsila*) of the nation, women were accorded a special role as "the educators of the [next] generation and its progenitors (*walidat al-jil*)." If women are ignorant and superstitious their sons will be so, but if they are educated and knowledgeable the homeland (*watan*) and its sons (*abna'uhu*) will be so too.[39]

The Woman Question Encounters Modern Science

Soon after *al-Jinan* first appeared, two other journals were launched almost concurrently in Beirut, *al-Muqtataf* and *Thamarat al-Funun*, and once again the debate concerning women attracted significant attention. *Al-Muqtataf* (*The Gleaning*) was a monthly journal devoted to the advancement of the arts and sciences founded in 1876 by Ya'qub Sarruf (1852–1927) and Faris Nimr (1857–1951), both graduates (and instructors) of the American Syrian Protestant College. In 1884, the editors and the journal's manager Shahin Makariyus left Beirut for Egypt, where they continued publishing the journal. The journal usually published a few original articles written in Arabic, summaries of the proceedings of scientific societies, as well as summaries, selections and translations of scientific news, articles and book reviews selected from a variety of journals such as *Scientific American*, *Science*, the *Nineteenth Century* and *The Times*.[40]

Although several women (including Yaqut Sarruf and Maryam Nimr Makariyus) had previously published scientific articles in the journal, the first article concerning women appeared in 1882. During the next few years the journal published several articles devoted to a variety of issues concerning women: women's education, women and the medical profession, their role in child education, summaries of lectures on dress and fashion, and biographical sketches (such as those of Mme Roland and Mme de Staël), written by readers using pseudonyms as well as by well-known intellectuals such as Salim al-Bustani, Wadi' al-Khuri, and Yaqut Sarruf. These articles, replete with intertextual references to the work of classical and Arab historians (such as Herodotus, Xenophon, 'Ali ibn al-Athir and Abu al-Fida'), discussions and allusions to notable women (such as Catherine the Great and philosopher Catherine Trotter Cockburn), more modern thinkers (Descartes, Pascal, John Stuart Mill, Mary Wollstonecraft, Elizabeth Cady Stanton, and François Xavier Joseph Droz), as well as references to articles published in other journals (such as *al-Jinan* and *Lisan al-Hal*), demonstrate that a lively community of readers read, contemplated, debated and wrote on various aspects of the "woman question." This phase differs from the previous one by the overt references to the texts that shaped the authors' thinking. While in previous years one can discern the influence of the work of American anthropologist Lewis Henry Morgan in Fransis Marrash's work, or hear the echoes of the notion of the "republican mother" in al-Bustani's and Kassab's writings, rarely were such works cited explicitly, as they were from this point onward.[41] A brief glance at the works cited and the examples of "women worthies" brought forth to bolster arguments suggests that these authors (as well many of their readers) were highly conversant with the work of the leading thinkers of their age, sharing an in-depth knowledge of both Arabic and European literary and historical texts.

Not all the articles were celebratory in tone, however. In 1883 Shams Shahada of Zahle wrote a piece in which she berated members of her sex for their indifference and failure to work hard enough to propel women further; she argued that instead of solely blaming men, it is women who are prepared to settle for very little.[42] Citing earlier articles by Salma Tannus and Maryam Jurji Ilyan as well as pieces by Ya'qub Sarruf and Salim al-Bustani, which called for women's education as a way of ameliorating their status, she argued that women have failed to take the path set out for them by these writers, but instead have contented themselves with trifles:

Where do you see a woman who has made use of her money to further her education [...] by creating her own library, with only a fraction of the amount she has spent on perfume and clothes? Which woman visits her friend in order to discuss matters of general interest to her sex or that which will better them?[43]

She continued by asserting that if one mistakes superficial mannerisms (such as the privilege of sipping one's coffee or entering a room before a man) for women's rights, one does not comprehend the truths of natural progress, which requires that women exert themselves and work hard, relying only on their own selves and God. It is important to note that Shahada was among a small but significant group of women and men (such as Hannih Yanni of Tripoli, Amin Abu Khatir of Zahle, and later Maryam Khalid of Deir al-Qamar, in Mount Lebanon) who lived outside Beirut who were drawn into the debate on women, establishing that this discussion had permeated well into the periphery.[44]

Many of the biographical articles on notable women in the journal were polemical in nature, and served as an opening for the author to develop the case in favor of women's education and rights. In 1885 Maryam Makariyus (1860–88) published a short piece on al-Khansa', the seventh-century poet, on whose life she had lectured previously to the female literary society *Bakurat Suriyya*. Here she did not just criticize biographers' practice of ignoring the role al-Khansa's mother played in her education; rather she complained that contrary to Europe, where the life of such a woman would garner great interest, "we will lay such a jewels (*jawahir*) aside." Given the important role Makariyus' own mother played in her upbringing, it is perhaps unsurprising that she displayed great sensitivity when it came to accounting for other mothers' impact on the intellectual lives of their daughters. Makariyus also used this opportunity to re-emphasize to her readers, women in particular, the importance of reading as a way to build moral character and gain useful knowledge of the world; accordingly she suggested that her readers peruse edifying texts, such as the lives of notable women, and not just entertaining ones, such as novels.[45]

The voices of men who were more critical of women's quest for equality were not absent from the pages of the newspaper. In 1886, Amin Abu Khatir of Zahle, who presented himself as a proponent of women's rights, argued that while women's demands for equality have increased they have neglected many of their domestic duties and have not demonstrated their ability to exercise restraint (especially when it came to spending money on frivolities). He admitted that a few exceptional women had combined new rights with older duties, however "it would be incorrect to reach a decision for all women based on their example."[46]

In the same year, in a debate on women's rights (*huquq al-nisa'*) between Najib Antunyus of Alexandria and Wadi' al-Khuri of Beirut, Antunyus raised arguments concerning women's supposed "limited energies." In an earlier issue, al-Khuri had argued in favor of greater equality for women, citing in particular their mental and intellectual prowess by giving examples of women rulers in ancient Egypt and in France and pointing out that some modern nations had recognized this by granting women the right to vote in municipal elections (in Britain) and state elections (in the western United States). Antunyus challenged him, arguing that as women's physiological makeup differed from that of men, full equality would never be achieved. He maintained that those who favor women's education ought to know that girls' mental powers cannot equal those of boys; if and when they succeed in doing so then surely the girls' bodies will be weak and disease-prone. Antunyus concluded that all those who tell women that they can equal men and permit them to step out of the home will live to see both the home and human society in ruins. Antunyus was echoing the views of several prominent European and American physicians of the 1870s, who insisted that male and female biological differences dictated, differences in their behavior and social roles. Arguing that females possessed only a limited amount of energy, most of which was diverted to the reproductive organs, they claimed that any re-direction of energy to other activities (especially intellectual ones) would sap women's energy, ruin their health, and perhaps even lead to sterility.[47]

This trend toward using scientific (or pseudo-scientific) arguments, especially biological and genetic ones, grew as time passed. In 1887 Shibli Shumayyil (1850–1917) argued in favor of male physical and intellectual superiority by drawing heavily on his medical training and on the work of European and American thinkers and scientists, such as mathematician and sociologist Adolphe Quételet (1796–1874), anthropologist and geneticist Francis Galton (1822–1911), and psychologist and sociologist Gustave Le Bon (1841–1931), whose findings were used extensively in conjunction with the work of Darwin and Herbert Spencer in discussions concerning women's education and political rights.[48] Shumayyil asserted that sexual dimorphism is the greatest in humans and argued that as a species advances or as a nation becomes more civilized, males gain precedence over females. He enumerated males' "superior" physical and intellectual attributes and compared them to women's, arguing that women's "weaker" bodies and "slower" mental cognition caused them to be more devious and cunning, able only to make use of the "weapons of the weak" (silah al-da'if). He claimed that women rulers existed in less advanced societies but had inherited the throne, rather than ascended to it on the basis of their leadership skills or intellectual qualities, and that this had no bearing on the status of ordinary women. He opposed those who called for the equality of the sexes, and who argued that the differences between them were the outcome of different education and physical activities. Shumayyil suggested that rather than denigrate women as Schopenhauer did or extol them like Diderot, "we need to situate her in her true place, as an important member of human society, who follows after man and his development and helps him, and this will regulate the human family."[49]

Women's responses were not slow in coming; four responses, appearing together in later issues under the general title "The Defense of Women by Women," point out just how widespread were the reverberations of this debate. The first respondent was M. A. Y. of Damascus, who while politely acknowledging Shumayyil's status and reputation, expressed reservations concerning his overall argument. She objected to his comparison of women to lower species of animals and reiterated that women must receive an education that will build up their bodies and minds. She insisted that even if women are not equal men in terms of physical strength, they will surely be able to exceed them in knowledge and morals.[50] Rahil Hajjar of Cairo criticized the validity of Shumayyil's biological argument, finding it faulty and counterfactual. She stressed that the "facts" that Shumayyil used to corroborate his case could be interpreted otherwise or were merely (his or other people's) opinions not facts. In her closing remarks, Hajjar hinted that this debate had attracted wider public attention: "I hope that it is indeed true, as some people have reported that he has retracted some of his views."[51]

Maryam Makariyus, the third respondent, was far more emphatic in her objections, perhaps due to her cultural status as a leading figure in intellectual life both in Greater Syria and Egypt. While she too paid nodding respect to Shumayyil, she stressed that men of his stature should be even more careful with their words. Finding his article disrespectful to women and even insulting, Makariyus claimed Shumayyil conflated "what is" with "what is good." Demonstrating a strong working knowledge of medical, biological and anthropological studies which purported to demonstrate women's inferiority through scientific and quantitative means, Makariyus expressed her "wonder" that findings of differences between the sexes were always interpreted as favoring men, since she too believed these interpretations were mere opinions and not facts.[52] Maryam Matar of Cairo adopted an even more forceful tone; laying niceties aside she demanded "I want someone to tell me what made Shibli Shumayyil attack us?" Noting Shumayyil's disregard of women's work in their "little kingdoms," she shifted the burden of proof onto men's lives and behavior, pointing out that while women were quite capable of doing the same work as men, men could not claim to exhibit the same proficiency in women's work.[53]

In a later issue Khalil Sa'd of Cairo joined in, and as the title of his piece indicates he positioned himself firmly on the side of Shumayyil's biological arguments, although he did concede that woman is a nobler creature than man.[54] Shumayyil himself felt compelled to defend his position and soon addressed the "ladies" challenging him. He adamantly maintained that the two sexes were different and that equality between the two was impossible. Although he did admit that education had an impact on women's status, he insisted that women had other duties. He likened any project designed to promote equality of the sexes to an attempt to equate the parts of the body despite their inherently different functions. In an analogy between the human body and human society, Shumayyil insisted that each sex plays a vital role in human society; woman's "natural place" however was that of man's helpmeet.[55]

The debate initiated by Shumayyil was the culmination of a gradual process during which more traditional modes of argumentation and justification based on philosophy and religion made way for more secular and scientific arguments; a shift that paralleled changes in the argumentation on these issues in Europe and America. Articles concerning women's education and their role in society appeared sporadically throughout the 1890s in *al-Muqtataf*; however the main thrust of the debate seems to have moved to the numerous women's journals (such as *al-Fatat* and *Anis al-Jalis*),[56] which appeared in the 1890s, and *al-Hilal* (*The Crescent*), founded by yet another Syrian émigré, author and novelist Jurji Zaydan (1861–1914).[57]

In 1894, for example, an argument regarding the capabilities and rights of women erupted among the readers of *al-Hilal* that bears a striking similarity to the debate that had appeared in *al-Muqtataf* close to a decade earlier, and one that the readers of *al-Hilal* invoked to support their arguments both in favor and against women's rights. The debate was sparked by an "op-ed" piece sent by "Zaki M. of Istanbul," who expressed surprise that no one had yet responded to an earlier reader's question: "Should women demand all the rights of men?" Zaki claimed that the more appropriate question was whether women have the ability and skills to do so; citing Bedouin and Spartan women's physical strength, the intellectual prowess of famous queens and women philosophers, and the achievements of contemporary women in Europe and the United States who earned degrees in law and medicine, he asserted that women had clearly demonstrated both their skills and intellectual abilities, and therefore could demand "all the rights of men."[58]

Zaki's piece immediately prompted numerous readers' responses (including in other journals) in a drawn-out exchange, with Dr Amin al-Khuri (of Damyat) arguing the case against women, and Jirjis Ilyas al-Khuri (of Tripoli), Bahiyya (of Alexandria), Maram Antaki (of Aleppo), Istir al-Azhari, Jabir Dumit, and two anonymous women (all of Beirut) in favor of women.[59] This debate resurrected many arguments found earlier in the exchanges in *al-Muqtataf*. Amin al-Khuri cited numerous biological and evolutionary studies and revived many pseudo-scientific arguments to bolster his case against women's education,[60] while the others adopted the discourse of rights to elaborate on the virtues of the educated woman and her contribution to home and society.[61] Eventually, as the debate showed no signs of abating after an entire year, the editors had to step in and terminate it.

These are crucial glimpses into the "community of discourse" debating these issues, flashes of which may be discerned in the journals and newspapers themselves. For example, Yaqut Sarruf's brief obituary of Nasra Ilyas of Tripoli (1862–88) provides a rare insight into the workings of one such community; a circle of female intellectuals (and friends) who met regularly to discuss women's issues and who were also the writers and readers of these journals. Sarruf (d. 1937) stated that after relocating to Egypt in 1885 together with her friends Maryam Makariyus and Nasra Ilyas, the three women lived nearby, and met regularly to talk about issues such as the "condition of the woman in the East," the importance of women's education, as well as to discuss new books and newspaper and journal articles.[62] Such regular meetings, both single-sex and mixed company, also took place in Beirut. 'Anbara Salam al-Khalidi (1897–1986), a writer and feminist from a distinguished Sunni-Muslim Beiruti family, recalls in her memoirs that in her grandparents' home (the al-Barbirs) in the 1860s and 1870s a weekly, mixed-company gathering was held to read and discuss the news and articles published in "the journals of the Bustanis [such as *al-Jinan*] and the Qabbanis [*Thamarat al-Funun*]."[63] Sisters and authors, Anisa (1883–1906) and 'Afifa Shartuni (1886–1906) also reported many such gatherings where, following the appearance of newspaper articles on the subject, the issue of women's equality, including political equality, was fiercely debated.[64]

Another enchanting glimpse, which brings an additional gathering of readers and writers to life, appeared in 1894 in *Lisan al-Hal* (*Voice of the Present*). A writer, publishing under the pen-name "Ibin al-Hakim" reported on the events at a mixed social gathering at his home after his first article on marriage was published. All his guests were fully conversant with the ongoing debate on marriage in the pages of the newspaper; indeed, one of the guests summarized the debate by saying that while all the writers of the articles agreed on the importance of marriage, many bachelors still did not want to marry. His audience was so fascinated and caught up with their debate that they waited impatiently until 2 o'clock in the afternoon, when the latest issue of *Lisan al-Hal* was brought into the salon by the parlor maid. "Ibn al-Hakim" proceeded to read out aloud his new article on marriage, to the great delight of his audience. "Ibn al-Hakim" confessed that he derived great delight from the fact that his friends did not know he was the author. One of the women at the gathering, who thought that the writer should lay the blame on lack of parental guidance and not on the bachelors themselves, asked why the writer chose to conceal his identity. She speculated that someone who called himself "Ibn al-Hakim" might be a doctor and have many social and professional connections that could be damaged by such opinions, and so chose not to disclose his identity.[65]

Another *Lisan al-Hal* writer, Dawud al-Naqqash, referred to an article written by Ibrahim Afandi al-Khuri published in the Maronite journal *al-Misbah* (*The Lamp*, 1880–1908), which described similar interactions with readers. Al-Khuri first acknowledged that he eagerly read the articles on marriage appearing in *Lisan al-Hal*, and then proceeded to describe a conversation he had during his visit to the home of a friend. While al-Khuri was waiting for his friend, his friend's wife saw him with the paper and asked him to read out loud the articles concerning marriage. When he finished, al-Khuri asked the woman for her opinion. She responded that these debates did not apply to most women since the majority could not read: "There are not more than five hundred women in the region who know how to read and write, so how is this going to affect women?" Arguing that male writers only wanted to see their names in print, she expressed her preference that such weighty issues be resolved by religious leaders. Al-Naqqash explained to his readers that it was incidents and views such as this one that prompted him to write his article in the first place.[66] This anecdote suggests that in spite of the rather conventional views the woman expressed, she was deeply engrossed in the debate, and even though she may not have been able to read she was able to participate in conversations on the issue as the articles were read out loud in public, semi-private, and private gatherings.

During these years several important books on women's issues, such as those by 'A'isha Taymur (1840–1902) and Princess Nazli Hanim, were published. Readers also attended or read reports of the speeches on the "woman question" delivered to literary and charitable societies, such as that of Amir Amin Arslan in 1892.[67] Readers were also familiarized with the organized struggle for women's suffrage elsewhere. In 1899 Yaqut Sarruf, a member of the International Council of Women, spoke at the organization's annual meeting and reported to her readers about the meeting, the presidential address of Ishbel Hamilton-Gordon (1857–1939), and that of American educator and suffragist May Wright Sewell (1844–1920) describing the advances in women's political equality in the United States.[68]

These journals and writers did not always look toward European or American writers and thinkers for inspiration. In 1899 *al-Muqtataf* ran a two-part article entitled "The Woman in Islam" written by the liberal Indian-Muslim jurist and politician Syed Ameer Ali (1849–1928). It is not surprising that the editors chose Ali and his work, as it fit in with the general tone of the pro-woman discourse in Greater Syria and Egypt. Ali was a strong proponent of women's education, and one equal to that of men's. Drawing heavily on the example of early and medieval Muslim women teachers, rulers, diplomats, intermediaries, and innovators, Ali showed that women could carry out all these activities in keeping with the Prophet's teachings.[69] These issues, such as the progressive education appropriate for Muslim women and their role in society, would be of more interest to the readers and writers of the last of the journals under consideration, *Thamarat al-Funun (Fruits of Knowledge)*.

From Equality in Difference to Women's Suffrage

The driving force behind *Thamarat al-Funun* (1875–1908) was 'Abd al-Qadir al-Qabbani (b. 1849), a well-established scion of a wealthy Beiruti-Muslim family. Al-Qabbani studied in al-Bustani's *al-Madrasa al-Wataniyya*. Later, with other Muslim notables, he established a philanthropic society (*al-Maqasid al-Khayriyya*), which sought to promote education among Muslims. The society founded elementary schools for boys and girls and in 1875 began the publication of *Thamarat al-Funun*, which enjoyed a large Muslim readership.[70]

In 1875, its first year of publication, Beirut-born author Maryam Nahhas (Nawfal) (1856–88) chose this forum to announce her forthcoming book *The Fine Woman's Exhibition of Biographies of Famous Women* (1879).[71] Even in this relatively short notice intended to secure subscribers for her book, Nahhas expounded her views on the condition of women. "After I saw the condition of my [female] compatriots (*banat watani*), who are not interested in progress, I decided to contribute to their advancement on this issue. I decided to write a dictionary." Nahhas compiled and wrote the biographies of famous Arab and Persian women renowned for their knowledge and courage.[72] Nahhas' notice was the sole reference to the "women question" in *Thamarat al-Funun* in the next 15 years, but once the debate began in the early 1890s it did not abate.[73]

The debate on women in *Thamarat al-Funun* had several characteristics that distinguished it from the debate in the other journals. First, readers were absent from the debate which involved the editor and the (mostly unidentified) writers in the journal, although at times they responded to articles and debates in other journals. It is possible that as one of the few Beirut-based journals it was wary of stirring up a more widespread (and perhaps uncontrollable) debate which would draw the attention of the ever-vigilant Ottoman censor. Second, the debate on women did not stand on its own but was embedded within a larger, general debate on the family, and the modern Muslim family in particular. Hence one does not find an abundance of specific writings on women's education, rights, and activities, but a variety of articles on breastfeeding, nannies and women's fashions, within which were inserted views and comments about women and their social roles. An in-depth reading of the issues of *Thamarat al-Funun* from the last decade of the nineteenth century indicates that the journal's writers viewed the family, rather than the individual, as the basic socio-political unit. These intellectuals did not conceive of women (or men for that matter) as individuals distinct from their instrumental, relational and sexually discrete social roles.

An example of how such general articles in *Thamarat al-Funun* led to comments on women can be found in an article on "Marriage and Family Life in Europe," which outlined the "breakdown" of the modern family because of men's and women's interests outside the home. The author noted that similar developments were now occurring in Arab society "especially among Christian families," therefore the "daughters of the east (*banat al-Sharq*)" and its sons should remain in their marriages come what may.[74] These kinds of comments resurfaced throughout the debate on women in *Thamarat al-Funun*, where the suggested reform measures concerning women would be unfavorably compared to rights Arab women already enjoyed.

Another such commentary appeared in the 1893–94 issues. An earlier report concerning the debate on dress reform at the Chicago World's Fair was reprinted from *Kawkab Amrika*.[75] The report noted that several American women viewed the corset as harmful to women and their health, and were advocating a looser fitting outfit for women that closely resembled "the dress of eastern women" (*malabis al-sharqiyyat*). The later report (also reprinted from *Kawkab Amrika*) concerned a group of suffragists who wore "the Bloomer costume" in public in Topeka. The editor of *Thamarat al-Funun* commented briefly: "this is proof for some of our women that our original dress was sensible."[76] This wary remark, which suggested that Arab women should examine imports from the West (be it dress or behaviors) cautiously and that seemingly novel ideas were already to be found in Arab and/or Muslim cultures, was echoed throughout the debate on dress reform in the press. In 1896, for example, an article on the corset in *al-Hilal* detailed and illustrated its debilitative effects on the body's internal organs. The author commented "it is strange that among us it [the corset] has been adopted by educated women, and even though they understand its harm, they continue to use and admire it."[77]

One of the most important thinkers receiving significant attention in *Thamarat al-Funun* was French dramatist and essayist Ernest Wilfred Legouvé (1807–1903), a highly influential writer on the "woman question." His major work, *Histoire morale des femmes* (1849), was later translated into several other European languages, and had a strong influence on Norwegian and German feminists. The *Thamarat* articles referred to a later, abbreviated version, *La question des femmes* (1881). Legouvé argued in favor of the "equality in difference" and called for "women's emancipation in the name of the very principles reclaimed for subjugation by its adversaries – tradition and sexual difference." Legouvé grounded his call for emancipation on women's differences from men and their social role as mothers. By insisting on linking the two sexes through the institution of marriage, he laid to rest the fear of the sexual emancipation of women.[78] Perhaps more importantly, Legouvé did not reject the important role religion played in the life of the family, in particular in the lives of women and children. Given the insistence on sexual difference and the complementarity between males and females, the need for restructuring the family, moral motherhood, and in particular the distancing from the doctrines of sexual emancipation, it is unsurprising that French feminist thought such as that of Ernest Legouvé was so appealing to many Arab thinkers and readers of the *Nahda* period.

Throughout 1899 to 1900, *Thamarat* ran an 13-part article which included translated excepts of Legouvé's work preceded by an introduction by 'Abd al-Basit Fathallah, who compared Legouvé's views and demands regarding women to the status of Muslim women under *shari'a* law.[79] Fathallah argued that in many instances under *shari'a* law women enjoyed a much higher status; for instance, married Muslim women were not required to turn over their earnings to their family, while European women were required to do so. He concluded his argument by stating that returning to the basic teachings of Islam would only increase human happiness for "there is no need to imitate the West and its women."[80] While Fathallah conceded that women play an important role in the happiness and development of the nation, he cautioned against excess and stressed that the advancement of women (which he favored) should follow *shari'a* law.[81]

Similar views can be found in the writings of an anonymous Muslim intellectual that appeared three years earlier in *al-Hilal*. The author claimed that the young educated woman of the present is able to join in conversations on culture and science because she understands the cause and effect of things; a reader of books and newspapers, she becomes cognizant of her rights and duties. She is a source of happiness to her husband, bringing wisdom and light to her family. He did, however, caution that there are women who exceed this role: "How should we react to this, as it happens in the homes of the most respected people?" The author suggested that as each culture and society had its own customs and pace of development, one should not try and imitate those of another.[82]

This fear that Arab women might imitate the forward and improper behavior of foreign women also seeped into the writing of another reader, Wadi' Abu Rizq of Melbourne, Australia, who wrote an "op-ed" piece for *al-Muqtataf* in 1896, reporting on a public meeting in Melbourne in which women demanded suffrage rights. Abu Rizq not only mocked this demand and viewed it as contrary to nature, but compared the destabilizing effect women would have on society to that of the Russian Nihilists.[83] While there was nothing particularly unusual about the style and content of this piece, the response to it certainly was, as it was destined to be one of the earliest articulations of the demand for female suffrage in the mainstream *Nahda* press. The anonymous author, styling herself "one of the readers," launched an outright attack on Abu Rizq. She did not remain content with a defense of her sex, but boldly demanded women's political rights and articulated a strong pacifist worldview. She outlined for her readers her vision of a world in which women participated in public life, a world where peace reigned, where government was free of corruption and vice, one where the money saved could be put to good use to combat poverty. In making her case, she taunted Abu Rizq: what proof is there that the "laws of nature" prevent women from exerting themselves in public life? Compared to their exertion at home at even the easiest of domestic chores, "what woman cannot write her name on a note and place it in a ballot box (*sunduq al-intikhab*) every two or three years?"[84]

***

In this chapter we sketched the outlines of a little-considered and far lengthier debate on women in the nineteenth-century Arab press and demonstrated the existence of a vibrant "community of discourse" (which included men and women), first in Greater Syria and later in Egypt, which discussed, refashioned and disseminated ideas on women, their roles and rights. By re-examining the chronology, geography, and sociocultural aspects of the debate, its terms, and participants, we established three points. First, that the "woman question" had deep roots in the early *Nahda*; it had percolated for some time in society before appearing in the press in the late 1850s, and spread well beyond the upper middle class; moreover it permeated into peripheral areas, and did not remain within the confines of the larger cosmopolitan cities of Beirut, Cairo, Alexandria and Istanbul.[85] Second, the debate was by all accounts condensed, especially when compared to similar ones in Europe, as barely within the span of 50 years it ran the gamut from a "defense of women" to a fully articulated demand for equal political rights for women. In the early stage, participants advocated more rights for women, in particular women's education, in order to advance women themselves (albeit in their future roles as wife and mother), but they did not subordinate the "woman question" to the debate on the nation state, as was the case in the early twentieth century. On the whole they did not anchor themselves within the discourse of individual rights (although they were conversant with it); rather they embedded their arguments within the discourse of social responsibility and conceived of women (and men for that matter) as individuals inseparable from their relational social roles. This may explain their partiality toward continental philosophers and feminists, such as Legouvé, who envisioned women's rights and roles in a similar fashion. Third, while the writers and readers of the *Nahda* period were influenced by a wide variety of ideas, texts, and authors, they sifted through them to mold a feminist world-view that was uniquely their own, and laid the groundwork for later works favoring women's emancipation, such as those by Qasim Amin, which inaugurated the second phase of the debate in the twentieth century. While Western thought often served as a template for modernization and Western feminists provided a compelling model of independent womanhood for emulation, Arab intellectuals of the *Nahda* period (readers and writers alike) were committed to constructing a local model through a lengthy and complex process of re-thinking, remolding and rearticulating these notions. Thus, the ideas they eventually came to express were the product of an intricate process of negotiation, adaptation and synthesis between foreign and Arab feminist texts, which only later would be complicated by competing discourses of masculinity and nationalism/imperialism, as in the much later debate on veiling.

By moving beyond the accepted chronological, geographical and socio-cultural boundaries of this debate, re-envisioning them and showing that the *Nahda* involved a major re-conceptualization of social relations whose core was gender and women's issues, we provide a new framework for rethinking the dynamics of the debate on women. Thus future interpretations of the *Nahda* and its significance in Arab historiography will need to go well beyond the focus on literary, linguistic, and historical concerns, and scholars of women and gender must re-examine this period in order to ground their understanding of later developments and engage in a multifaceted analysis of the place and rights of women in modern Arab societies.

CHAPTER 2

LOVE, MARRIAGE AND SOCIAL REFORM IN THE EARLY ARABIC NOVEL

In 1873 Salim al-Bustani, one of the leading nineteenth-century Arab intellectuals, sometimes considered to be the "father of the modern Arabic novel,"[1] published his serialized novel *Asma* in his family-owned periodical *al-Jinan* (*The Gardens*).[2] Although it was al-Bustani's fourth novel, *Asma* represents a shift from the themes and settings of his three earlier novels. The first, *al-Huyam fi Jinan al-Sham* (*Passionate Love in the Gardens of al-Sham*, 1870), takes place in a pastoral setting at an unspecified time. The second, *Zanubya* (1871), was a historical novel, relating the story of the third-century Queen Zenobia and her rebellion against the Roman Empire. The third, *Budur* (1872), another historical novel, takes place in eighth-century Andalusia. The action in *Asma*, however, takes place in a contemporary urban setting and focuses on the manners and morals of the newly established Arab bourgeoisie, in this case two merchant families of Beirut and the marital decisions of their children. This new and divergent setting and plot were to become the prototype for many of his later short stories and novels such as *Bint al-'Asr* (*Daughter of the Age*, 1875), *Fatina* (1877), *Salma* (1878–79), and *Samya* (1882), as well as for the social novels of later writers.[3]

During the nineteenth century (and well into the twentieth) the Arabic novel was perceived as a lower or non-canonical genre, especially when compared to poetry.[4] Only in the second half of the twentieth century did prose writing, especially novels, become the leading genre. As a result, the works of the early Arabic novelists such as Salim al-Bustani have not garnered much scholarly attention. Although the place of al-Bustani in modern Arabic literature is akin to that of Fielding and Richardson in English literature, his novels, though popular in his lifetime, have sometimes been disregarded,[5] not studied in depth, only mentioned in passing,[6] and at times even derisively dismissed by later scholars.[7] We believe that it is important to understand the crucial role al-Bustani's novels played in the development of the Arabic novel, since a failure to do so leaves both readers and scholars with a skewed view of the history of modern Arabic fiction.

This decline in contemporary lay and scholarly interest is the result of both textual and extra-textual reasons. The didactic tone, twisting sentimental plots, unsophisticated narrative and minimal character development in the novels themselves fostered the perception that these novels were mere "amusements" (*fukahat*) and fell short of the stricter rules of the later modern novel. In addition, unlike the works of other early novelists, al-Bustani's novels were never reissued in book form; hence they remain unavailable to readers without access to a research library. In recent years, however, a handful of contemporary scholars have begun to re-examine the works of Salim al-Bustani and re-evaluate his role in the emergence of the modern Arabic novel. They claim that his popular and influential novels set the pattern for years to come, contributing to the emergence, development and form of the modern Arabic novel.[8]

In this chapter we examine *Asma* (1873), one of Salim al-Bustani's early novels, in which bourgeois women and the marriages they contract are of crucial social importance. Building on the new appraisal of al-Bustani's *oeuvre*, we highlight al-Bustani's contribution to the development of the Arabic novel as a genre. We examine the plot and illustrate how al-Bustani deliberated on serious contemporary social issues, such as the challenges facing a society undergoing rapid modernization, and in particular the role of women in the formation of a modern Arab family. After a brief introduction to Salim al-Bustani and his work, we consider the mid-nineteenth-century Arab reading audience and its literary tastes. We then examine al-Bustani's stylistic techniques and narrative, and most importantly the new social themes he introduced into the Arabic novel; mainly the Arab encounter with modernity, a theme which has prevailed to the present day.[9] We demonstrate that while al-Bustani was indeed well aware of the more recent developments in the genre (for example Romantic and Gothic novels), he had to adopt a style suitable to this readership. His novels can thus be seen as a transitional phase in the evolution of the Arabic novel during which he reshaped the tastes of a new generation of the reading public, laid the groundwork and prepared his readers for a more widespread acceptance of the conventions of the modern novel and its focus on social issues. We believe that this re-evaluation of Salim al-Bustani's work will enable scholars to re-envision the Arabic novel's formative period in more innovative ways.

Salim al-Bustani – A Brief Biography

Salim al-Bustani was the eldest son of Butrus al-Bustani (1819–83) and Rahil ('Ata) al-Bustani (1823–94), members of a Beiruti Christian family. Both his parents were highly educated and well-versed in Arabic and Western literatures (especially English and French). His father, an author, translator, publisher, and educator, was a major figure in the Beiruti intellectual scene of the *Nahda* period. Butrus al-Bustani started a preparatory school (*al-Madrasa al-Wataniyya*) for a college founded by the American missionaries (one which would later become the American University of Beirut); he also wrote the first Arabic encyclopedia and dictionary, and established among others the periodical *al-Jinan* (1870–86; a bi-weekly publication). *Al-Jinan*, the first pan-Arabic publication, circulated throughout Greater Syria, Iraq, and Egypt. American missionary Henry Harris Jessup claimed that it had a local circulation of about 1,500;[10] it even reached subscribers in the various European capitals. It published translations of French, Italian and English fiction, and was the venue where all of Salim al-Bustani's novels were first serialized.[11] Rahil al-Bustani, his mother, was raised by American missionaries and studied in the 1830s in the first school for girls established by them. After her marriage not only did she manage her household and raise nine children, but she was actively involved in running the preparatory school, where she was in charge of the students' diet, health and hygiene. Her biographer claimed that she was an avid reader of philosophy and literature in both Arabic and English and instilled her love of literature in her children.[12]

Salim al-Bustani followed his parents' social and literary footsteps. In 1863 he was named assistant principal of the preparatory school, where he headed the departments of history, nature and English, and upon his father's death took up his work on the encyclopedia and *al-Jinan*. He was also involved in local politics and was later elected to the Beirut City Council. In the course of his literary career he published political and economic essays, reviews, short stories, novels, historical novels, and three plays (which have been lost); he also translated numerous European (mainly French) novels into Arabic.[13] However, although al-Bustani was closely attuned to his audiences' tastes he did not hesitate to introduce them to new forms and employ the novel to disseminate and promote his social vision of a modern Arab society.

The Early Arabic Novel and Its Audience

The first novels that appeared in Arabic were translations of an assortment of European novels. Many were marginal works that are all but forgotten today; some cannot even be traced back to their source as the translators often "Arabized" the texts to such an extent that they are unidentifiable. These translations usually appeared in serialized form in newspapers, such as *Hadiqat al-Akhbar* (1858–1911), and periodicals such as *al-Jinan*.[14] In these translations, which began appearing in the mid-nineteenth century, translators exhibited great affinity for the works of Alexandre Dumas *père*, Sir Walter Scott, and a range of lesser known romances, adventure stories, historical, detective and mystery novels.[15]

First, however, we need to attend to Salim al-Bustani's reading public and its literary tastes. As Hans Robert Jauss argued "the historical life of a literary work is unthinkable without the active participation of its audience. For it is only through the process of communication that the work reaches the changing horizon of experience in continuity in which the continual change occurs from simple reception to critical understanding."[16]

M. M. Badawi argued that the *Nahda* period witnessed the emergence of a new kind of reader, a graduate of the missionary schools (in Greater Syria) or the more secular schools (in Egypt), and one who sought to read and be entertained but was not deeply grounded in classic Arabic literature and hence was more open to a more direct, less formal, and simpler style.[17] The Arab reading public was accustomed on the one hand to poetry, which was highly stylized, rhymed and metered, and used a literary Arabic (*fusha*), and on the other to the themes and oral techniques of the more popular *maqama* (session) and *sira sha'biyya* (popular tales). The translated material filled a certain literary void, as most of the items were either technical and scientific books or popular fiction. The translated popular novels reflected the prevailing tastes among this "newly-but-marginally literate" readership.[18] Not surprisingly, the works of more canonical authors such as Dickens, Thackeray, and Tolstoy were translated into Arabic only during the second decade of the twentieth century.

The choice of the translated novels suggests that the translators were closely attuned to readers' tastes and were aware of what literary styles and themes would be amenable to them. Echoing the traditional *sira sha'biyya* (popular tales), *ustura* (legends) or the tales of a *Thousand and One Nights*, these translated novels are often set in mythic or historical times; their heroes are involved in adventures and have dealings with mysterious beings or magical creatures. The plots themselves are formulaic in nature, and stock characters are frequent. Both the advent of journalism and the publication of the translations (both fictional and non-fictional) fostered a gradual change in the style of modern Arabic prose; by eliminating excessive rhetorical devices, using colloquial idioms, and simplifying its syntax and style, often in conscious violation of grammatical rules; they not only transformed prose into a genre where matter was privileged over manner, but ushered in the modernization of Arabic.[19] Thus, it is important not to dismiss this popular literature, as it set the stage for the appearance of writers such as Salim al-Bustani.

In his study of early English novels, J. Paul Hunter argues that the novels of this period have been ignored by contemporary readers and less systematically studied by scholars not only because of their closeness to popular literature and responsiveness to historical tastes, but due to a "pervasive modern resistance to their insistent didacticism."[20] A similar argument may well be made regarding the early Arabic novel. One of the main reasons why the novels of al-Bustani have suffered a similar fate is that they are closely attuned to the "horizon of expectations" of his original reading audience. In his explanation of his term the "horizon of expectations," Jauss argued that:

A literary work, even when it appears to be new, does not present itself as something absolutely new in an informational vacuum, but predisposes its audience to a very specific kind of reception by announcements, overt and covert signals, familiar characteristics, or implicit allusions. It awakens memories of that which was already read, brings the reader to a specific emotional attitude, and with its beginning arouses expectations for the "middle and end," which can then be maintained intact or altered, reoriented, or even fulfilled ironically in the course of the reading according to specific rules of the genre or type of text. The psychic process in the reception of a text is, in the primary horizon of aesthetic experience, by no means only an arbitrary series of merely subjective impressions, but rather the carrying out of specific instructions in the process of directed perception, which can be comprehended according to its constitutive motivations and triggering signals.[21]

Jauss claims that each successive text in a particular genre alters this horizon and "evokes for the reader (listener) the horizon of expectations and rules familiar from earlier texts which are then varied, corrected, altered, or even just reproduced."[22] In al-Bustani's case the modern readers' "horizon of expectations" not only shifted considerably but to such an extent that al-Bustani's originality, especially when it came to his subject matter – the personal (and political) ramifications of modernization – remains hidden from the modern eye.

All the earlier (linguistic, stylistic, and thematic) developments in Arabic narrative fiction set the stage for the work of Salim al-Bustani. Al-Bustani was not only one of the first to write original novels (*riwaya*) in Arabic, he was the first to try his pen at social novels. While the plots and the chain of events in his novels such as *Asma* (1873), *Bint al-'Asr* (1875), *Fatina* (1877), *Salma* (1878–9), and *Samya* (1882) bear an outward resemblance to non-canonical Arabic traditional adventure tales involving a love story with its trials, tribulations, and happy ending, the themes of al-Bustani's narratives are similar to those of European sentimental and domestic novels. They take place in a contemporary urban setting and focus on courtship and marriage. He posed new moral dilemmas to his youthful protagonists that mainly involved reconciling traditional Arab customs and values with those introduced by modernity.

Al-Bustani's novels employ a new and dynamic language (*wusta*), a mixture of classical Arabic and its colloquial form. Unlike earlier literary works that were often part of a cycle of tales (focused on the same character) or a frame story, his novels have a well-defined and recognizable structure (namely a beginning, middle and end) and a plot. These novels shift between sections in which the plot is revealed through an omniscient narrator and those where the author interjects himself into the texts and addresses his readers directly. While al-Bustani preferred to expound directly in a philosophical and didactic fashion on his main theme, he sometimes conveyed these views by the use of interior monologues.

Salim al-Bustani's novels border on realism but often present an idealized view of society. They are set in a specific place and time, while "in traditional Arabic literary discourse, place was frequently almost as general and vague as time,"[23] and indeed in his first novel *al-Huyam fi Jinan al-Sham* all the reader is told is that the action takes place in an unspecified desert at an unspecified time. In *Asma* and the other social novels the reader is not provided with an exact date and location. However, al-Bustani openly acknowledged the importance of the temporal information and vouched for its veracity to his readers. Although he claimed that he did not reveal this information for fear of disclosing the characters' "real" identities, he went on to say that he himself had witnessed events similar to those described in the novel in his own social milieu; in so doing, al-Bustani in effect revealed the novel's contemporary setting.[24]

Another factor that gave readers a clue as to the time and place of the action in the novel was the accompanying illustrations (see pictures from the novel in Appendix 1). Both *Asma* and his earlier novel *Budur* contained illustrations; these were the first to appear in an Arabic novel. But contrary to *Budur*, the figures in the illustrations in *Asma* wear fashionable contemporary European dress (although some minor concessions are made to Arab/Turkish items, such as the fez) and are situated in a domestic setting with European furniture, just as one would expect to find in the homes of the urban bourgeoisie. While these illustrations may present an idealized and far more homogenous view of the domestic life of the local middle classes, they nonetheless provided readers with a clear indication of the time and place of the action.

The Plot Thickens

Incorporating elements from both the didactic and sentimental novel, *Asma* tells the story of the families of two business partners. Nadir and Sadir are merchants and each has two children, a son and a daughter. Nadir, the father of Jalil and Asma, is wealthy but unassuming and charitable. His friend and partner Sadir, the father of Badi' and Badi'a, is his opposite: he brags about his wealth and is overly concerned with appearance and his family's status. Jalil and Asma are a reflection of their father; they are well-educated, well-mannered and modest, yet strong minded and honorable. Badi' and Badi'a are uneducated, foolish, self-centered, and their behavior often borders on immodest or downright criminal (in the case of Badiʻ). Sadir and his children have long assumed that the two families' business relationship will be cemented by marriages with Nadir's children. At this stage of their lives enters Karim al-Baghdadi, a well-educated and upstanding young merchant who is visiting the city. Asma and Karim soon find that they have similar views and share many interests, and fall in love. Meanwhile Jalil comes to realize that Badiʻa is not the sort of woman he would have wished to marry; he tries to reform her behavior and manners, but fails. He then turns his attention to a modest and shy young girl named Saʻda, and by the end of the novel marries her.

Badiʻ, who has always assumed that he would marry Asma, is jealous of Karim and decides to ruin Karim's reputation by framing him for a crime he did not commit. Although Karim is arrested, Asma remains convinced of his innocence. During this period Asma is pursued by another suitor, Farid, who is also courting four other young women (Nabiha, Jamila, Farida and Latifa). Karim is soon released, but he realizes that someone has set him up and decides to leave until matters clear up. After learning of Karim's decision, Asma asks her brother and father to help clear Karim's name and refuses all her other suitors' offers of marriage. Badiʻ understands that in order to remove Karim from the scene he will have to take more drastic measures, and hires men to follow Karim and murder him. The assassins do manage to shoot Karim and his servant rushes to Asma to deliver the news of his master's death. When the authorities accompanied by Nadir and Jalil appear on the scene the body has disappeared.

Badiʻ, impersonating Karim, sends word to Asma telling her that he is alive and asks her to meet him. When Asma arrives at the meeting she finds out that it was a subterfuge designed to draw her out of her home and that Badiʻ intends to marry her against her will. Miraculously, Karim (who has finally identified who framed him) appears and rescues Asma from the clutches of Badiʻ, takes her home and the two become engaged to be married. After several more failed attempts to ruin Karim's reputation and a few days before Asma and Karim's wedding, Badiʻ kidnaps Asma in yet another attempt to force her to marry him. Karim rescues Asma after shooting Badi', and the two lovers are finally united in marriage. When she gets to her new home, Asma discovers that Karim is a well-respected and wealthy merchant himself, who hid his true identity in order to find a worthy and virtuous bride. Badi', who was sentenced to prison for two years, marries the beautiful but diabolical (*shaytana*) Jamila after his release, whereas his sister ends up with the lazy and devious Farid.

It should be clear by now that this novel's plot is indeed as convoluted and unsophisticated as its critics have claimed (certainly when compared to twentieth-century Arabic novels). It draws on a multitude of literary conventions and its series of mini-climaxes were inserted (often abruptly) to retain readers' flagging interest from one issue of the magazine to the next.[25] In the past these elements distracted scholars' attention from al-Bustani's major contributions to the evolution of the modern Arabic novel, which range from technique and style to his choices of plot, characters, setting and theme.

Gender, Genre and the Constitution of a "Modern" Arab Family

Salim al-Bustani's most important contribution to the Arabic novel and the expansion of his readers' "horizon of expectations" was his choice of theme; namely, the encounter of traditional Arab culture and values with those of the modern world and their reconciliation. This choice of theme was by no means exclusive to al-Bustani; it can be found, for instance, in the plays of 'Abdallah Nadim (1845–96), the short stories of Khalil al-Khuri (1836–1907), and the essays of Fransis Marrash (1836–73) that also appeared during this period. Like many other Arab writers and intellectuals of the *Nahda* period, al-Bustani insisted on distinguishing between modernization and Westernization. The exposure to Western ideas, culture, and technology inspired great admiration, but with it came a growing sense of the need to preserve the Arab heritage. Similar views reverberated through the private letters, speeches delivered before assemblies of the cultural societies, newspaper and periodical articles of the period, all produced by and for the bourgeoisie. These writers and intellectuals saw themselves as "the generation of light and knowledge" and believed they were on the brink of a new era (al-'asr al-jadid); an era in which the East would regain its former prominence and hopefully even transcend the West.[26] In order to do so, they argued, it was necessary to reshape their "traditional" society and transform it into a more "open" or "advanced" and egalitarian one. However, this transformation was not to be a mere imitation of the West, but one in which certain (selected) Western ideas and institutions would be used as a tool to advance their society.[27]

Salim al-Bustani cautioned his readers time and again against mistaking the superficial mannerisms of Western culture (tamaddun khariji) for a truly (haqiqi) advanced and modern society, one reformed from within (tamaddun dakhili). The latter sensibly combines the "good" values of two distinct cultures including the universally valid ideas and values of modernity such as freedom, individual dignity, orderliness, equality and tolerance, with what he perceives to be "Arab values" such as non-materialism, humility, charity and respect for tradition and the Arab cultural heritage.[28] The task of reconciling or perhaps sifting through the different values and creating a coherent value system and world view was not an easy one. Indeed, this process unsettled the peace of mind of several characters in Asma.

Introducing Asma and Karim: The Prototypes of the Modern Husband and Wife

In Asma (and his other social novels), al-Bustani chose to work out the socio-political issue of modernity on gendered bodies, both male and female. Many of al-Bustani's characters, including women such as Badi'a and Nabiha or men such as Badi' and Farid in Asma, conflate superficiality with authenticity and thus are subject to censure and ridicule by the author and some of the other characters in the novel. Early in the novel al-Bustani provides the reader with a list of characteristics and practices (many of them imported) which he associates with the superficial appropriation of Western culture and its values, such as materialism, greediness, ostentatious clothing, grandiose homes and carriages, ballroom dancing, makeup, and lighthearted conversation. For example, the reader is informed that Badiʿa has a great fondness for parties and the pleasures of life.[29] While she seeks to imitate Western dress and etiquette, she has absolutely no interest in literature or knowledge; she is in effect a hollow shell.[30] Just in case the reader has failed to understand Badiʿa's true nature, al-Bustani likened the movement of her body and the train of her dress to the undulations of a snake across a floor "strewn with her father's money which could have been given to the needy and the poor."[31]

Although Nabiha is more educated, and not quite as willful, like Badiʿa, she also confuses the superficial adoption of Western clothes and mannerisms for true culture. She judges and values people according to their appearance and wealth; a trait which often leads her to make serious misjudgments. The narrator concludes that if Nabiha could correct her flaws, she would be one of the leading female figures of her society.[32] In a similar manner, both Badiʿ and Farid are described as handsome but vain, self-centered, un-educated, lazy, immoral (perhaps also criminal) men. Both have a strong sense of self-entitlement deriving from their families' social position but do nothing to improve their minds and characters. Especially in Badiʿs' case, the reader is given to understand that his parents did nothing to check his behavior; instead they often defended him and laid the blame on others.

Asma, in contrast, serves as a model of a member of the true, internally-reformed society; she embodies the spirit of the age (ruh al-ʿasr). She personifies someone who has successfully blended the values of two cultures in that she is honest, modest, humble, non-materialistic and loyal. Not only is Asma educated in the arts and sciences and well-read (al-marʾa al-ʿaqila), she is also well-versed in the domestic arts.[33] Salim al-Bustani constantly equated body and mind, especially when it came to his female characters; Asma's balance of mind is reflected in her serene countenance and well-proportioned body.[34]

The man Asma seeks for her future husband will not only share her mental and moral qualities, but will be well-respected by his society. Both Karim (her prospective husband) and Jalil (her brother) personify the masculine aspect of al-Bustani's idealized, reformed society. Contrary to his detailed physical descriptions of the female characters, al-Bustani provides only the briefest physical description of his male characters and focuses on their thoughts and characters. Karim is pointedly described as "not handsome" but in possession of "good qualities"; although wealthy he is not materialistic and in fact conceals his actual status because he wishes to be judged on his merits. Karim is intellectually curious and seeks to associate himself with people who share his values. In his first meeting with Asma, she immediately recognizes his true character and concludes "it is clear that you despise *tamaddun khariji.*"[35]

Contrary to the widely-held perception, al-Bustani's characters are not "fully developed symbols of vice or virtue."[36] Rather, while virtue may be absolute, there are various degrees of vice; some characters have the potential to change, although very often they choose not to do so. Badi'a could perhaps reform herself and the readers are given to understand that Jalil (her intended fiancé) would have supported her endeavors; however, her pride and haughtiness do not permit her to acknowledge the error of her ways. She is convinced that her adoption of Western fashions and manners is absolute proof of her transformation into a European.[37] Sa'da (the young woman Jalil eventually marries) does choose to reform herself. She too comes from a merchant family, although her mother is described as lazy and neglectful of domestic affairs. In fact Sa'da's mother is so self-centered that she ignores her children's doings and is jealous of her daughter's youth and beauty. It was Sa'da's formal schooling that instilled in her a love of cleanliness and orderliness, and as a result she runs her parents' household. Thus al-Bustani intimated that people do have the capability to correct their manners and morals and transcend the teachings of their parents.[38]

In a modern society an individual's true value does not devolve from birth, title, or social status, but resides in the essential qualities of mind, which are manifested in behavior. Salim al-Bustani expected his characters to tackle another important issue, that of marriage on the basis of these qualities of mind.[39] Al-Bustani shifted the locus of the socio-cultural work of reconciling two distinct cultural traditions and laying the foundation of a modern Arab society onto the family, and in particular the married couple. It is their mutual affirmation of each other's character which will give birth to the modern family, the building-block of al-Bustani's ideal, reformed, modern Arab society. Nearly all of al-Bustani's young characters (in all of his social novels) need to decide who to marry, or more precisely to determine the nature of their marriages. Are wealth and family status more (or less) important than individual character? Should one abide with the long tradition of an arranged marriage contracted by the parents or should a person be guided by love and individual choice? Jalil, for example, considers his impending marriage to Badi'a early in the novel. While he is often bothered by her inappropriate behavior and loose conversation, he is kind and reluctant to break off their relationship. Even after witnessing the loving, respectful and intellectually compatible relationship evolving between his sister Asma and Karim, and realizing that there is no hope for Badi'a's reform and that marrying her will make them both miserable, he clings to the hope that she will improve her behavior. He agonizes that severing the relationship will ruin Badi'a reputation, be contrary to the wishes of their parents and perhaps even damage the two families' business partnership.[40] Only upon witnessing firsthand Badi'a's immodest behavior with another man and faced with her mother's reluctance to correct this behavior does Jalil inform Badi'a of his decision not to marry her.[41]

Thus, while al-Bustani clearly supported shifting the decision-making regarding marriage from the hands of family to the individual, this choice should not be made for capricious reasons or selfish motives but after serious and rational deliberation. The individual's choice should not totally disregard family concerns and values or disrespect tradition. While love may oil the wheels of marriage, mutual respect, compatibility, understanding and shared interests are its primary components. More importantly, a prospective spouse's virtues and moral character may outweigh status and family fortunes. The choice of an appropriate marriage partner has far-reaching social (and eventually political) consequences, because it is the basis of a virtuous, civic-minded family; such a family will always act in the best interests of its people (*qawm*) and homeland (*watan*).[42]

The Ideal Modern Marriage in Non-fictional Essays

Although descriptions of the requisite qualities of the desired modern couple were found in the 1870s and 1880s mainly in novels, by the 1890s their figures had become a permanent fixture in essays and op-ed pieces in the *Nahda* press. Writers debated the desired qualities of wife and husband and their roles in society; they also sought to understand what kind of education or upbringing could foster the emergence of the modern wife. In one of the most fascinating articles, *"'Ilaj al-Zawaj"* ("Dealing with Marriage"), Dawud al-Naqqash defended women vigorously and blamed men and the system of education for their reluctance to marry and their unpreparedness for their main role in life. Al-Naqqash accused men (fathers and prospective husbands alike) of sending mixed messages to young women; these men provide young women with a confusing education (music, foreign languages, etc.) that fails to teach them how to manage a household or its finances and does not educate them concerning the mutual obligations of husband and wife, and then they in turn blame women for this failure. Al-Naqqash also rebuked young men for turning away from their wives and taking less care of their children. He ended his article by asking how many men talk about women's good character or praise the women they know, concluding that this is one of the reasons why women do not want to be married in the first place.[43]

Some of the writers who defended women preferred to remain anonymous and signed with pen names. One of these writers who called himself "a contemporary researcher" (*al-Bahith al-'Asri*) felt that some of the writers "were harsh toward women."[44] Another, known as "The wise man's son" or "the physician's son" (*Ibn al-Hakim*), placed the blame once again on men. In his opinion many young men are single because they are looking for rich brides. He warns them that when they reach 40 they will start to think about marriage but by then it will be too late.[45] Such responses by men were indicative of a growing awareness and sensitivity on their part towards the institution of marriage and towards women. They also reveal a deep anxiety that this institution would not withstand the changes of modern times and demonstrates their concern over the increase in the number of single men.

Other writers placed the blame for this unhappy state of affairs on women. Khatir Iliyas Samaha, a doctor, expanded on the importance of marriage as a social and religious institution. He blamed women for neglecting their duties in the home and attributed their behavior to their "hysterical attitude, attraction to fashion, the reading of novels and squandering of money."[46] Mayy's (a pseudonym) witty response challenged all such writers by saying that parental education is the most important thing for a successful marriage. She argued that since these young women's fathers or brothers aspire to be modern they want their daughters to look fashionable, thus they dress them in fancy clothes. Though Mayy did not approve of this, she hoped that women would return to an earlier simplicity and men would not find fancy dresses appealing.[47] The responses to Mayy's article varied greatly. One of the writers asserted that Mayy (and women in general) should mend their ways and that silence would be more appropriate;[48] other writers defended Mayy and encouraged her to write.[49]

Some of the writers tried to instruct their readers about the true meaning of marriage and the reciprocal duties of men and women. Some listed the virtues of a "good" woman needed to contract a good marriage. For example, an anonymous writer calling himself "One of the Esteemed Intellectuals" (*Ahad al-Udaba' al-Fadil*) explained that the main objective of marriage is to raise children to serve their *watan*. He suggested that a prospective bride should be educated, be aware of her duties and her obligations, and argued that wealth, beauty and dowry are less important than character and virtues.[50] He rejected the common attitude that the main purpose of the family is the accumulation of wealth and defined three types of marriage: a rational marriage, which is the most desirable; a marriage for love which is less desirable; and a marriage for economic reasons, which corrupts society and is the least desirable.[51]

In a rare instance, *Lisan al-Hal* published two articles signed by Salwa, a middle-class woman who utilized her own autobiographical story to instruct women about their choices in marriage and their economic requirements. After describing how she lost her father at the young age of 12, she depicts her own struggle to rebuild her life. Like Mayy she emphasizes the importance of parental education. Salwa believes that the knowledge her father, whom she refers to as 'aqil (educated), provided to her at a young age, helped her persevere when the family's economic situation deteriorated after his death.

She describes how her father taught her to pay the servants, oversee the cooking and cleaning, and calculate and supervise domestic expenses. Her story emphasizes the importance of both the father's and the mother's involvement in their daughter's domestic education. Later, after her father's death, her family was forced to move from their large house to a smaller one, yet despite their difficult economic situation, her mother sent her to school where she also learned sewing. Thus, when she reached marriageable age with the skills and knowledge of a good housewife, she did not have to rush into marriage. She decided to find a good husband, who knew the duties of marriage, which she defined as "one who will love her and her family." The process took several years, since she saw marriage as a very "important and practical decision to take."[52] Finally she found a suitable husband, a factory owner, and she then proceeded to describe her happy life with him in which he works and diligently manages the factory while she efficiently manages the home.[53]

Like al-Bustani before her, Salwa challenged the contemporary view of what constituted a strong foundation for marriage. The basis of a modern marriage is not the couple's background, title, or socio-economic status; rather it is their mutually compatible individual qualities of mind, expressed in their behavior, which provide the basis for an affectionate marriage. Salwa insisted that people do not understand the true meaning and purpose of marriage, which is why it is in such dire straits. She advised her readers that before entering into marriage they should attempt to comprehend its meanings and terms.

Salwa viewed the decision of a marriage partner as a rational and calculated decision tempered by love. For her, marriage is a mutual relationship, providing companionship. "Marriage is an expression of a partnership [. . .]. This partnership between spouses is governed not only by religious law (*al-shari'a al-ilahiyya*) but also by human laws (*qawanin bashariyya*) since it concerns the family and human society."[54] Salwa was careful to inform her readers that marriage was not always sunshine and light; there were good times and bad times, in which marriage may seem a "burden." Thus couples should invest both emotions and time in their marriage.[55]

Salwa was not alone in her concerns. In another article written earlier that year, *Ibn al-Hakim* expounded on the virtues of a good husband and the components of a successful marriage. He believed that a husband should be educated, cognizant of his obligations and take responsibility for women's education. He should be a good provider and spend his money on things the family needs. He should be kind to the needy and an excellent host. He should be interested in culture, know how to forgive, love his country (*dawla*) and follow the straight and narrow by preserving order and discipline in society. Thus *Ibn al-Hakim* expected men to be full and active partners in marriage by being dutiful husbands, and attentive fathers devoted to their family.[56]

The Novel as a Social Compass

In his novels Salim al-Bustani presented his main theme of modernization but not Westernization in various modes. While the sentimental, convoluted, and overlapping plots exemplify his main theme, he presented them in a diluted (or perhaps a more palatable) form to his readers; the sections in which he directly addressed his readers were designed to deliver his message in a condensed form in a more abstract manner. Thus even if potential readers were only interested in the sentimental parts of the novel they would be unable to avoid his main message. However, the latter sections contain a more serious and theoretical discussion of the impact and consequences of modernization for Arab society and culture. Throughout *Asma* (as well as the other social novels), al-Bustani discussed issues such as the education of women, the institution of marriage, and parents and their influence on their children's upbringing, and connected them to the rise and fall of nations.[57]

Virtually echoing the works of Enlightenment philosophers, al-Bustani argued that a truly reformed society rests upon truly reformed individuals. These can only be produced in reformed families, a union of like-minded men and women bound together by affection, who are committed to modern ideals such as freedom, individual dignity, orderliness, equality, and tolerance, combined with "Arab values" such as non-materialism, humility, charity, and respect for tradition and the Arab cultural heritage. The basis for such reform is education, especially female education. This education includes not only developing a woman's intellect but also her domestic skills. Women must realize the importance of their own education, as it will bring them happiness and prestige in their roles as mothers and wives; they (together with their husbands) will instill these values in their children.[58]

Almost anticipating the kind of charges that would be leveled against his writing, Salim al-Bustani also used these sections to launch an all-out defense of the novel, in particular the new role of the novel as a guide or a vehicle for conveying the values of a society reformed from within (*tamaddun dakhili*). Al-Bustani first argued in favor of the ideological power of the novel. He claimed that the reading of novels and histories cultivated the readers' moral judgment and served the nation as it stimulated public debate on a variety of social issues of both a public and private nature. Al-Bustani asserted that there was no reason why such serious issues could not be presented in a pleasing and entertaining fashion, since the ultimate goal was to promote the interests of "our homeland of Syria (*biladuna al-Suriyya*)."[59]

In *Asma*, Salim al-Bustani not only dealt with the morals and manners of the new urban bourgeoisie, but introduced issues that had serious socio-political implications. He envisioned his novel as a kind of a social compass in a period of transition that would guide his readers through the erratic currents of the encounter with modernity, as well as the West. Al-Bustani's style enabled him to appeal directly to his readers' sentiments, elucidate his views on reforms, and at times even preach and moralize. His choice to fuse elements from earlier literary traditions into his novel let him appeal to a larger readership and furthers his mission to reform Arab society by a selective combination of Arab and modern values.

***

This reconsideration of Salim al-Bustani's work raises an entire set of questions for further consideration. First and foremost is the fate of the Arabic social novel in the latter years of the nineteenth century. After al-Bustani's death in 1884,[60] novelists such as Fransis Marrash, Nu'man 'Abduh al-Qasatli, Alice al-Bustani (Salim's sister), and even Jurji Zaydan continued to write social novels; however, historical novels took on greater prominence. Al-Bustani's undertaking was only pursued in earnest in the early twentieth century when the social novel came into its own. Early twentieth century novelists such as Farah Antun (1874–1922), Niquala Haddad (1872–1954), and in particular Muhammad Husayn Haykal (1888–1956) would re-stimulate the reading public's interest in social novels. But although female characters abound in the later novels, a subtle shift seems to have occurred (especially in novels written after Haykal's *Zaynab*, published in 1914) in that issues of nation and class (especially the urban/rural and rich/poor divide) tend to prevail over the issues of gender that al-Bustani emphasized so greatly.

It is possible that this movement toward the historical novel was one outcome of political changes in the Ottoman Empire and its Arab provinces, which coincided with the ascension of Abdul Hamid II (1876–1908) to the throne. In the twilight years of the Ottoman Empire, with the rise of the Young Turk movement in Turkey and Arab secret societies in the provinces (the hotbeds of Arab nationalism), the waning of the imperial identity resulted in the need to cultivate an alternative, Arab national identity;[61] a need responded to by the Arab novelists following Salim al-Bustani, who brought issues of nation and class in the novel to the fore.[62] The growing censorship restrictions from the 1880s onward (in Greater Syria) and the British occupation of Egypt from 1882, meant that these topics could not be discussed in a direct manner, but rather were raised within the context of the historical novel that displaced the action and the debate of these issues into a distant time. In the years leading up to World War I, however, social issues including debates over gender, nation and class resurfaced.

Re-examining the groundbreaking cultural and ideological work of the early Arabic novelists, especially Salim al-Bustani, clearly demonstrates their importance, not only in terms of literature but also in explicating the encounter with modernity, assessing its impact, and envisioning its future. The insistence on distinguishing between modernization and Westernization hints at the underlying anxieties that accompanied the encounter with modernization and the West: the unease concerning changing gender roles, the concern over a loss of cultural uniqueness, and the fear of engulfment or perhaps even self-erasure by a foreign culture. Just as importantly, this work also posited the individual (male and female) as an important (if not yet ultimate) source of authority, thus fostering a mindset both suited to and necessary for the still unarticulated claims of the bourgeoisie for a greater say in the political and economic affairs of their society.

Salim al-Bustani's social novels were among the early fictional articulations in Arabic literature that charted these issues and anxieties and mapped a possible future course for society and its individual members. Al-Bustani recognized that gender issues were crucial to the project of a new kind of individual (and perhaps even civic) identity and to the formation of a reformed, modern society (*tamaddun dakhili*), but just as importantly he understood in what form to present such notions to win the hearts and minds of his readers and introduce these ideas into public discourse. Admittedly, at times his novels are overloaded with sub-plots, ideas, and philosophical discussions which al-Bustani did not always manage to integrate into a seamless narrative. This, however, should not blind contemporary readers to his uniqueness and originality as a writer and intellectual who placed the Arab encounter with modernity at the heart of his works and understood the power of the novel as a means of tackling this issue.

CHAPTER 3

REPAVING THE PATH OF *MURU'A:* MANLY VIRTUE AND THE EMERGENCE OF A MODERN MASCULINITY IN GREATER SYRIA

Shepherding is inappropriate for a man, as it does not generate fame (*shuhra*) resulting from courage (*jasara*), or physical feats (*iqdam*), or valor (*batsh*), of which a man may boast, especially if he was of noble birth (*sayyid al-qawm*) and inherited honor (*sharaf*) from his father and his forebears.[1]

You should be very proud of your wounds as they demonstrate your nobility of mind (*shahama*) and manly virtue (*muru'a*).[2]

In Chapter 1 we established that during the second half of the nineteenth century there were lively discussions in the Arab press concerning women, their social status, education and rights. Readers and writers, most of whom were men, heatedly debated various educational reform schemes, appropriate reading material for women, women's proper role within the family, and even political rights. Modern studies of gender and the formation of gendered identities have corroborated the close link between the identity-formation processes of masculinity and femininity. Thus, if women and femininity were so passionately discussed during the second half of the nineteenth century, what was the parallel discussion regarding men and masculinity? What terms did it employ? In what literary genres was it best expressed? And why has it escaped scholarly notice? Most studies focusing on Arab masculinities in the modern period have examined them in connection to early nationalist discourses (e.g. Egypt and Iran) in the opening years of the twentieth century[3] or regarded them as a more minor theme appearing in discussions on women and their rights or representations of the "New Woman" in the late nineteenth century.[4] Even Hoda Elsadda, who engages in a sophisticated examination of constructions of masculinity and its connection to nationality, focuses on the early decades of the twentieth century (in Egypt), whereas Linda Jones elegantly skirts nineteenth-century articulations of masculine ideals in Egypt and Greater Syria.[5] Thus, there is a gap in the scholarly literature on the discourse of modern Arab masculinities that has both neglected the emergence of an earlier discourse on masculinity during the middle of the *Nahda* period (1870s–90s) in Greater Syria and has overlooked its unique vocabulary. In this chapter we examine the ways the modern Arab discourse of masculinity made use of the pre-Islamic concept of *muru'a* (manly virtue).

"Pro-feminism" or a New Masculinity?

In her article "Paradoxes of Masculinity," Deniz Kandiyoti raised a series of provocative questions regarding the psycho-developmental origins of the "pro-feminism" of several male Arab thinkers and writers in the late nineteenth and early twentieth centuries. She speculated about their deeper motivations and wondered "if they were being self-serving by manifestly bemoaning the subjection of women while in fact rebelling against their own." Kandiyoti concluded that this pro-feminist discourse was the product of "the emergence of a novel male agenda which did not necessarily have as its main concern women's liberation, but rather their own." Writing several years later about an early twentieth-century magazine *al-Mar'a fil-Islam* (*Woman in Islam*) that was founded, edited, and almost entirely composed by men, with a predominantly male readership, Marilyn Booth argued that this journal also "focused ostensibly on women, [but] was in fact talking about men."[6] These two thought-provoking essays propelled us first to consider closely the ways in which discourses of masculinity and femininity were entwined, and to examine those rare instances in which men chose to speak directly about themselves and not filter their thoughts about masculinity through a discourse on femininity.

Scholars and historians in particular have drawn attention to the fact that "'masculinity' and 'femininity' are constructs of specific historical time and place." These are categories that "are continually being forged, contested, reworked and reaffirmed in social institutions and practices as well as a range of ideologies."[7] As gender identities are formed both vis-à-vis other genders and within a gender, it is crucial to examine how masculinities are shaped in relation to femininities and in relation to other masculinities. American anthropologist Stanley H. Brandes, for example, argues that even if women are not physically present or reflected in men's thoughts, their "presence" remains a significant factor in men's perception of what it means to be a man.[8]

As men do not constitute a homogenous, internally coherent gender, certain masculinities are subordinated by the practices and discourses of hegemonic ones. R. W. Connell maintains that at any given time, one form of masculinity is culturally exalted over others. Yet, this fact does not necessarily entail that the "most visible bearers of hegemonic masculinity are always the most powerful people. They may be exemplars [...] or even fantasy figures." However, "hegemony is likely to be established only if there is some correspondence between cultural ideal and institutional power, collective if not individual." The majority of men (who may or may not display the characteristics of hegemonic masculinity) have an interest in supporting hegemonic masculinity in that they benefit from the overall subordination of women; the benefits of this "patriarchal dividend" can be translated into terms of "honor, prestige, and the right to command," as well as into material wealth and political power. Hence the support of hegemonic masculinity is a means of defending their dominant social position vis-à-vis women.[9] Scholars have shown that masculine subordination may be the product of class, race/ethnicity, or sexual orientation, but if, as psychologist Frank Pittman so succinctly puts it, "masculinity is different for each generation,"[10] it is also necessary to examine how masculinity is constantly being fashioned, challenged, modified and reaffirmed from one generation to the next.

The term *muru'a* is perhaps one of the more complex and elusive concepts in Arab culture. The list of the qualities of *muru'a*, detailed in the opening quotes to this chapter, was enumerated first by Fitna, the female protagonist of Nu'man 'Abduh al-Qasatli's (1854–1920) serialized novel *Riwayat Murshid wa-Fitna* (*A Novel about Murshid and Fitna*, 1880–1), and then by Hind, a minor female figure in the novel. The term can be found in almost any dictionary entry or scholarly article discussing *muru'a* since it was first consolidated among Arab tribes in the *jahiliyya* (pre-Islamic) period. While the nuances of this pre-Islamic concept underwent significant modification in the intervening centuries, the concept itself retained much of its persuasive powers well into the nineteenth century. Scholars concur that it is a conjunction of two elements; it describes the sum of the ideal physical qualities of a man (such as strength, bravery, fortitude, military prowess, and leadership abilities) and his moral virtues (such as loyalty, chastity, dignity, politeness, hospitality, compassion, religious observance, resolve, truthfulness and generosity).[11] In both instances the women address their comments to their main love interest, Murshid, a young man seeking to carve out a position in society. The two young women and Murshid's father are constantly exhorting and advising him on how he should proceed on his quest for distinction and fame. The path they chart for Murshid is the path of *muru'a*.

In the Arabic novels written during the second half of the nineteenth century, two models of masculinity, an older generation's and that of a younger generation, competed for hegemony. Perhaps unsurprisingly, given that the authors were in their 20s and 30s, the younger generation's version of masculinity emerged victorious. The authors posited two paths or modes to the victory of modern Arab masculinity: a "revolutionary," confrontational mode, and an "evolutionary," sequential one. In the first, the two generational models of masculinity are at odds with each other: they collide, clash, and eventually the younger generation's version triumphs. In the second mode, the younger generation's version also prevails, but the two generational models partially overlap. They are positioned on the same continuum, where the more recent model is seen as a modified, updated, version of older ones, and draws mainly on the logic of *muru'a*. The texts we discuss here demonstrate that in order to mitigate the anxiety produced by this struggle, these novelists took up the primordial concept of *muru'a* in their novels, imbued it (explicitly and implicitly) with a new gender significance and posited it as the model for modern Arab masculinity. Concomitantly, they deployed the figure of the young "new woman" as a vehicle to enable this shift to a modern masculinity.

This unfolding of a modern Arab masculinity is best seen in the plots of several novels and novellas written by the three leading novelists of the *Nahda* over a period of 20 years. These include Salim al-Bustani's (1846–84) *Asma* (1873), *Bint al-'Asr* (*Daughter of the Age*, 1875), *Fatina* (1877), *Salma* (1878–9), and *Samya* (1882),[12] Nu'man 'Abduh al-Qasatli's (1854–1920) *al-Fatat Amina wa-Ummuha* (*The Faithful Young Woman and her Mother*, 1880), *Riwayat Murshid wa-Fitna* and *Riwayat Anis* (*A Novel of Anis*, 1881–82),[13] and Jurji Zaydan's (1861–1914) *Jihad al-Muhibbin* (*The Lovers' Struggle*, 1893).[14] All these novels written by the first generation of young Arab novelists were originally published in serialized form in two of the leading journals of the period, *al-Jinan* (Beirut: 1870–86) and *al-Hilal* (Cairo: 1892–).[15] They were an integral part of a much larger debate concerning the impact of modernity, scientific knowledge, emerging proto-national sentiments, and the role of women in modern society.

Although the discourse regarding women and femininity was carried out openly in both non-fictional and fictional texts, views and reflections concerning men and masculinity were overwhelmingly expressed in fictional texts. While these novels have been studied previously, as most have not been reissued in book form they have remained the domain of literary scholars. These scholars, who have focused mainly on the female characters, often view the early novels as a milestone on the path of the development of twentieth-century modern Arabic novels, and do not consider them to have great intrinsic value.[16] Thus, these early texts have not yet been examined as a site for the construction or renegotiation of masculinities.

Nevertheless, other scholars have adopted an approach that considers fictional texts as a key to the mindset of a time and place. For example, inspired by Benedict Anderson, who pointed to the continuities between nation-building and the print communities formed around newspapers and novels, Doris Sommer used nineteenth-century Latin American romance novels to explore the formation of national ideologies and their role in national consolidation. In a similar fashion, Afsaneh Najmabadi examined the ways in which central concepts of Iranian modernity were gendered in a range of cultural texts (including newspaper articles, novels and paintings) from Qajar Iran (1785–1925). We too approach these novels as historical tools that enable us to reconstruct the contours of this gender discourse and re-evaluate its significance for modern Arab gender relations.[17]

The juxtaposition of these fictional texts reveals a complex generational gender discourse in which masculinity and femininity were reworked. We point out the nuances in the novelists' views on gender and its form and function in a modern Arab society, which were mostly absent or obscured in non-fictional texts. We demonstrate that a re-visioning of masculinity and the role of the "new man" lay at the heart of their literary project. It was both embedded as a subtext within the discourse of femininity and the "new woman," and stood on its own (in *Riwayat Murshid wa-Fitna*). Studying these texts not only adds to the scholarship examining the ways in which Arab men themselves responded to the twin challenges of modernization and feminism, but enables readers to consider the ramifications of the regional and class variations of masculinity on the study of gender in Arab societies in the nineteenth and early twentieth century.

The Novelists and *Muru'a*

Salim al-Bustani, Nu'man 'Abduh al-Qasatli, and Jurji Zaydan were the leading novelists of the *Nahda* period and members of a vibrant and influential intellectual circle in Beirut. Al-Qasatli, one of the period's least studied intellectuals, was born in Damascus and raised in Beirut, although he divided his time as an adult between the two cities. He was al-Bustani's protégé and had a brief but significant literary career; besides the three novels examined here, he also published two other important works: a history of Damascus and a travelogue of Syria and Palestine. His contemporary, Jurji Zaydan, started out as journalist and war correspondent and later founded and edited *al-Hilal* (*The Crescent*) in 1892. His literary *oeuvre* ranges from 23 novels (all, save one, historical novels), two monumental histories, and numerous journal articles.[18]

All these social novels ostensibly involve the marital choices facing a young woman, the main character, whose name most often figures prominently in novel's title. All these young heroines are beautiful, virtuous and highly educated and put greater store in virtue and merit than in inherited wealth and social status. Al-Bustani's Asma seems to have served as a prototype for these heroines. Not only does she embody the spirit of her age (*ruh al-'asr*), but she is also described as beautiful, honest, modest, humble, non-materialistic and loyal. She is educated in the arts and sciences and well-read (*al-mar'a al-'aqila*), but she is also well-versed in the domestic arts. Very similar qualities are attributed to Amina, the heroine of al-Qasatli's *al-Fatat Amina wa-Ummuha*.[19] These young women are at an important crossroads in their lives and must decide which young suitor to marry.

In many of the novels, the young women's parents (especially their mothers) attempt to convince their daughters (at times by physical force) to marry the men they would have chosen, or men with whom marriage had been contracted in childhood.[20] These "unsuitable suitors" favored by the older generation are wealthy and have considerable social standing but conceal numerous vices. Some are prone to gambling or have fallen into bad company, while others have been seduced by the wiles of the West, mainly by new ideologies (such as the radical socialism espoused by Fa'iz in al-Bustani's *Samya*), or have adopted the repugnant and superficial aspects of "Western culture" such as materialism, greediness, ostentatious clothing, grandiose homes and carriages, ballroom dancing, and lighthearted conversation (Badi' in al-Bustani's *Asma* and Anis in *Bint al-'Asr*). The illustrations in al-Bustani's *Asma* also portray this "unsuitable suitor" as an effeminate dandy. It is important to note that it is not merely the "unsuitable suitor's" acquisitiveness or modern ideas that make him an inappropriate partner, but rather the fact that he has not tempered or balanced them with what the authors see as "Arab" ones, such as charity and true scholarship.

While the older generation is dazzled by these suitors' wealth and rank, their daughters see through this guise and favor the less wealthy but virtuous and educated (at times professional) young men. In al-Qasatli's *al-Fatat Amina wa-Ummuha*, for example, the older generation is represented by Amina's mother, who is described as impudent, selfish, cruel, ruthless, and insulting. She gossips about trivial things, and is totally oblivious and uncaring with regard to her daughter's wishes; worse, she is described as careless with her daughter's honor (*'ird*). When Thabit, the young lover, expresses his frustration at her interference, he sets her up as representative of the entire older generation, and accuses them of failing to understand "the spirit of modern times" (*al-tamaddun al-'asri*) and not recognizing the "personal rights of the fair sex" (*huquq al-jins al-latif al-shakhsiyya*). While Thabit accuses Amina's mother of interfering and insensitivity to her daughter's feelings, he also perceives her behavior as an insult to his honor, and even goes so far as to say that despite his love for Amina there are limits to his ability to accept her mother's behavior.[21] Once again, al-Qasatli did not depict a simple dichotomy between the supposedly more "traditional" values of an older generation and the "modern" values of a younger generation; rather he praised the individual who consciously adheres to "good" Arab values.

Although the path to true love is never straightforward and the lovers have to struggle to overcome a series of melodramatic obstacles to be united, either in a happy marriage or in death, the authors highlight the social price the young women often have to pay for their choice (an issue we shall return to in Chapter 6). Al-Qasatli's Amina is imprisoned by her mother and denied food and water until she relents; al-Bustani's Fatina is almost driven to madness, whereas Zaydan's Salma (in *Jihad*) has her reputation sullied. These young women and their struggles have a generational significance. They are not just struggling for their own personal happiness, but for their own and future generations' freedom and happiness, and as such are willing to sacrifice their lives to advance their cause. During her imprisonment Amina boldly states: "my death will be of great service to the young men and women of my beloved homeland (*watan*) ... and history will mark my passing with honor."[22]

The "unsuitable suitor," as described by the novelists, is almost a grotesque caricature of the kind of man and masculine qualities supposedly favored by the older generation. It is difficult to believe that the readers of these journals (in which the novels appeared), who read and heatedly debated scientific theory, women's rights, and the merits of different philosophers, would find such a stock character credible, unless something in this stock character (and its counterpart) struck a chord in the hearts and minds of the growing reading audience, many of whom were young men and women from the urban middle classes.[23]

Even a brief glance at the other pages of these two journals (*al-Jinan* and *al-Hilal*), as well as other journals reveals that the difficulties of young marriageable men who lacked sufficient funds to pay the ever-rising bride-price demanded by prospective in-laws were a common topic of discussion during this period. For example, in *Lisan al-Hal* (1877–1959), another leading newspaper, a letter which appeared in late June 1894 generated an intense two-month debate with responses appearing until late September. The letter deplored the avariciousness of young women (and their parents) who craved a wealthy future husband who would enable them to live a life of idleness and luxury. Historians have indeed shown that "ordinary men were encumbering increasing amounts of money to 'marry up' to women from families whose daughters would bring a 'dowry' of social prestige and connections."[24]

While the readers who carried out a lively debate on the journal pages clearly sympathized with young marriageable men, the focus of their displeasure was young women, whom (they believed) had to be taught to reject wealth and material goods. In countless letters and articles to the journals of the period they described their ideal young woman. This woman bears an uncanny resemblance to the heroines of the social novels. For example, in an article by Fathallah Jawish concerning "Woman in Human Society," he describes such an ideal young woman in great detail, crowning her "the sovereign of the house" (*hakimat al-bayt*) and the "pillar of human society" (*qiwam al-hay'a al-ijtima'iyya*).[25]

Other readers argued that young men also shared the blame for this deplorable situation: "You want her father to educate her as a *femme de salon*, and then demand [. . .] that she be a good housewife (*imr'at al-bayt*)."[26] This recurring concern that undue Western influences, symbolized by a superficial education (a few phases in foreign languages, tinkling on the piano, dancing, and reading foreign novels) would undermine the basis of Arab society hints at the underlying anxieties accompanying the encounter with modernization and the West. This unease was expressed in concerns about changing gender roles and the potential loss of one's cultural uniqueness to a foreign culture.

Up to this point, young women were positioned by the novelists and the journals' readership as both the symbols and preservers of Arab society and heritage. The role of men, in particular those of the younger generation, remained unarticulated. It is thus unsurprising that historians have not dealt with the discursive modes of Arab masculinity in this early period. One author, al-Qasatli, however did rise to the challenge and attempted to formulate quite explicitly what the model of masculinity for a new generation of Arab men should be.

Although al-Qasatli used the term *muru'a* in both his other novels, the clearest and most detailed expression of the concept is found in *Riwayat Murshid wa-Fitna*. The novel is set among the Bedouin tribes in the rural areas of nineteenth-century Greater Syria[27] and concerns the romantic trials and tribulations of two young couples, Murshid and Fitna, and May and Huwaydil. In the brief frame-story the elderly Murshid sits and reminiscences about his exploits as a young man, his quest for leadership and love. Murshid is the son of the leader of his tribe (*shaykh*), yet despite his prominent position he seeks to establish his own reputation to deserve the leadership position which will eventually be his. One day while herding, Murshid meets Fitna, a young girl from a rival tribe, and is attracted to her bravery as much as to her beauty and innocence.[28] Overcoming parental disapproval, previous marriage engagements, conniving rivals, and death-defying encounters the two eventually marry.[29]

This convoluted plot aside, the novel's main concern is to define what qualities Murshid should embrace in his quest to be a man of *muru'a*. The first to kindle Murshid's desire for fame and distinction is his father, who stresses that before a young man from a distinguished family can marry he must prove his military prowess (*ghazu*), heroism (*'aza'im*), and horsemanship.[30] However, only after meeting Fitna while herding the sheep does Murshid go off to try and be a fearless hero (*sanadid al-rijal*). Fitna is described as bright, beautiful, strong and healthy, and as a person who speaks intelligently about practical and serious matters (e.g. the natural world and Arab heritage and history), contrary to the idle talk of city-women.[31] In the course of their first conversation, in one of the most crucial sections of the novel, Murshid inquires about his reputation and standing among "the daughters of the Arabs"; when he hears that he has none as yet, Murshid swears upon the *Zamzam* (the sacred spring) and the *Ka'ba* that he will set out on a quest to gain fame.[32] Upon hearing of this quest, Fitna berates him and says:

> Shepherding is inappropriate for a man, as it does not generate distinction (*shuhra*) resulting from courage (*jasara*), or physical feats (*iqdam*), or valor (*batsh*), of which a man may boast, especially if he was of noble birth (*sayyid al-qawm*) and inherited honor (*sharaf*) from his father and his forebears.[33]

Fitna's role in goading Murshid into action mirrors the social approbation of these actions, and imbues them with value (by eventually choosing him as her husband). Goading was an important role played by Arab women in the *jahiliyya* and the early Islamic period. Through poetry and songs of praise they urged men into battle (and cursed their enemies), sang of their glorious deeds and passed on these values to future generations. Fitna enjoins Murshid to go in search of fame, and promises that "the daughters of the Arabs will view it as *muru'a*" and will "elevate you to a high position."[34] The fact that Fitna has already distinguished herself through her acts of bravery, which are retold by the elders in the tribal council (*majlis*), further prompts Murshid into action and kindles his desire to win her hand in marriage. In the following pages, Murshid goes off to raid other tribes and though wounded in battle he demonstrates great bravery. He avenges the death of his brother, helps a widow and her orphaned child, and eventually acquires great wealth. It is only then, after proving himself worthy, that Murshid can win Fitna's hand in marriage.[35]

Lest his readers assume that these values were appropriate and applicable only in a rural, Bedouin society, al-Qasatli made use of *muru'a* in another novel published that year, entitled *al-Fatat Amina wa-Ummuha*, that takes place in an urban setting. The imprisoned Amina has asked her sister Da'd to pass a letter to Thabit, the young man she loves. In order to identify Thabit (whom she knows only by his letters to her sister), Da'd openly asks Thabit: "Are you the virtuous (*muru'a*) one, the noble (*shahama*) one, the principled one?"[36] In his later novel, *Anis*, al-Qasatli does not resort to such an overt use of the term, but it is implicitly present throughout. Anis (a merchant) and his friend Adib (a military officer) are educated and have earned their social position through merit and hard work; they are described as principled, steadfast, truthful and sensitive to their beloveds' wishes. Their rivals are full of vices and are intellectual dilettantes. The rivals rely upon tradition (e.g. marriage between cousins) and the backing (perhaps even enforcement) of the older generation in the hope that through their intervention they will marry.

As far as we have been able to discern, only two women novelists toward the end of the period made explicit use of the term *muru'a*: the feminist writer and intellectual Zaynab Fawwaz (1846 or 1850–1914) in her novel *Husn al-'Awaqib aw Ghada al-Zahira* (*Good Consequences, or Ghada the Radiant*, 1899) and author and journalist Labiba Madi Hashim (1882–1952) in her novel *Qalb Rajul* (1904). In both novels *muru'a* is invoked by the authors as a manly quality elicited to protect the defenseless, especially women. In Fawwaz's novel, when Shakib, one of the leading characters, finds out about his cousin's (Tamir) dishonorable behavior towards their mutual cousin the Princess Fari'a, he exclaims in horror: "Where is his *muru'a*? Where is his consideration? Where are his *shahama* and the honor of his ancestors?" Shakib is shocked that Tamir behaved in such a dastardly fashion towards a cousin whose honor and protection he has been entrusted to protect, and regards such a disregard of family honor (*al-sharaf al-'a'ili*) as an earth-shattering event.[37] As both of these novels were set during the sectarian strife in the 1860s in Mount Lebanon, when women were highly vulnerable, the authors' invocation of the term is perhaps unsurprising. These women authors, however, use the term to depict a form of male attentiveness or sensitivity to women, but they do not deploy the term or develop their use of it, and they certainly do not invoke it as a blueprint for appropriate male behavior.

Another male author who set his novels among the emerging urban bourgeoisie but made an implicit appeal to the values of *muru'a* was Salim al-Bustani. In his novel *Asma* he provides a clear indication of the contemporary Arab location of the action, yet here as well the qualities of *muru'a* are invoked indirectly. The novel's main male character Karim, a wealthy merchant from Baghdad who comes to Beirut, is also on a quest. It may not be framed in Murshid's pre-Islamic terms of military prowess (*ghazu*) and heroism (*'aza'im*), but it remains nonetheless a quest to establish his independent standing as a merchant and his reputation as virtuous man (which here also is validated by a woman's choice). Karim is pointedly described as "not handsome" but in possession of "good qualities." He is intellectually curious, compassionate, hard-working, honorable, and seeks to associate himself with people who share his values. Although wealthy and a member of a highly respected family, he is not materialistic and in fact conceals his true social status until the novel's end, since he wishes to be chosen (by Asma) on the basis of his character and not his wealth, and indeed in his first meeting with Asma she immediately recognizes his true nature. In this novel, Asma's parents approve of her marital choice, despite the fact that their business partner has long assumed that the two families' relationship will be cemented by their children's marriage. Thus they demonstrate their preference for the characteristics of modern *muru'a* (which at times bears much similarity to middle-class values) over those of an older model that emphasized wealth and birth.

In these novels, in particular those of al-Qasatli, readers are presented with an "old-new" view of masculinity; masculinity was not an aggregate of essentialist qualities a human male was born with, and becoming a man did not merely mean attaining adulthood. Rather, the active and conscious pursuit of *muru'a* makes a true man. In essence, al-Qasatli seems to have been articulating a rather modern argument, which to rephrase de Beauvoir may be expressed as "One is not born, but rather becomes, a man." For al-Qasatli to have suggested that "oppressed" or "backward" women were in need of reform was one matter, as men remain as though unmarked by gender (and hence normatively human). But to suggest that men themselves were in need of reform (and hence are implicitly marked by gender) was another matter altogether. Such a man achieves manhood not merely through his family's fortune and name but by cultivating good qualities of character and advancing through merit. By articulating this modern model of an Arab masculinity through the age-old concept of *muru'a*, al-Qasatli adhered to the *Nahda* intellectuals' project of reshaping their "traditional" society and transforming it into a more "open" or "advanced" and egalitarian one, but not through imitation. This transformation cannot be completed just by women; men must play an active role as well.

Al-Qasatli's demand echoed earlier hints by other writers for masculine reform. For example, in an 1877 article entitled "Husband and Wife," Salim al-Bustani argued that if a woman remains uneducated her husband will lose interest in his family and seek pleasure elsewhere, such as many married men did in the packed coffeehouses of Beirut of his day. He claimed that this situation was indicative of the worsening state of marital life. He did not lay the blame solely on women, however, but argued that men also bore a responsibility. Citing extensively from an anonymous article written by a woman who "wonders" at the absence of articles concerning men's behavior, al-Bustani suggested that perhaps men should demand the same kinds of reforms (in character and behavior) from themselves that they demand from women; namely, "the patience of Job, the wisdom of Solomon, the generosity of David, and the strength of Samson."[38]

However, al-Qasatli and others insisted that this transformation should not be achieved through a wholesale adoption of "Western" models of gender, which could unmoor individuals (men and women alike) from their families and their familial responsibilities. In a rare article entitled "Women and Our Laws," published in 1882, al-Qasatli explicitly expressed his views regarding the social and political roles of men and women. Despite men's and women's biological differences, al-Qasatli acknowledged their shared humanity and virtue and viewed their roles as complementary. Al-Qasatli approved of women's educational rights, and recognized their important social role as mothers and educators; he also granted them some economic rights (as petty traders). While he was adamant that women should never be treated as menial servants, he insisted that they must not forget their duties to men, and thus rejected full political membership in society. He claimed it was inappropriate at that time to grant them full political rights, and expressed concern that such equality would diminish men, and set women up as men's opponents rather than retain them as supportive and encouraging allies.[39] Thus once again the implicit topic of an article devoted ostensibly to women and their rights was men and their role in a modern Arab society.

Other journalists and intellectuals voiced very similar arguments in their writings in the journals and newspapers of the period. For example, one reader, Yusuf Afandi Shalhat, who was very mildly supportive of women's education, claimed that: "if we look at what has happened in the West, we see that women's rights have diverted them from their duties, which are home management and child-rearing." Even author Wadi' al-Khuri, who came closest to supporting women's political rights, viewed them ultimately as a means through which women would truly be able to fulfill their roles in the family, as mothers in charge of educating their children and as partners and "true supporters" of their husbands.[40] Thus, in these articles (and a host of others) published over three decades, the authors insisted time and time again that a social compromise had to be reached that would preserve men's leading role in society, but at the same time afford women greater personal freedom (e.g. choice in marriage) and rights (e.g. education). The authors and intellectuals were highly conscious of the socio-political impact of their writings and deliberately set out to impress their vision of a new society on the minds of their young readers. In the closing pages of *Anis*, for example, al-Qasatli stated that he wrote the novel "so that young men and women [will be able] to differentiate between good and bad."[41]

***

In this chapter we demonstrated that in the Arabic novels of the *Nahda* two competing models of masculinity struggled over the hearts and minds of their readers, and that the younger generation's version emerged victorious. In a bold stroke of imagination they suggested that one path to this victory was the path of *muru'a*. Second, by articulating their new masculine model along the lines of *muru'a* they both mitigated the anxiety which may have accompanied such a struggle, and adhered to their principle of distinguishing between modernization and Westernization. Their vision was of a modern society that selected from among both Arab and Western norms and mores, discarding the unwanted and outdated, but did not subordinate one to the other. Thus while the process did raise concern (perhaps even consternation), it was not viewed as something to be feared. In their attempt to formulate a "new," modern masculine role, they harked back to the "old" morals and masculine values of the pre-Islamic period as a potent source of revitalization of Arab society. By imbuing *muru'a* with both ancient and modern meanings, they shaped it into a vibrant and attractive model for the sons of the rising middle class.[42]

The significant social and economic changes in the second half of the nineteenth century in Greater Syria, which propelled the new urban middle classes to prominence and witnessed the rise of a wide range of new professions and occupations (teachers, lawyers, doctors, journalists, and entrepreneurs), necessitated a reshaping of both class and gender identities. As in other places, the novel became an important site for the reworking of these new gender identities and the re-establishment of the home and family as a private sphere shared by like-minded virtuous men and women.[43] However, by calling for a reworking of masculinity and femininity, the writers and intellectuals of the *Nahda* were also calling attention (perhaps unconsciously) to the social construction of gender. If men themselves were in need of reform, if masculinity was something that had to be acquired and cultivated, it could no longer remain unmarked. This may explain why so many of the authors (of the novels and the journal articles) chose to embed their comments and views on men and masculinity within a discourse on the reform of women's rights and education.

The authors and intellectuals of this early period deployed the figure of the young "new woman" as a vehicle to facilitate this move from one masculine model to the next. These novelists employed marriage plots that involve a daughter's perseverance regarding her marital choices, at times even rebelling against (although not openly disobeying) her parents' choice of husband. They celebrated not only the daughter's triumph but the success of her favored virtuous suitor, who overcomes the machinations of his virtue-less rival and the objections of the tradition-bound older generation. The young woman was the arbiter between these two competing models and her decision validated the model based on virtue and merit (*muru'a*). Thus, the struggle for women's independence and rights turns out in fact to be a struggle for the independence and privileges of a younger generation of men.

This examination of the rearticulating of one model of modern Arab masculinity reveals the highly flexible, perhaps even "protean" nature of hegemonic manifestations of gender. While the emerging hegemonic models of masculinity (and femininity) discussed are clearly prescriptive and not descriptive, they reinforce Connell's argument that "hegemony is likely to be established only if there is some correspondence between cultural ideal and institutional power, collective if not individual." The socioeconomic changes, the rise of the urban bourgeoisie and the exchange of ideas and ideologies necessitated the updating or remodeling of the dominant model of masculinity. Although individual members of a society need not actively identify with this model, "the hegemonic must continually evolve so as to recuperate alternative hegemonies."[44] By adopting and even embracing some of the new demands made by Arab women of the upper and middle-classes (regarding marital choice, education, and the importance of motherhood), the potentially destabilizing effect of the demand for women's rights may have been contained.

Thus the (implicit or explicit) discourse concerning the "new man" which first emerged in Greater Syria during the middle of the *Nahda* period (1870s–90s) or even before, may have predated a similar one, which several scholars suggest appeared only later in Egypt. Mona Russell, for example, argues that the discourse concerning the "new man" in Egypt emerged during the Urabi Revolt of 1880–1 and British invasion of Egypt which came on its heels.[45] "The revolt," she claims, "was about the New Egyptian Man, and the resulting occupation brought about his emasculation." Elizabeth Thompson, who examined later gender discourse in Syria and Lebanon during World War I and the Mandate period (1920s to late 1940s), argues that a similar sense of emasculation or crisis in masculinity occurred only much later.[46] However, in Greater Syria the emergence of the discourse on the "new man" (in the 1870s–90s) seems to have been a response to significant socioeconomic changes and modernizing impulses and was not the result of direct colonialism or an emerging discourse on nationalism.

This suggests that in the future scholars need to pay close attention to the articulation of gendered identities within literary texts (here, novels) and keep a close eye on regional gender differences which are the product of very different historical contexts, and not gloss over them. In this chapter, we focused on the formulation of an Arab masculinity in a new-old form within the novels of the period, and we stressed the necessity of integrating the study of literary texts into the study of gender history, as these texts provide invaluable information and insights into the complex working of an emerging gender discourse on femininity and on masculinity. Studying the novels of a place and time known for the scarcity of personal primary sources (diaries, autobiographies and letters) expands our data sources far beyond the traditional ones (such as the records of the *shari'a* courts) used for the study of gender. Clearly there was no monolithic "Arab masculinity" or "Arab man" in the historical discourse of the past, just as there was no one model of "Arab femininity" or "Arab woman." What can be found are traces of competing models of masculinities and femininities struggling for hegemony. As the identity-formation processes of masculinity and femininity are so closely intertwined, any historical discourse revolving around a "new man" or a "new woman" is sure to reflect its hidden counterpart.

CHAPTER 4

"LIKE A PLANET WITHOUT A STAR":[1] THE GLOCALIZATION OF DOMESTIC DISCOURSE

In the winter of 1893, Salma al-Nawfal sent a brief humorous sketch to *al-Fatat* (*The Young Girl*), one of the leading women's journals of the period. It tells of a married man who asked his wife to sew back a button which had fallen off his shirt; the wife, however, was far too engrossed in her books, as she was preparing for her medical board exams. The wife suggested that he ask the nurse, the cook or the maid to help him out. The husband did as she suggested, but found the nurse far too absorbed in the study of astronomy, the cook in the midst of a chemical experiment, and the maid hurrying off to a suffrage meeting. The frustrated yet good-natured husband left home to place a newspaper ad for "an illiterate French maid." The newspaper editor laughed at him, saying that if such a woman could be found he would want her as his wife. The husband finally found a sympathetic tailor and told him about his adventures; the husband summed up his tale by saying (perhaps sarcastically): "Thank God we have reached a time when women compete with men in the field of knowledge and culture rather than being engrossed in pride, vanity and the lavishness of their dress."[2]

This seemingly trivial anecdote conjures up a series of deep-seated anxieties regarding the changing role of modern women in society and the home shared by many both in Europe and the Arab world; anxieties we wish to explore further. In previous chapters we argued that a key component of *Nahda* involved the encounter of Arab culture and values with those of the modern world and their reconciliation. While the *Nahda* intellectuals greatly admired Western ideas, culture, and technology they also felt a growing need to preserve the Arab heritage; the modernization of Arab society was not to be a mere imitation of the West, but one in which certain (selected) ideas and institutions from the West would be used as a tool to advance their society. The advancement of women and their new role in reshaping Arab society is a case in point. The disconcerting question remained how to foster such advancement without destabilizing Arab society; or, as our anecdote would have it, how does a society arrive at an intelligent and rational wife and mother, but one who is still capable and willing to sew on her husband's shirt button?

In her influential study of the American middle class, historian Mary Ryan stated that "a careful reading of nineteenth-century literature on femininity has revealed a significant escalation in the volume and intensity of domestic sentiments."[3] Domesticity, as a product of nineteenth-century middle class ideologies, was imbued with the values associated with rationality, order, efficiency, and science. These themes and values had to be translated into the practices of the daily domestic life of the middle class. The person entrusted with this interpretative project and seen as most suited to the ordering of home and family life was the wife and mother, who had to become the shining, warm, life-giving "star" around which revolved the social solar system, which included her family and society at large. The wife and mother now also had to face ever-increasing housekeeping standards: How often to wash and change the bed linen? How best to decorate and arrange the home? To what extent should a mother be involved in the education of her children? A woman was expected to know not only how to set a formal table and how (and whom) to entertain, but to understand how to convert this knowledge into maintaining her family's social status. Thus domesticity was also used as a means to create, define and police class boundaries.

This domestic discourse, which arose in Europe and North America, went global over the course of the nineteenth century though a series of cultural and economic exchanges and colonial relationships. Historians have devoted considerable attention to the variety of forms of domesticity during the nineteenth century in Europe, North America[4] and in the European colonies overseas.[5] Historians of the late nineteenth- and early twentieth-century Middle East have focused mainly on the practices and discourse of domesticity in turn-of-the-century Egypt.[6] While a few have noted the prominent role played by émigré writers, journal editors, and publishers from Greater Syria, their main focus has been to connect the discourse of domesticity to the emergence of an Egyptian national discourse. As less attention has been paid to the origins of this recently-arrived discourse in Greater Syria itself, it appears somewhat as a *deus ex machina*.

In order to make better sense of the historical emergence of the Middle Eastern domestic discourse, we turn to Edward Said's concept of "traveling theory." Said argued that the movement of ideas or theories from one culture, period, or situation to another is never unimpeded. When an idea "travels" to a new context it confronts a set of conditions that first enable the introduction of the idea and then negotiate its ultimate (full or partial) acceptance or rejection. Even if accepted, the end result is an idea that has been "to some extent transformed by its new uses, its new position in a new time and place."[7] This concept of the movement of ideas and texts in a global arena is strengthened by Stuart Hall's contentions in two landmark essays. He argued that although global mass culture has a homogenizing impact on local values, local culture plays an important role in reshaping global "imports." Hall maintained that global culture is a particular form of "capital" which can only "rule through other capitals, rule alongside and in partnership with other economic and political elites. It does not attempt to obliterate them; it operates through them."[8]

Thus, we view the domestic discourse emerging on the pages of the novels, journals and newspapers of Greater Syria in the second half of the nineteenth century as a hybrid, complex, processual, and dynamic cultural creation in which power relations were negotiated and re-inscribed, and which drew on multiple sources (both Arab and Euro-American) to constitute a unique discourse, albeit one which bore an outward resemblance to similar discourses emerging worldwide. Marwan Kraidy argued that "a critical hybridity theory considers hybridity as a space where intercultural and international communication practices are continuously negotiated in interactions of differential power." Thus, Kraidy suggests that "glocalization" is a far more flexible conceptual framework for researchers that enables them to depict the complexities of international cultural exchanges.[9]

Although one cannot deny the impact cultural mediators such as missionary women teachers must have had in introducing and transmitting a "Western" brand of domesticity to their Arab women students, Marilyn Booth, who engaged in a close reading of the biographies of many leading women writers and intellectuals, suggested that this "Western" brand of womanhood underwent significant modification. Students were appreciative of their teachers' educational efforts, but this did not necessitate the abandonment of an Arab education which was often supplemented in the home or after graduation. Elizabeth Thompson confronted a similar issue when considering the usage of the "private/public" terminology with regard to the Middle East. Thompson acknowledged that scholars' avoidance of "normative European categories that might distort local experience" makes good sense, but it "may also incur steep costs to historical understanding." Such avoidance or even rejection of universal categories may encourage cultural exceptionalism and essentialism, but more significantly it "denies the reality of transnational historical experience."[10]

Judith Walsh eloquently argued in her study of domesticity in colonial India that "by midcentury, domestic discourse no longer had a port of national origin, a national citizenship. It was a transnational creation, equally at home and equally foreign in England, America, Africa and India."[11] We concur and show that the same applies to the Middle East. We demonstrate that the domestic discourse as it first emerged in Greater Syria was first and foremost the product of a complex negotiation and interweaving of Arab notions concerning the management of the well-ordered household (*tadbir al-manzil*) and "Western" or Enlightenment notions of progress and technology, new bodily disciplines and middle-class femininity fostered by the rise of global consumer culture. Like other women worldwide (Europe and North America included), women in the Middle East had to learn and internalize the new values, practices and performance associated with domesticity. This domestic discourse was a product of the rise of the middle class and only much later did it become enmeshed with the discourses of nation or colonialism.

In order to focus on the discourse of domesticity in the late nineteenth-century Arab press, the era when the hybrid message of domesticity/*tadbir al-manzil* reached the middle-class households of Greater Syria through the print medium, we examine the prescriptive messages circulated by the novels and journals of the period. We first take a brief look at the ideal woman promoted in the early lectures of the cultural societies, and then engage in a thematic examination of domestic advice columns and articles which first appeared in *al-Muqtataf* (Beirut: 1876–84; Cairo: 1885–1914), *Thamarat al-Funun* (Beirut: 1875–1900), *Lisan al-Hal* (Beirut: 1878–1900) and later those of *al-Fatat* (1892–94) and *al-Hilal* (Cairo: 1892–1900).[12] We chart the contours of the new discourse concerning domestic health and hygiene, the spatial reorganization of the home, and the role women had in implementing both. We also examine the closely-related debate on Western fashions. We show that although women were encouraged to expand their social horizons through a variety of communal and familial activities, this expansion did not entail the crafting of independent identities or agendas.

Tadbir al-Manzil Meets the Ideology of Domesticity

Modern scholars studying the ideology of domesticity in late nineteenth-century Arab society have often paired domesticity with the Arabic term *tadbir al-manzil*. However, *tadbir al-manzil* is a centuries-old term that goes back to the medieval period when Muslim philosophers translated the Greek *oikonomia* (one of the three subdivisions of practical philosophy) into *'ilm tadbir al-manzil* (the science of household management). Texts by Islamic scholars such as al-Farabi (c.872–950/1), Ibn Taymiyya (1262–1328) and Ibn Khaldun's (1332–1406) *Muqaddima* (1377; also known as the *Prolegomena*) deal with the organization of the household and the roles of the various individuals within the household (the head of the household, wife, children, servants, etc.).[13]

Nineteenth-century discussions of *tadbir al-manzil* suggest that contemporary readers and writers also relied on *Oikonomikos*, the work of the second-century neo-Pythagorean philosopher Bryson.[14] This work was addressed to the man of the house and viewed the wife/mother at best as a helpmeet; it stressed that a woman's most important quality was her obedience to the wishes of the head of the household: "For he is the head over all the others in the household and all others follow and obey him."[15]

Khalil Ghanim's 1879 collection *Kitab al-Iqtisad al-Siyasi aw Tadbir al-Manzil* is another example of such texts concerning *tadbir al-manzil*. While most of the texts are devoted to the general economic development of the nation (imports and exports, taxation, banking, manufacturing concerns and their management, and how to increase business profits), there are occasional references to more specific issues such as the morality and usefulness of employing child labor and women's paid work outside the home.[16] Three years later, however, when the first *tadbir al-manzil* column appeared in *al-Muqtataf* in 1881, the term was much narrower in scope and referred to the home and its management. A summary of a later work on *tadbir al-manzil*, probably Jurjis Qusah's *Kitab Tadbir al-Manzil* (1889) found in *al-Fatat* suggests that this book dealt with the role of the wife and mother in the management of the home and family, and the implications of the well-ordered household on the well-being of the nation.[17] Thus in a rather brief period the meaning of the term *tadbir al-manzil* changed.

While it is difficult to recapture the lost world of the texts that served as sources for the domestic discourse in the early *Nahda*, fragmentary evidence does suggest that its scope was quite wide. Besides the Arabic texts mentioned above (which were cited by readers), only a few readers mentioned which foreign texts had influenced their discussions on domesticity/*tadbir al-manzil*. Some simply noted that "before writing" they "read books in English" and consulted "*Ifranji* books,"[18] while others made a passing reference to well-known texts such as the novels of the Countess de Ségur,[19] or to once-influential texts such as Dr Mary J. Studley's manual on health and hygiene for young girls.[20] Surprisingly, the more influential texts on domesticity and women's moral role, such as those written by Catherine Beecher and Isabella Beeton, were only mentioned in passing in the press, although it is quite possible that they had a greater influence. However, as discussed in Chapter 1, the intellectuals, authors and many of readers during the *Nahda* period were highly conversant with the works of the leading thinkers of their age, and had an in-depth knowledge of both Arabic and European literary, philosophical and historical texts. In fact, a variety of French texts from the Enlightenment and the post-Revolutionary periods seem to have been the other main sources of influence for the increasing importance attributed to women's roles in the home.

In 1894, for example, *al-Fatat* published a reading list suitable for educated women, both to satisfy their interests and intellectual curiosity and to steer them away from the immoral influence of cheap novels.[21] The list included novels such as Madame de La Fayette's *La Princesse de Clèves* (1678), Germaine de Staël's *Corinne ou l'Italie* (1807), George Sand's *La Petite Fadette* (1849) and *Marquis de Villemer* (1860), and works of poetry such as those of Marceline Desbordes-Valmore, Louisa Seifert, and Delphine Gay (de Girardin). Also included in the list were letters and memoirs, such as the letters of Madame de Sévigné to her daughter (1671–96) and those of Eugénie de Guerin, and the memoirs of Madame de Maintenon. A place of honor was given to educational treatises and tracts, such as Albertine Necker de Saussure's *L'education progressive* (1828) on women's education, and Pauline (de Meulan) Guizot's *L'education domestique ou lettres de famille sur l'education* (1823), which won Guizot her second prize for moral theory from the Académie Française, and to the work of women historians, such as Henriette Guizot De Witt's histories (for adults and children).[22]

Whether this list reflected the reading tastes of a miniscule set of women intellectuals or whether it was the product of a much broader intellectual consensus cannot be established with certainty; however, a closer examination of the names and works on the list provide some intriguing hints. Not only were many of the women authors highly educated and prolific writers, they also chose to write on "feminine" themes such as motherhood, family matters and female autonomy. Topics such as the relationship between mothers and daughters, sisters' influences on their siblings, mothers' educational influence on their children, and women's education in particular were the main subjects of the philosophical essays and the works of fiction and poetry. Other writers paid homage to the women intellectuals who preceded them; for example, poet Delphine Gay de Girardin (1804– 55) credited the influence of her female contemporaries Germaine de Staël, Claire de Duras and Marceline Desbordes-Valmore. The list also emphasized that motherhood did not conflict with intellectual endeavors (especially those geared towards strengthening the family) by selecting women writers who were the mothers or daughters of other women writers. For example, Delphine Gay (de Girardin) was herself the daughter of novelist Sophie Gay (1776–1852), whereas journalist and author Pauline (de Meulan) Guizot (1773–1837), the wife of historian and French politician François Guizot (1787– 1874), was the mother of historian and children's author Henriette Guizot de Witt (1829–1908). Thus, very subtly, the compiler of the list not only opined that wifehood and motherhood were not incompatible with a sustained engagement in an intellectual project, but also established intellectual as well as flesh and blood feminocentric lineages.

"Especially for the Members of My Sex":[23] The *Tadbir al-Manzil* Columns

The issue of women's (especially mothers') educational influence and women's education became important early on. The writers focused both on women's academic training and intellectual achievements and their practical domestic skills. In private letters, speeches delivered before assemblies of cultural societies, newspaper and periodical articles, intellectuals, writers and readers expounded their views on these issues. As early as January 1849 Butrus al-Bustani delivered *A Lecture on the Education of Women* to a meeting of the Syrian Society for the Acquisition of Sciences (*al-Jam'iyya al-Suriyya li-Iktisab al-'Ulum wal-Funun*). In his lecture, he advocated providing women with a broad and solid education to enable them to carry out their marital, maternal, and domestic duties for the benefit of their family, society and nation. However, he also bemoaned their lack of knowledge concerning domestic practices: "What do women know about raising children, the arrangement of the house or attending to the sick?"

Later in the lecture Butrus al-Bustani was quite explicit as to what he included under the broad title of "care of the home": cleanliness, needlework, cooking, and caring for the sick. Moreover, he advocated that women should receive formal schooling in these subjects "which many consider despised [topics]." Al-Bustani ended the lecture with a paraphrase of the well-known refrain that "the hand that rocks the cradle is the hand that rules the world."[24]

The novels and early articles dealing with the gendered impact of modernization and women's education did outline the characteristics of the educated, yet domestically-oriented, young woman and stressed her usefulness to social progress. However, they did not go into the details of the domestic arts she needed to master, or engage in an in-depth discussion of the newly-emerging standards of housekeeping and mothering. Such discussions were to be found in the *tadbir al-manzil* columns of journals and newspapers. These columns reasoned that a woman's role was not only to exert a civilizing influence on her family through her formal knowledge, but to ensure the smooth running of her household through her practical knowledge. Her main role was to establish order in the home and family, and through her good and rational care of them to ensure the peace and harmony of the household. It is through these activities (more than any other intellectual pursuits) that she derives her dignity and honor.

Perhaps unsurprisingly, given its scientific orientation, the first *tadbir al-manzil* columns emphasizing the scientific knowledge and rationality inherent in the role of housewife and mother appeared in *al-Muqtataf* in 1881.[25] For example, an early column, entitled "Soap and Water rather than Rouge and Cosmetics," outlined the new regime of bodily cleanliness and stressed the ties between an ever-vigilant mother and a disease-free home. The anonymous female author's professed goal was to teach "women how to keep their home and family clean." According to the author, the wife and mother charged with maintaining the health and hygiene of her family must recognize the importance of fresh air, clean water, and exercise in this project. The author claimed that while soap and water were readily available and inexpensive, "ignorant women" shun them precisely for that reason and rather than achieve a natural, clean and healthy complexion resorted to the use of rouge and white face powder. Two years later, another such column stressed the importance of a healthy and varied diet, adequate sleep, and seasonal clothing for the maintenance of family health.[26] These articles stressing domestic cleanliness and personal hygiene were supplemented by others dealing with the removal of stains from soiled clothes, silks, or leather gloves, how to wash marble floors, or the comparison of the qualities of various soaps.[27]

Just like household hygiene, cooking was invested with additional meanings beyond the functional ones. While food (and its preparation) became a medium thorough which a woman expressed her love and commitment to her family, dining and entertaining became a way to display the family's social and cultural capital. Some journal articles sought to enlighten housewives regarding the chemical composition of various foodstuffs and their nutritional properties; they extolled the virtues of olive oil and recommended the consumption of fresh fruits instead of sweetmeats. Other writers provided women with detailed recipes for salting beef and for preserving tomatoes and pears with sugar, and outlined the appropriate diet for the sick.[28]

Although the *tadbir al-manzil* columns appeared only from 1881 onward, one can find several earlier (and later) lengthy medical articles addressed to women, and often written by women (e.g. Yaqut Sarruf and Maryam Nimr Makariyus), explaining the workings of the human body (accompanied by detailed illustrations), refuting superstitions regarding childbirth and newborns, and arguing in favor of women studying medicine. These articles provided women with a broader, even scientific, understanding of the importance of their work within the home and family. Read together, such columns and articles suggest that, similar to Europe and North America, the belief in the notion of "scientific motherhood," i.e., that women required expert scientific and medical advice in order to raise their children and run their households, was rapidly gaining ground in Greater Syria as well.[29]

The debate concerning childrearing and children's education in Arab society was by this time centuries-old,[30] but new educational theories incorporating both the work of Enlightenment thinkers and nineteenth-century physicians were added into the mix. A growing number of the *tadbir al-manzil* columns as well as later articles such as those by Salim Kassab in *Lisan al-Hal* and those authored by women writers in *al-Fatat* were devoted to both children's and girls' education. Emphasizing that all education began at home, the authors devoted considerable attention both to the mother and to the values she should instill in her children. Her role as a filterer of correct information and behavioral norms was stressed; her responsibility was not merely to instill knowledge but to inculcate a moral code of behavior because "the child learns more in one year from his mother than he does over a period of years from his teacher." The mother was expected to select appropriate clothing for her children, feed them a healthy diet, and care for them when sick, but her most important function was to serve as a moral exemplar for her children. Salim Kassab for example stressed that girls, the mothers of the future, should receive a formal and structured domestic education; in essence he called for the establishment of classes in home economics.[31]

"The Little Kingdom over Which God Made You Queen":[32] Women and the Creation of a Modern Arab Home

The issues of home arrangement and organizing the family's routine and leisure activities also occupied the journals throughout the second half of the nineteenth-century, and numerous articles and columns discussed the changing physical appearance and organization of the modern Arab household and the shifting styles of daily living. These changes to the interior and exterior of family houses were the product of both an emerging modern Arab discourse of domesticity and an official project to rationalize the urban space in the large cities of Greater Syria and plan their expansion in advance following the *Tanzimat* (lit. re-ordering; 1839–76), the provincial reforms (1864) and the ensuing efforts at centralization and modernization.

During this period (in particular 1864–1918), countless municipal buildings, police stations and law courts, transportation hubs (tram and train stations) and grand private homes were built, new water and sewage systems were put in place and gas and electrical streetlights were installed. Old streets were enlarged and new ones were paved in the newer urban and suburban areas. Shopping, leisure and entertainment areas were planned, and would soon come to include department stores and marketplaces, hotels, coffeehouses, theaters, and parks.[33] In recent years, historians studying the architectural developments and changes to the major cities of Greater Syria such as Beirut, Aleppo, and Damascus,[34] as well as the major Ottoman centers such as Izmir and Istanbul,[35] and those of Egypt[36] have found increasing material evidence for these interior and exterior changes. As elite and bourgeois families began to move out of the courtyard houses into apartment buildings and suburban villas in the latter half of the nineteenth century, they increasingly adopted and combined old and new architectural features, furniture and decorative items. However, the social and gendered meanings of this reorganization of the interior domestic space, which went hand in hand with the architectural changes, have only received scant attention.[37]

Articles and columns discussing the changing social organization of the modern Arab household, the physical appearance of the house and the shifting styles of daily living occupied the middle ground between the grand philosophical articles extolling the moral and political role of the well-ordered household, and the nitty-gritty *tadbir al-manzil* pieces advising the housewife on the intricacies of stain removal. Only a handful of articles devoted themselves to outlining the spatial expressions of this tranquil and ordered household. These articles were extremely detailed; their authors walked the reader through the home and provided comprehensive explanations of the rationale behind the design and arrangement.

The best example of such an early article was written by Rujina Shukri, who told of visiting "a friend's house," which although clean and tidy, did not live up to her standards of household décor; thus, she proceeded to tell her readers how to better organize and decorate their homes.[38] Shukri emphasized to her readers that it was a woman's responsibility to turn her home into a tranquil and welcoming place and cautioned them that if the woman failed it ran the risk of becoming a place of desolation. Shurki acknowledged the limited finances at the disposal of many middle-class families, but claimed that the ideal house she was about to describe was the suitable abode for "ordinary people of the middle class."[39]

Rujina Shukri's characterization of the Beiruti middle-class home was one with "many rooms" (*ghuraf*) and her first recommendation that the woman of the house should assign different rooms for different activities (each with its appropriate furniture) suggests that she was referring to a new type of house. Jirjis Hamam, writing a few years after Shukri, also suggested that an educated and distinguished bourgeois family should have several rooms at its disposal, including a nursery, a guest bedroom and a kitchen.[40] The "central-hall house," as it came to be known, appeared in Beirut in the second half of the nineteenth century and was designed for the use of one nuclear family. With their red-tiled roofs and triple-arch windows, these houses that opened onto a front garden and the street were constructed in Beirut and the towns and villages surrounding it. In contrast to earlier residential styles, especially the traditional courtyard houses (the *dar* and the *hara*), where rooms were built around a central court, in the new "central-hall house" rooms were organized along a rectangular central hall.[41]

Shukri devoted considerable attention to the public portion of this central hall (the vestibule) and to the first public room it opened onto, the main receiving room or parlor (*ghurfat al-majlis*). Although relatively small, the vestibule should boast several multi-colored rugs, and paintings and prints should be displayed on the walls; for the comfort of guests waiting to be received, there should be several chairs and a large stand where they could deposit their walking-sticks, parasols and hats.[42]

Next came the main receiving room, or parlor, which historian Karen Haltunnen has described as situated between "the urban street where strangers freely mingled and the back regions of the house where only family members were permitted to enter uninvited."[43] As the main receiving room was both the first room guests would encounter and one which "reflects the skills of the woman of the house," it had to be appointed with great care and furnished with the best furniture and decorative items. Shukri once again provided precise directions for the décor and layout of this room, as well as a detailed list of the items to be displayed: flower arrangements, candelabras, chandeliers, handsomely bound books, carpets and light, airy curtains.[44] Archeological and architectural case studies of "central-hall house" interiors which served as vestibules and reception rooms have found evidence of the widespread usage of light green, pink and blue wall paint, stucco ornaments, cornices, *trompe-d'œil* paintings, decorated ceilings, mosaic tile or marble floors and glass windows.[45]

Shurki as well as other columnists also turned their attention to semi-private areas, such as the dining room and the library, and the private family rooms, such as the bedroom and the nursery. Like the reception room, the dining room became a place a woman could both demonstrate and enhance her family's wealth and cultural capital by displaying the china, the silverware and other table decorations correctly. Arguing that "the table is the mirror of the level achieved by the lady of the house (*rabbat al-bayt*)," Arab women were instructed on how to furnish their dining rooms, how to present food dishes, and columns devoted considerable attention to the setting of a formal dining table. They explained the fine points of dining etiquette, provided detailed instructions on how to create and decorate an epergne (a tiered centerpiece), and compared the older

الشكل الاول

الشكل الثاني

Figure 1   Sketch showing the appropriate table setting.
Source: Farida Hubayqa, "Adab al-Ma'ida," *al-Muqtataf* 9 (1884), p. 370.

service à la française with the virtues of the newer *service à la russe* (*al ma'ida al-Muskubiyya*).[46]

The parlor and the dining room became the main locations for events (or the planning of events) designed to foster the social and familial ties between bourgeois families. It was here that women enacted the emotional work needed to maintain these ties during visiting hours and afternoon teas and planned a host of social activities for leisure hours, such as outings to the beach, charity bazaars, and children's parties. These birthday parties (*'id al-awlad*) were new to middle-class households in Greater Syria, and were entrusted primarily to the organizational skills of the mother. While many cultures celebrated the birthdays of religious figures and secular rulers and coming of age ceremonies, celebrating "regular" middle-class children's annual birthdays become increasing popular during the nineteenth century. The anonymous author of a short 1894 article favored such parties as they instill a sense of importance in the child; however the author cautioned against over-spending and overindulging the young children with sweets.[47]

As books were noticeably present in all the rooms discussed (except for the dining room), it is clear that reading had become an important social activity cultivated by the Beiruti middle-classes, and one much preferred over idle card or backgammon games.[48] Thus, it is unsurprising that home libraries were increasingly present in descriptions of modern Arab homes. Contrary to the other rooms, however, few if any details are given as to how this room ought to be furnished. It is possible that in Beirut, as in Europe and North America, the library was considered a masculine space where a man retires after dinner to work or "read a newspaper or a novel."[49] Although a man's wife may have been welcome to join him occasionally and keep him company while he worked, it was not hers to leave an imprint on.

Similar to Europe and North America, Arab middle-class housewives had to create suitable home conditions to enable their husbands to recuperate from the hustle and bustle of work. Thus the writers put a premium on responding to the needs (and demands) of husbands and fathers for privacy and quiet after a day's work, and the home library/office was designated a male area, off-limits to the activities and the noise created by children and servants. The assignment of different rooms for different functions was not only "rational" and maximized each room's use; it also shielded the head of the household from the turmoil of housework and childcare, whereas the housewife had to resort to creative combinations of space and time to create "a room of her own."[50]

Last came the bedrooms (*ghurfat al-nawm*); these were supposed to cater both to the inhabitants' physical needs (such as sleep) and the emotional ones (to withdraw from the world and let one's guard down). Thus, they had to have a bed for each person, a washstand and a mirror, as well as a chest of drawers and a clothes closet. No less important, however, the bedroom had to be restful and pleasing to the eye; thus, a few pictures should be hung on the walls, a "nice rug" placed on the floor before a comfortable armchair and a side table with books on it. Other writers recommended separate rooms for younger and older children and urged mothers to see that the nursery was clean, sunny and airy, and maintained at a steady temperature.[51]

It is important to note the three areas in the house which were not described in great detail: the kitchen, the bathroom, and the servants' quarters. Given the great focus on bodily hygiene and clean and healthy food on the one hand, and the proper management of servants on the other, it is rather surprising that these areas were neglected. However, this may be the result of the on-going separation of the living and service areas. In traditional houses many service activities (such as cooking and laundry) took place outside the house (or on a different floor) and were carried out by servants belonging to a lower social class; this may account for the neglect of these areas in articles appearing in the periodical press. Given the known "invisibility of housework" and especially the "invisibility" of servants performing such work, perhaps such surprise is unwarranted. In the case of central-hall houses these activities were carried out both outside and on a different (housekeeping or mezzanine) floor. While this housekeeping floor is not mentioned in the press, it is found in certain houses that are still standing today, as well as in blueprints and photographs.[52]

These detailed descriptions of the organization of different rooms, their functions, and the items placed in them suggest that this spatial reorganization had a strong consumer and class aspect. In the Arabic periodical literature of the period, there was a marked increase in the number of advertisements for new consumer goods such as ready-made clothes, furniture, household goods and appliances, clocks and watches, pharmaceuticals, cosmetics, detergents, soap and chocolates, as well as services such as housekeepers, French and English teachers and piano instructors. With the opening of local merchandise depots (such as al-Kaff al-Ahmar and Makhzan Suriyya) and the launching of European department store outlets (such as Au Bon Marché and Le Grand Magasin au Printemps) at the turn of the century, these consumer desires could be amply satisfied.[53]

This consumer facet of the spatial reorganization of middle class houses in Beirut suggests that bourgeois men, and in particular women, were using these newly-acquired items and services to gain and broadcast their class status to the world. Historian Deborah Cohen has argued that for middle class Victorians such items (e.g. furniture, paintings, carpets, and curios) conferred status to such a degree that "things preceded identity; what you owned told others (and yourself) who you were." As domestic interiors and their personal bodies (dress) were two of the main sites where women could express their tastes, values, and class identities, perhaps it is no coincidence that the Arab periodical press of the late nineteenth century began to devote considerable attention to them and to advise women on how better to do so.[54]

All these columns and articles attest to the ongoing project of redrawing the interior of modern Arab homes and investing them with new social and gendered meanings. First, the columns attended to the emergence of the public areas of the home, often occupied by both female and male guests. They established the reception room and the dining room as spaces which a modern and educated, but respectable, woman could safely occupy and where she could demonstrate her family's status. They also called for shielding the home, and in particular the private rooms, from the outside world; fences, hedges, front gardens, shutters, windows and curtains created a visual and acoustical barrier between the outdoor noise, dirt and disorderliness, and indoor quiet, cleanliness and order. Taken together, both these features may be reflective of a shift from a home organized around a male–female principle to one organized around a public–private one.[55] Similar to Europe and North America, Arab middle-class housewives in Beirut had to create suitable home conditions to enable their men folk (in particular husbands) to recuperate from the turmoil of "a heartless world." The writers in the late nineteenth-century Beiruti press invested this spatial reorganization of the home with emotional and political meaning. As early as 1877 Salim al-Bustani stressed that an untidy, noisy and disorderly household would drive a married man away to seek the pleasures of the coffeehouse rather than spend time with his family. According to al-Bustani, this masculine abandonment of the domestic space had far-reaching consequences, as it was an indicator of the deteriorating state of the home and nation; conversely, readers could understand that strengthening familial bonds would also reinforce those of the nation and further the cause of *tamaddun dakhili*.[56] Thus, by preserving the tranquility and orderliness of her household, a woman could also ensure the wellbeing of her nation.

A good wife was not just one who kept a clean house and provided hot, tasty meals to a hungry husband, but rather one who was his friend and partner in life. "Don't serve him food as if he were at an inn, but sit by his side, be his friend and show interest in his affairs."[57] A woman's real task was to convert a house into a "pleasant and inviting" home, which would appeal to the men of the house and keep them away from the temptations of the "coffee-houses and casinos."[58] As women were encouraged to adopt and cultivate this "modern" conjugal ideal and were entrusted with accumulating and expressing their families' cultural capital, the journals and newspapers of the period were only too glad to guide them in their journey. At the same time, however, and sometimes on the same page, women were strongly cautioned against the excessive consumption of "foreign" goods (especially "Western" fashions) lest such intemperate spending lead to the financial ruin of their husbands and families and contribute to the economic deterioration of their nation.[59] Thus the locus of balancing between the "modern" or "Western" and the "Arab" was the home and the main burden of this balancing act was placed on women.

"Enslaved to Western Fashion": The Dangers of Western Fashion

This analysis of *tadbir al-manzil* columns and other articles on the topic indicates that writers and readers were fairly open to incorporating modern educational philosophies, ideas concerning household organization and management, and the values of bodily hygiene, cleanliness, exercise and healthy food. However, the incorporation of modern consumer items, and especially "Western" fashions, became a highly contested issue. In his early novella *Way...Idhan Lastu bi Ifranji (Alas...I Am Not a Foreigner*; 1859–1861) Khalil al-Khuri directed his attention (and ridicule) toward the increasing adoption of foreign manners and dining styles. The novella's protagonist, Mikhali, an Aleppo merchant affecting Western manners, wants to marry off his young educated daughter to Edmond, an Arab imposter posing as a foreigner. In order to impress the prospective suitor, Mikhali invites him home for dinner.

Mikhali stresses to his guest the importance of using a knife and fork and of serving coffee with milk, and he becomes increasingly annoyed when his wife fails to keep up appearances and neglects to serve the dinner courses in the "correct" order.[60]

As the years passed, however, the main focus of this critique was women's fashions. Writers readily expressed their views about women's dress both on the pages of the journals and in novels, and readers chimed in as well. For example, in al-Bustani's 1873 novel *Asma*, the novel's heroine Asma is fashionably, yet modestly, dressed (see Figure 2). Her counterpart (Badi'a) in contrast displays a far more revealing décolletage, and she is depicted as coquettishly wielding her fan (see Figure 3). Al-Bustani informed his readers that Badi'a's "entire focus is on clothes, luxuries, food, sweets, and sherbets." More importantly, she used make-up and "when she left her house it seemed that all her dress was for display."[61] Just in case the readers failed to understand Badi'a's true nature, al-Bustani likened the movement of her body and her trailing dress to the undulations of a snake across a floor "strewn with her father's money which has been deprived from the needy and the poor."[62]

Comments of a similar nature echo throughout his later novel, *Bint al-'Asr* (1875), another social novel devoted to the life and morals of the Arab bourgeoisie; al-Bustani acerbically describes Jamila's dress and comments that the frills and flounces of her dress alone "could sustain a poor family for two months and the dress itself for a whole year" and later expresses the fear she will waste all of her future husband's money by constantly buying new clothes in an attempt to keep up with fashions.[63] Such comments established the connection between women's excessive consumption of goods and social decadence, and gave voice to concerns that such intemperate spending could lead to the financial ruin of their husbands and families.[64]

Thus, similar to other writers, al-Bustani linked the love of finery and "Western" fashions with moral corruption. In the course of a party (*ma'duba*) attended by the protagonists, Majed and Jamila discuss at length the social impact of the newly-imported manners and fashions, especially Western women's fashions and ballroom dancing. Majed explicitly connects these two practices as they both draw unwarranted attention to a woman's body and in effect put it on

Figure 2   Asma, the heroine of the novel *Asma*.
Source: Salim al-Bustani, "Asma," *al-Jinan* 4 (1873), p. 29.

display for a male gaze and lead to licentiousness. Ballroom dancing affords women an opportunity to talk with (and undoubtedly be held and touched by) men they are not engaged to marry and with whom their families may even be unacquainted. This kind of behavior he says "may lead to matters I am unwilling to mention." While Majed does not disapprove of all imported manners and fashions, he argues that they have to be adopted discriminatingly, as not all are suited to the ideals of an Arab society.[65]

This issue also underlies later newspaper articles regarding clothes and fashion. Although ostensibly devoted to instructing women on how to achieve a neat and tidy appearance, their main concern remained how Arab women should incorporate "Western" fashions in a very selective manner.[66] Journal articles explicitly aimed to educate women how to match colors in a tasteful way, how to choose materials that can be washed easily, as well as how to choose clothes that enable a woman to move around and breathe easily.

أسما
(من قلم سليم افندي البستاني تام الترجمة الآتي)

بديعة

Figure 3   Badi'a, the villain of the novel *Asma*.
Source: Salim al-Bustani, "Asma," *al-Jinan* 4 (1873), p. 65.

Several articles concerning modern dress stressed it should be healthy and rational in contrast to the newly-imported "Western" fashions. The main "culprit" was the corset ("that infernal device") and its adverse impact on women's health, especially on their internal and reproductive organs (see Figure 4). For example, in 1896 in *al-Hilal* ran a detailed and illustrated article on the corset and its debilitative effects on the body's internal organs.

At the same time numerous articles decried women's alleged obsessive preoccupation with the latest fashions and the economic toll and moral consequences of such behavior.[67] These articles often associated women's love of finery with immodesty and women's fashion extravagances with debt and the financial weakening of the family and nation.[68]

Thus as long as the woman's consumption of services and goods was for the benefit of the family, it was viewed as benign; however, when this consumption was directed toward the woman herself, and

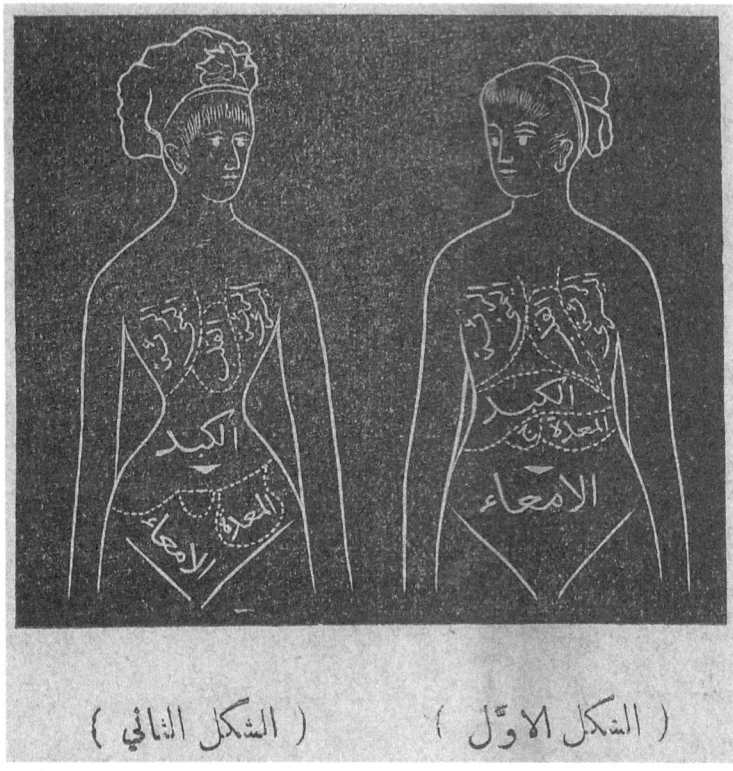

(الشكل الثاني)   (الشكل الأول)

Figure 4   Sketch showing the detrimental effects of the corset on the internal organs.
Source: Anonymous, "al-Mishadd," *al-Hilal* 5 (1896), p. 136.

her body in particular, it was viewed with increasing disfavor. In novels and journal articles, writers often conflated the desire for fashionable items of clothing with declining morals. Taken together with the pseudo-scientific arguments on the physiological and psychological inferiority of women (see Chapter 1), the writers' insistence that women's consumer energies be directed toward the family suggests they believed that unless these were channeled into domesticity they posed a threat to the social, moral and even sexual order.

The rhetoric of blaming women for the excesses of fashion was hardly a new phenomenon and was often accompanied by expressions of nostalgia for a simpler fashion. As early as his 1869 lecture, Butrus al-Bustani engaged in a general comparison between "Western" and Arab fashions, bodily practices, and food, and argued that the local, Arab practices were healthier and better suited to the local climate.[69] Later writers argued that the traditional Arab women's dress was not only more sensible as it enabled women to breathe and move with greater freedom, but was in many ways more "modern" than the cumbersome hoops, petticoats and corsets adopted by bourgeois Arab women seeking to emulate "Western" fashions.[70] Several of the leading intellectuals of the period, such as Ya'qub Sarruf, Hanna Kurani and Hannih Yanni (from Tripoli), 'Abd al-Basit Fathallah, as well as readers such as Shams Shahada (from Zhahle), repeatedly raised and discussed the threat of the rapidly growing consumer appetite for foreign goods (of which women were a symbol) to the local economy, as well as its social impact. These writers praised the importation of "Western" ideas and institutions, but argued that this came at a price; namely the backwardness of local manufactories, profits accrued mainly by foreign merchants, and the overreliance of Arab women on imported fashions.[71]

Hanna Kurani also argued that the decline of the East was the direct result of the decrease in exports and the preference for Western consumer goods over those produced in the East. She called upon all her readers (and women in particular) to cease this practice or else be forever "enslaved to Western fashion." Focusing in particular on the declining fortunes of the silk industry of Mount Lebanon, Kurani yearned for both a past and future time when "women will weave their family's garments with their own hands," and echoing Sarruf she expressed intense longing for the Phoenician period, when "the shores of Syria" teemed with "so many ships that the sea was invisible."[72]

Literary critic Svetlana Boym has argued that social (as opposed to personal) nostalgia is a defense mechanism that tends to appear in times of rapid changes or upheaval; it represents a desire "to obliterate history and turn it into private or collective mythology, to revisit time like space, refusing to surrender to the irreversibility of time that plagues the human condition." Indeed, Greater Syria was undergoing a series of rapid economic and social changes throughout the second half of the nineteenth century. Kurani's (and to a lesser degree Sarruf's) longings for an Eden-like past/future highlights the arguments of contemporary scholars of gender, who note the ways in which modernity was associated with masculinity while femininity was linked with the pre-modern, thereby making women "a symbol of non-alienated, and hence non-modern, identity."[73] Kurani's nostalgic sentiments positioned women as the key to this period; they needed to resist the tempting products and the comforts of modern life, as well as the personal freedoms and new social identities it offers. In essence, Arab women had to embody a model of modern domestic femininity while retaining an explicit link to the Arab past. Kurani's suggestion that Arab women use their domestically-oriented consumer activities both to re-establish "Syrian industries" (*al-sana'i' al-Suriyya*) and to demonstrate their "love and passion for the homeland" (*al-hubb wal-ghayra lil-watan*) anticipated the role that would be offered to women within the future national discourse as a "boundary and metaphorical limit" of the national body politic.[74]

***

Our examination of the domestic discourse as it emerged during the second half of the nineteenth century in Greater Syria, using Said's concept of "traveling theory," demonstrates that this discourse was the product of a complex interweave; it merged an earlier Arab discourse concerning *tadbir al-manzil* with "Western" or Enlightenment notions of progress and technology, new bodily disciplines and middle-class femininity fostered by the rise of global consumer culture. We showed that, like other women worldwide (and at the same time), women in the Middle East had to learn to internalize the new values, practices and conduct associated with domesticity; the end result bore an uncanny outward resemblance to the discourses and practices of domesticity emerging around the globe. However, a closer examination of the discourse on domesticity as expressed in the novels, journals and newspapers in Greater Syria also reveals the social context which changed and was changed by the "traveling theory" of domesticity. The Arab domestic discourse of the second half of the nineteenth century was a very "glocal" discourse, which became yet another site for the negotiation and reconciliation of Arab culture and values with those of the modern world. It was deployed both to stimulate local economic activity and consumerism and to establish the bourgeoisie's class boundaries, as well as to buttress the family as a value against competing "Western" ideas regarding individual freedom and women's rights.

Intellectuals, writers and readers worked hard to distinguish the "modern" from the "Western." A modern, educated wife and mother, who exerted her benevolent influence on her household and family and represented it through a tasteful consumption of goods, was highly desired; the woman who destabilized family and nation by her unrestrained pursuit of the latest fashions, or one who adopted new practices (such as dancing) enabling her to subvert social mores, was not. While the calls for women's education were legitimized by expanding the scope and meaning of their domestic roles, these calls were tempered by the belief that women should not (and could not) abandon their sacred role as wives and mothers. For example, an 1899 anonymous article published in *Anis al-Jalis* (most probably authored by the journal's editor, Alexandra Khuri Averino, 1872– 1926) argued that the term *tadbir al-manzil* was far too narrow to encompass all the work and activities carried out by women or to convey its actual social meaning, and suggested that it be renamed *tadbir al-dunya* (world management) or *tadbir al-haya* (life manage- ment). Despite this, the author quickly backtracked and returned to discuss women's domestic chores and emotional labor.[75] Thus although women were encouraged to expand their social horizons through philanthropic organizations, cultural salons, and a variety of communal and familial activities, this expansion was not to entail the crafting of independent identities or agendas.[76] When such boundaries were crossed (even within the confines of a literary text) women were to pay a very high social price for their transgressions. In short, a woman could be free to pursue an education, and perhaps even prepare for her medical board exams, so long as she still made time to sew on her husband's shirt buttons.

CHAPTER 5

THE "MISSING LINK"? THE *NAHDA* NOVELISTS AND INTELLECTUALS FROM SOCIAL COMMENTARY TO POLITICAL CRITIQUE AND ACTIVISM

In the years following the death of Salim al-Bustani (1884), while many leading male novelists were attracted to the historical novel, other novelists, women in particular, continued to cultivate the tradition of the social novel. Over the years the social novel shifted from a critique of social practices, such as cousin-marriages, to an overt political analysis of current events, such as the rise of the Young Turks (1908), the Armenian massacre in Adana (1909), and open criticism of Abdul Hamid II's rule. This literary shift toward social and political commentary was also reflected in the growing debate in the press concerning women's suffrage (see Appendix 2 for an example of one of the earliest letters on this issue). Both of these trends were reinforced by the emergence of a group of women philanthropists and activists who broadened the scope of women's social and political action. These women's political, social and literary work is the link between *Nahda*'s two overlapping facets: the cultural facet, which included a resurgence of linguistic, literary, and journalistic activity; and the political facet, which focused on issues of political identity and nationhood. Unfortunately for women, the growing focus on the national did not bode well for them. As Elizabeth Thompson suggested, women did not anticipate "the gender anxiety and conservative backlash" that would surface during the postwar period and the French Mandate.[1] This anxiety and backlash enabled their opponents (Muslim and Christian alike) to portray women's suffrage as a revolutionary threat and an unpatriotic desire that was allegedly the product of "Western" influences rather than the outcome of a century-long Arab debate. After 1920, the opponents of women's demands for equality and citizenship "sought to project women's suffrage as a revolutionary threat to the entire gender hierarchy," and despite women's attempts to rally and keep the suffrage issue alive in regular articles in the women's press, women were denied suffrage both in the Lebanese and Syrian constitutions (1926 and 1930, respectively).[2]

By linking the two phases of the *Nahda* we are able to focus on the early years of the twentieth century, a period which has been somewhat overlooked in cultural and gender studies of the *Nahda*. We first examine the late *Nahda* novelists and the way they extended the social and political boundaries of the novel. We argue that these writers, in particular Zaynab Fawwaz (1850–1914), Labiba Hashim (1882–1952) and Farida 'Atiyya (1867–1918), used their novels as a space in which to formulate questions and posit a critique of existing social, cultural, economic, legal, and political practices including, but not limited to, women. We then discuss one fin-de-siècle debate on the issues of the right of women to paid work and their political rights, which developed between Fawwaz and Hanna Kurani. Last, we focus on women such as Imily Sursuq (1861–1932), Julya Tu'ma al-Dimashqiyya (1882–1954), Mari 'Ajami (1888–1965) and Nazik Khatim al-'Abid Bayhum (1887–1959), who emerged both as activists and political writers during this period. Thus the gradual progression of the literary project from a discussion of social (even familial) issues to a political critique was intertwined with a similar shift of focus in women's social and political activity.

Nahda Novelists and the Critique of Social
and Political Practices

The work of these social novelists of the turn-of-the-century has been sidelined to a certain extent, as they and their work are often considered precursors to the work of later authors, in particular Muhammad Husayn Haykal's novel *Zaynab* (1914), which is often considered the first modern Arabic novel.[3] The fictional work of these writers from Greater Syria, which was viewed as overly influenced by European literary traditions and focused on the lives of the urban bourgeoisie, is perceived as somehow less "authentic" than that of the fiction of twentieth-century Egyptian writers, which was dominated by a romantic view of the peasantry (*fallahun*). Scholars have noted that such views have obscured the cultural contribution of the earlier novels. Elliot Colla, for example, who traced the emergence of this interpretation, argued that "the canonization of *Zaynab* as the first Arabic novel cannot be explained by the work itself, but rather by subsequent developments – most especially, in the film adaptations of the novel and in the nationalization of university curricula during the Nasserist period." He showed that at the time of its publication, audiences did not see anything "uniquely 'novel'" about it.[4] Rather it could be argued that *Zaynab* follows a fairly sentimental plot (love and its complications) encountered in countless earlier novels, though relocated among the Egyptian peasants. Michael Ezekiel Gaspar suggested that the Egyptian intelligentsia and middle classes "cast the peasant as the timeless repository of Egyptian-ness and then linked that repository to their own political and social aspirations," as an essential move in the legitimization of their own dominant position.[5] Thus historians and literary scholars should be wary of viewing a novel set in rural Egypt among the *fallahun* as necessarily more attuned to social and political issues than one set among the urban bourgeoisie.

As discussed in Chapter 3, the "feminocentric fictions" written by men were not necessarily female or feminist in impulse or origin.[6] These texts did not question the hierarchical relations between the sexes, or the necessity of women's submission to the patriarchal order (albeit in a much modified form); rather their focus was on masculinity and men's status. By adopting and even embracing some of the new demands made by Arab women, the potentially destabilizing effect of the demand for women's rights may have been contained. However, a handful of other novelists, women in particular, were not content with a rephrasing of the sentimental marriage plot, but used it to broaden the social and political boundaries of the novel. This literary activity was accompanied by and reflective of a surge in women's social and political activities that culminated in the period before and during World War I. Women became heavily invested in a range of philanthropic and educational endeavors, and during the period of the war itself engaged in overt political activities, such as caring for war orphans, aiding political prisoners and their families, and verbal confrontations with the Ottoman authorities. Thus, rather than viewing this period as a minor transition phase, it can be seen as a stage during which a group of women writers and activists formulated their own intellectual and activist feminist agenda and eventually attempted to introduce it into the national project.

Before turning our attention to these turn-of-the-century writers, it is important to mention another female member of the al-Bustani family. In 1870 Idlid al-Bustani published a short story (uqsusa), "Hanri wa-Imilya," which was probably the first work of fiction written by a woman in Greater Syria. The story, set in an unnamed seaside resort, revolves around a love triangle composed of an engaged couple, Hanri and Imilya, and Martha, who is attracted to Hanri herself. Martha engages the help of Hanna to sully Imilya's reputation by insinuating that she was seen with another man. Hanri breaks off the engagement, without even asking Imilya what really transpired, and decides to marry Martha. Only after Hanna has a change of heart does he return to the arms of Imilya.[7] The theme of this short story, namely the ease with which a woman's reputation can be tarnished, is one which would recur in the writings of later authors such as Alice al-Bustani, whose works we explore in depth in Chapter 6.

This interest in marriage and the different ways men and women articulated their views of it could also be glimpsed from time to time in the press. Men (both intellectuals and readers who responded to articles) tended to reiterate very abstract principles and voiced idealized notions of marriage. Fathallah Jawish, for example, waxed poetic in his article "On Woman in Human Society," addressing "woman" as "the soul of the house, ruler of the home," but otherwise only enumerated her domestic roles.[8] In contrast, the handful of women who joined in spoke from a grounded personal experience and drew upon it when illustrating their points. For example, in 1894 a woman referring to herself only as Salwa launched into an autobiographical narrative of her own marriage, through which she critiqued the prevailing notions and the views of the men debating the issue. Salwa described her childhood and the prominent role both her parents had played in her education (both general and domestic) and her preparation for married life. She recalled the pains she took to determine whether her suitors wished to marry her for her own qualities or for her generous dowry. Salwa was not so interested in the general principles of marriage, but rather in how marital relationships worked out on a daily basis, i.e. the partnership and emotional support husband and wife provide each other. In short, she grounded her comments within a discussion of a "real" woman and her life.[9]

Several women novelists of the period, such as Zaynab Fawwaz and Labiba Hashim, also wrote from personal experience. The feminist writer and intellectual Zaynab Fawwaz (1846 or 1850– 1914) was born in Tibnin, in the heart of what is known as Jabal 'Amil, to a Shi'ite family.[10] As a young girl she was a domestic in the house of the local ruler 'Ali Bek al-As'ad, where his wife Fatima Khalil took Fawwaz under her wing and provided her with an extensive Arab-Islamic education. Much later she traveled to Beirut and then to Cairo (around 1870), where she became known both for her writings and for her political activism; during her third marriage to Adib Nazami she moved back to Lebanon and then to Damascus, where she began a literary salon. She was a prolific writer, publishing numerous journal articles, a biographical dictionary of famous women, *al-Durr al-Manthur fi Tabaqat Rabbat al-Khudur* (*Scattered Pearls on the Generations of the Harem Dwellers,*

1895), a play, *al-Hawa wal-Wafa'* (*Passion and Fidelity*, 1893), and two novels, *Husn al-'Awaqib aw Ghada al-Zahira* (*Good Consequences, or Ghada the Radiant*, 1899) and *al-Malik Kurush Awwal Muluk al-Fars* (*King Xerxes, First of the Kings of Persia*, 1905). Her essays and poetry were published in *al-Rasa'il al-Zaynabiyya* (*The Zaynab Letters*, 1906).[11]

Fawwaz's *Ghada al-Zahira* once again tells the tale of a love triangle set in the recent past. Fawwaz situated the novel during the social and political unrest of the early 1860s, and based it on events she had probably heard about during her childhood in the al-As'ad household where she was raised. Two Druze princes from south Lebanon, Shakib (based on the figure of the historic 'Ali Bek al-As'ad) and his paternal cousin Tamir (the historic Tamir Bek Husayn), each seeking to marry their cousin Princess Fari'a, begin to fight each other.[12] While the convoluted plot, the kidnapping, shootings, disguises, and bandits are familiar features utilized in earlier novels, Fawwaz used them to take the novel one step further. By engaging in a social commentary on the practice of primogeniture and the struggle for feudal leadership, she also contemplated the qualities of the ideal ruler. Through a blending of fact and fiction in the novel, and the constant comparison between "good" and "bad" rulers, she argued for the consent of the governed and honor, rather than order of birth and tradition, as the basis for political (and marital) rule. Marilyn Booth claimed that this novel succeeds in refracting "a local politics of succession through a narration of feminine authority" and delegitimizes "political practice premised on force, competition, and sequestration."[13]

A far more penetrating account of the personal consequences of political events was provided by author and journalist Labiba Madi Hashim (1882–1952) in her novel *Qalb Rajul* (*A Man's Heart*, 1904). Born in Beirut, Hashim graduated from the Syrian Protestant College for Girls and immigrated with her family to Cairo in 1900. She began her publishing career at a very young age; she published several works in *al-Diya'*, including a serial novella "Hasanat al-Hubb" ("Merits of Love," 1898/9), and a short story, "al-Fawz Ba'da al Mawt" ("Victory after Death," 1899–1900), and later published two novels *Qalb Rajul* (1904) and *Shirin* (1907). Hashim was also a gifted painter and musician. In 1906 she founded and edited the journal *Fatat al-Sharq* (*Girl of the East*), which ran until 1939. She was the first Arab woman to lecture at the Egyptian University in 1911/12 and was appointed the supervisor of girls' schools in Damascus in 1919. Hashim subsequently immigrated to Latin America in 1921 (Brazil and Chile), where she founded the magazine *al-Sharq wal-Gharb* (*East and West*). After returning to Cairo in 1924, Hashim continued to edit *Fatat al-Sharq* until her death in 1952.[14]

Like Fawwaz, Hashim also set her most famous novel *Qalb Rajul* in the 1860s, the years of violent sectarian strife in Mount Lebanon between the Druze and Christians, and even harked back to the tumultuous years of 1841 and 1845; she also interwove historical figures from the region's leading families (such as the Junbalats) into the plot.[15] While this novel's plot also revolves around a love triangle (this time a man and two women), Hashim focused on the chaos and hardship brought about by war. She recognized war's long-lasting impact on individuals, whose lives were irrevocably marked by them through displacement and emigration. By echoing the turmoil and confusion of war within the narrative structure of the novel, she linked several plotlines and followed several characters, providing the readers with the protagonists' family histories, which are to a great extent a product of earlier political upheavals.

It is remarkable how the historical memories of communal strife in Mount Lebanon remained so embedded in the minds of two women who left Greater Syria when young adults. The fact that both chose to work through these painful and raw memories in the context of a sentimental novel should not obscure the significance of their attempts to incorporate the recent past and ground their novels within the recent historical experiences and memories of their readers.

These works represent a milestone in the development of the Arabic social novel. The early social novels (such as those of Salim al-Bustani) border on realism but are often didactic in tone and present an idealized view of society. They are set in a general place and time, usually the home of a bourgeois family in a city in Greater Syria in the late nineteenth century, but they lack references to specific historical events and characters. Such historical subjects were considered the province of historical novels, whose authors chose almost invariably to refer to events in the distant past, such as Jurji Zaydan's historical novels (1891–1913), or those of Farah Antun (1904–6). Zaydan and Antun sought to fictionalize historical events from the distant Arab past for their readers' edification and to construct a burgeoning national identity.[16] Fawwaz and Hashim, however, used the novel set in the recent past to reflect on human nature, comment upon it (even though indirectly) and contemplate alternative options (such as the possibility of non-sectarianism in Hashim's novel). Thus while all were engaged in a project of "inventing continuities,"[17] Zaydan and Antun sought to connect the past with the present, whereas Fawwaz and Hashim did so in order to bond the present to the future.

The civil war of 1860–1 and the events which led up to it were also the main topic of *Amir Lubnan* (*Prince of Lebanon*, 1907), a novel written by journalist, author and publisher Ya'qub Sarruf (1852–1927). Throughout the fictional plot, Sarruf injected information concerning historical events, such as the causes of the sectarian strife in Mount Lebanon, descriptions of the massacre itself and the social and political structures of the region (such as *majalis umara'*). At times the plot appears to be a pretext for a social and political commentary; Matti Moosa pithily remarked that "the novel reads like a social tract."[18] Perhaps because Sarruf was living in Egypt at this time, he was able to write (and publish) such a critique of the Ottoman government's ineptitude and mishandling of minorities.

The least known of this group of novelists was Farida Yusuf 'Atiyya (1867–1917). Born in Tripoli, she most probably lived there her entire life. A graduate of the Evangelical School for Girls in Tripoli, 'Atiyya trained as a teacher and wrote several journal articles and short stories for various periodicals; in 1889 she loosely translated into Arabic Edward Bulwer Lytton's hugely popular 1834 novel *The Last Days of Pompeii*.[19] Her novel *Bayna 'Arshayn* (*Between the Thrones*, 1912) is the most politically oriented of these novels

and deals with very recent events, most importantly the rise of the
Young Turks (1908), the removal of Sultan Abdul Hamid II and
ascension of Mehmed V to the throne (1909), and the Armenian
massacre of Adana (1909).[20]

'Atiyya was not the first to attempt to render a fictional account of
the events of 1908. The Young Turks' rise to power initially aroused
great hopes for constitutional reforms and greater equality for
minorities in the Arab provinces.[21] Tripoli-born poet and novelist
Labiba Mikha'il Sawaya (1876–1916) dealt with these events in her
novel *Hasna' Salonik* (*The Beautiful Lady of Salonika*, 1909) and
Zaydan did so in *al-Inqilab al-'Uthmani* (*The Ottoman Coup d'Etat*,
1910–11).[22] Despite this, 'Atiyya was the first to address the far
more contentious (and potentially far more dangerous) issue of the
Armenian massacre of 1909.

In *Bayna 'Arshayn*, 'Atiyya picked up on two themes which had
also appeared in Lytton's *The Last Days of Pompeii*: the decadent
culture of a doomed empire and the treatment of minorities (such as
Armenians and Jews) within the empire. The novel, which follows
the lives of several characters, provided 'Atiyya with an opportunity
to expound on her interpretation of recent political events. The love
story in fact serves as a pretext for 'Atiyya's historical interpretation of
the causes of the decline of the Ottoman Empire; her descriptions of
historical events and characters are far more vivid and persuasive than
the flat descriptions of the fictional characters and their doings.
'Atiyya began by describing the political violence, chaos and famine
at the beginning of the 1908 coup (*ba'da al-inqilab*). Immediately
thereafter she introduced her main characters, members of the
Armenian community in Adana and Tripoli, and described them in
very positive terms as proud, brave, kind, honest and hardworking,
but as vulnerable to harassment.[23] 'Atiyya then provided her
readers with countless examples of the decadence and ruthlessness
of the ruling dynasty. For example, relying on an article by Shibli
Shumayyil (a psycho-medical character analysis of Abdul Hamid II),
she claimed that Abdul Hamid II's upbringing (similar to that of the
other sultans) instilled selfishness and a flagrant disregard for the
people of his realm. She concluded that the end result was a

bloodthirsty, mad tyrant, and wondered why it took so long to overthrow him.[24]

'Atiyya was at her harshest describing the violence that occurred during the Armenian massacre in Adana. She did not mince words when recounting the events of the massacre and labeled the killings "atrocities" (*fazi'a*) and "barbarities" (*wahshiyya*). She described the bloodshed, casualties, orphans, destruction of property, as well as the ensuing famine, poverty and dislocation in detail. In her view, the Ottoman Empire would have been much better off had it promoted a policy of greater tolerance toward religious and ethnic minorities.[25] This is the reason she endorsed the Young Turks, who sought to re-establish the people's trust in their rulers, and hoped that with the ascension of a new sultan reform would be at hand.[26]

The growing political boldness of women novelists as well as the increasing visibility of the activities and assertiveness of women activists and reformers soon attracted the attentions of both detractors and supporters, who began to debate the appropriateness of these activities and their social impact. Surprisingly enough, even these women activists were not always in favor of expanding women's horizons beyond those of the family and household.

To Work or Not to Work – To Vote or Not to Vote: The Debate on Women's Activities Outside the Home

One of the more notable lengthy and heated debates in the press concerning these issues commenced in 1891 between Zaynab Fawwaz and Hanna Kurani. This debate over the issue of women's work outside the home soon escalated into one concerning their right to universal suffrage that involved several writers and readers. While this debate has often been interpreted as a clash between "conservative" (Kurani) and the "liberal" (Fawwaz) views concerning women's work and suffrage rights,[27] this interpretation tends to disregard the different conceptions of citizenship that inspired these suffragists and women activists. In her study of the history of women's suffrage, historian Jane Rendall emphasized that women in the early suffrage movement utilized a complex language that promoted individualist aspirations, but also argued in favor of women's unique (and different) civilizing or moral mission. Virginia Sapiro stated that such women "ask not only that citizens who happen to be women be represented, but that women be represented *because* they are women."[28] In effect, many of these women challenged the liberal conception of the separation of public and private spheres, but at the same time accepted it on the basis of women's difference.

Thus, Hanna Kurani's presumed opposition to women's work outside the home should be read both within the context of the gendered changes of employment patterns in the silk industry in Mount Lebanon and her association with the women of "organized womanhood" during the time she spent in the United States (1893–5). The Kurani–Fawwaz debate translated these different conceptions of citizenship into local terms. This heated debate also suggests that the link between citizenship and "patriotic mother-hood" was forged well before the Mandate period, when this debate was renewed in earnest.[29]

Hanna Kasbani Kurani (1871–98) was born in Kfarshima, Mount Lebanon; she attended the American missionary school in Kfarshima and in Beirut. After her graduation in 1885 she taught at the American School for Girls in Tripoli, and in 1887 she married Amin Kurani. Subsequently she published several articles in the local press, translated novels and began her career as a public speaker. She is also known to have written a play and two novels as well as a non-fiction work, *Manners and Habits*, which was translated into English. Kurani traveled extensively in Greater Syria, and toured Malta, France, England, the United States and Egypt. After attending the Columbian World Exposition in Chicago (1893), Kurani set out on a lecture tour around the United States, eventually settling down for two years in New York City. There she involved herself with the work of several women's groups and lectured to them. During her stay in the United States, Kurani continued to contribute articles to the Arab press and published several articles in the American press.

According to one source, Kurani's extended visit to the United States was more on the lines of a forced exile, as "the Syrian Government" was displeased with the feminist opinions she voiced: not only was her property confiscated but "she was informed that if this did not produce the desired result her father and mother would also be exiled." Only after the intercession of the American government, at the instigation of several prominent women (especially philanthropist and socialite Bertha Honoré Palmer, wife of Chicago businessman Potter Palmer), was she allowed to return. Unfortunately, by then Kurani had contracted tuberculosis and soon after returning to her home in Mount Lebanon she died (1898).[30]

Kurani's activities and the close friendships she forged with women such as May Sewell and Bertha Honoré Palmer shed a new light on her views on women. For example, in February 1894 she lectured to a meeting of the New York City chapter of Sorosis (est. 1868), the first professional women's club in the United States, and she was a member of its board. Sorosis was part of the women's club movement which promoted the idea that women had a moral duty to improve society, and sought to provide its members with the political experience and leadership skills necessary to shape civic public affairs.[31] Thus it is highly unlikely that Kurani was adamantly opposed to women's work outside the home, or their attempts to exert an influence on social and political affairs.

Kurani strongly favored a broad liberal education for women, supplemented by a "domestic education" (al-tarbiyya al-baytiyya), both of which were especially necessary in her opinion during "the time of the awakening" (zaman al-nahda). In a two-part article published in the fall of 1890, she outlined a basic curriculum for girls, which included mathematics, science, history, geography and gymnastics. Kurani was insistent that girls be well-versed in Arabic, and ridiculed "Westernized women" (mutafarnijat) who preferred to teach their daughters a smattering of French rather than provide them with a solid grounding in their native tongue. She asserted that "Syria will not generate patriotic women (nisa' wataniyyat) if they do not strengthen [their bonds] to their language and homeland (bilad), and favor their language over all others." As to the domestic facet of this curriculum, Kurani suggested that it include an acquaintance with the principles of bodily and domestic hygiene, sewing and other handwork, and a general knowledge of a variety of domestic chores. The end-product of this educational regime should be a young woman who contributed to her society and homeland (*watan*).[32]

Although Kurani expected this young woman to exert a social and moral influence on the world, it was to be carried out through the family. She expressed a rather ambivalent view of women's paid work outside the home, as she believed that women had a different path laid out before them. In an 1890 article in *Lisan al-Hal*, which she later presented in her speech to the Congress of Women in the Columbian World Exposition in Chicago (1893), she argued that:

> It would never do to have them labor in the same field of action. This is against the law of nature which provides a sphere for everything. Equality between the sexes is not the equal portion of the same work, but the equality of their whole to the welfare of the race. Woman should glory in womanhood, in being the mother of men, the doctor of moral and mental illnesses, in offering to mankind the fruits of her labors and experience.[33]

Kurani had no doubts as to women's intellectual capabilities to pursue independent careers, but she believed that their roles as wives and mothers had greater importance. She insisted: "I do not think it is right for them to go into business among men. The country is not ready for it." Indeed, in later interviews published in the *New York Times* during her visit to the United States, she stated that although she did not doubt that women had the right to vote, she did not believe in universal suffrage.

> I do not believe in universal suffrage even for men. A qualified suffrage for both sexes I believe to be the best. Put the ordering of the Government into the hands of those men or women who are best fit by education to say what it shall be.[34]

Judith Tucker, in her analysis of the changing role of Egyptian working-class women in the textile industry, noted that "social perceptions of the conflict between work and family responsibilities, especially that of child care, continued to plague women who worked outside the home." A similar comment can be made regarding women in the silk industry in Mount Lebanon. As the silk industry on Mount Lebanon grew in the second half of the nineteenth century, the peasants sent their daughters to work in the factories to supplement the household income. Historian Akram Khater, however, argued that while this income was indispensable, "socially this work had repercussions." Women's paid work outside their homes tarnished their reputations, and families faced immense social pressure from neighbors and the Maronite church to prevent young women from working outside the home.[35]

Given that Kurani was a native of Mount Lebanon and traveled extensively in the area, it may have been in response to these conflicting social expectations that she found a greater affinity with the ideas and goals of the Progressive-era women activists of "organized womanhood" in the United States and shared the motivations behind their campaign against the exploitation of women in the labor market. These women believed that American women laboring in factories faced a crisis, as factory work "devalued what they did and, therefore, who they were." Taking a holistic view of women's work, they argued that "all duties, paid and unpaid, were valuable so long as those tasks fulfilled women's moral responsibilities towards home and society."[36] Many of these women viewed "womanhood" and "motherhood" as powerful integrating forces with the potential to enable women to transcend the boundaries of class and race.[37] Kurani's support of these aims may have encouraged her in 1894 to join the National Industrial Union, an organization whose aim was "to furnish women with employment suited to their abilities."[38]

According to notices and reports following her mission to the Columbian World Exposition on behalf of Syrian women, as well as later articles referring to this debate (such as a 1909 article by Anisa Shartuni), Kurani did not lack supporters in Egypt and in Greater Syria.[39] Thus, despite attempts to read Kurani's views as "conservative" or an expression of gender essentialism, they were in line with the views of many in Greater Syria as well as in Europe and the United States, who believed that women's citizenship should be exercised through personal influence and moral suasion. This view valorized women's personal and moral influence over and beyond their formal political equality.

Kurani's views were vigorously opposed by Zaynab Fawwaz, who launched an all-out defense of women's unlimited right to work and to vote. Fawwaz argued that "woman was not created to remain within the household sphere, never to emerge"; on the contrary, "the practices to which women are accustomed permit them to acquire and work in all arts and skills." She scorned both the attempt to "domesticate politics" and efforts at "rationalizing" household management, and dismissively commented:

> Indeed, whoever wants to learn the laws of household management and childrearing can gain this knowledge from women without much difficulty, whether those women are in a state of primitiveness or not, for even primitive women manage their households and raise their children to the best of their abilities and circumstances.

Attacking Kurani directly, Fawwaz asserted that women who were against suffrage "are more deserving of censure than are the others, for they have chosen isolation and sloth."[40] In retrospect this acrimonious debate is saddening; Kurani and Fawwaz seem to be working at cross purposes in this case, and with Kurani's untimely death their debate was destined to remain unresolved.

Women Philanthropists and Activists

This growing confidence and assertiveness of women novelists and journalists, who demonstrated increasing readiness to voice their political sentiments in their writings, paralleled the self-assurance of women activists and reformers. One of the earliest was philanthropist Imily Sursuq (1861–1932). Born in Beirut and educated in Alexandria, in 1881 Sursuq together with Labiba Jahshan founded a school and orphanage for girls called the Zahrat al-Ihsan (Flower of

Charity), which she headed for many years. She became so well known for this and her generous financial support of convents, churches, and hospitals, that many viewed her as the emblematic virtuous woman. While Sursuq's activities may have been the culmination of the activities of an earlier generation of women, it did, as Elizabeth Thompson argues, reflect "a new spirit." By 1912, her activities had taken on a clear political tone; she donated money for military uniforms, formed a benevolent society for the aid of the wounded, and a medical aid society.[41]

In the coming years several women extended the scope of what were considered "suitable" social activities for women. The early activities of educator, journalist and author Julya Tu'ma al-Dimashqiyya (1882–1954) closely resembled those of other young, educated and socially conscious Arab women of her period. She taught in girls' schools and later directed the first girls' school for the al-Maqasid Islamic Charitable Association (founded in 1914). Tu'ma became known as an eloquent speaker and published numerous articles on the educational mission of women (whom she described as cheerful "angels") and on children's education.[42] During the war she gathered several women together to provide charitable aid for the needy. In 1917 she established the Women's Association and the Women's Club in Beirut, which met monthly in her home. Tu'ma made a concerted effort to reach out to women of all faiths and sects, in order to in order to elevate "women's cultural level" and to foster patriotic sentiments. Soon after the commencement of the French Mandate she began to raise political issues in meetings and on the pages of the new magazine she founded and edited: al-Mar'a al-Jadida (1921–8). On its pages she advocated granting women political rights, removing the veil, and promoted the cause of Syrian national unity as a means to gain independence.[43]

Educator, translator and journalist Mari 'Ajami (1888–1965), a graduate of the Syrian Protestant College in Beirut, was the founding editor of al-'Arus (The Bride; Damascus: 1910–14, 1918–25), which soon became a forum for the defense of women's rights. 'Ajami also established the Literary League in Damascus (1921) and hosted an intellectual salon in her home. Just as significant was the fact that

'Ajami soon turned her newspaper into an important venue for criticism of the Ottoman regime. After visiting political prisoners she published several exposés on the squalid living conditions in the prisons and detention centers. In numerous speeches and articles 'Ajami not only demanded that Jamal Pasha (1872–1922), the military governor of Ottoman Syria and commander of the Ottoman Fourth Army, release the Arab political prisoners but also attacked him personally. After the execution of several of these prisoners in Damascus on May 6, 1916 she composed several elegies in their honor. The ferocity of her attacks on Jamal Pasha was so virulent that some "began to wonder how was it that the tyrant did not include her among the martyrs of al-Marja Square."[44]

Just as politically active was the social activist and philanthropist Nazik Khatim al-'Abid Bayhum (1887–1959). Born in Damascus to an influential Muslim family, the highly educated Nazik al-'Abid took up fairly conventional charitable activities, such as the establishment of a women's society, and occasionally wrote articles for the women's press, helped set up a public library and encouraged women to donate money for the education of poor Muslim women.[45] During the war her family was exiled to Izmir and 'Abid volunteered in a hospital treating wounded Arab soldiers. When she returned to Damascus she threw herself into political activities. In January 1919, soon after her return, she set up yet another philanthropic society to aid the poor, *Nur al-Fayha'* (Light of Damascus), as well as an orphanage and school for the daughters of the war dead, and a women's journal (all bearing the name *Nur al-Fayha'*).[46] In July 1920, with Prince (later King) Faysal's support, she founded the Red Star Association (the Red Crescent's forerunner) and was awarded an honorary military rank as "honorary president" of the Arab Army. Later that month she led the nurses' battalion into the famous Battle of Maysalun during which the Syrian Arab Army was defeated by French forces on the outskirts of Damascus (July 23, 1920). In recognition of her wartime contributions and her participation in resistance activities against the French, the public hailed her as the "Joan of Arc" of Syria and compared her to the early Muslim warrior-poet Khawla bint al-Azwar.[47] After the defeat al-'Abid was forced into exile, and when the French granted a general amnesty in 1921 she was permitted to return only after she agreed not to be involved in political affairs. Al-ʿAbid continued her public activities in the years to come, mainly supporting the social demands of working women, but these were far more limited in scope.[48]

***

In this chapter, we saw that the gradual progression of the literary project from socio-familial issues to political critique was intertwined with a similar shift in women's social and political activities from the charitable to the political. These writings and activities, however, were curtailed from the 1920s onward. We continue this discussion in the next chapter, concentrating on another set of writers who emerged during the same period, whose texts focused mainly on the re-examination of the gender status quo, especially as played out within and without marriage; a reconsideration which was accompanied by intense deliberation on the prevailing sexual norms. As we will show, this literary project also came to an abrupt halt in the early years of the Mandate period.

CHAPTER 6

BEYOND THE MARRIAGE PLOT: MARRIAGE, SEXUALITY AND THE RISE OF "OUTLAW EMOTIONS" IN TURN-OF-THE-CENTURY NOVELS

In the closing paragraphs of Jubran Khalil Jubran's short story "Warda al-Hani," in which both spouses tell the tale of the breakdown of their marriage, the narrator, who has just left the home of Warda, the runaway wife of Rashid Bey Nu'man, reflects on this encounter and directs a series of questions to the reader:

> Did that woman wrong him when she left him and followed her free spirit, or was it he that wronged her when he forced her body to yield to marriage while her spirit was inclined towards love? Which of them is the oppressor and which the oppressed? Indeed, who is the guilty one and who the innocent?[1]

This set of questions, and others like it which appeared in several fin-de-siècle novels, novellas and short stories, disrupt the conservative lessons that lay behind the standard marriage plot found in the Arab novels of the early *Nahda*. Rather than focusing on the periods of courtship and the nature of a good marriage, these later texts deal with the breakdown of marriage or its psychological price: the painful sacrifices demanded of married women, who have to eschew autonomy and individuality in order to avoid social censure and maintain their reputations, or the social consequences that befall a woman unable to enter into marriage, or an unfaithful wife.

Moving from Alice al-Bustani's *Riwayat Sa'iba* (1891), which rejects a happy ending to a marriage plot, to Niqula Haddad's *Hawwa al-Jadida* (1906), in which a "fallen woman" finds that she can never hope to marry and dies brokenhearted, to Jubran Khalil Jubran's early short stories and novellas that openly challenge the institution of marriage itself (not just its textual representation), the texts undermined the lessons put forward in novels employing the marriage plot. These deliberately thought-provoking texts, which have been neglected by scholars, were widely read and heatedly debated by fin-de-siècle Arab readers, who attested to the great emotional and intellectual resonance of these texts even years after they were published.

In her influential article, "Love and Knowledge," feminist philosopher Alison Jaggar argued that "critical reflection on emotion is not a self-indulgent substitute for political analysis and political action. It is itself a kind of political theory and political practice, indispensable for an adequate social theory and social transform-ation." She singles out a particular set of emotions that she terms "outlaw emotions," which are incompatible with dominant perceptions, norms and values. Jaggar claims that these emotions "provide the first indications that something is wrong with the way alleged facts have been constructed." Such "outlaw emotions," which precede "conscious recognition that accepted descriptions and justifications often conceal as much as they reveal the prevailing state of affairs," may well lead to "subversive observations that challenge dominant conceptions of the status quo." Although individuals feeling such emotions may experience confusion and self-doubt when these emotions are shared with and validated by others, "the basis exists for forming a subculture" opposed to the dominant values; thus, Jaggar concludes "outlaw emotions may be politically because epistemologically subversive."[2]

In this chapter we examine a set of novels, novellas and short stories written by a group of late *Nahda* novelists who questioned and perhaps even sought to challenge the prevailing societal and sexual norms by drawing their readers into an intimacy with the fictional characters. We also look at their readers' emotional responses and self-reflections that questioned status quo beliefs regarding marriage and sexuality. We were particularly fascinated by these texts, which are often overlooked, but on close reading reveal a textual richness and narrative complexity. All these authors offer their readers a reconsideration of their society's prevailing social structure by rethinking gender relations, in particular within marriage. By providing a discursive or a "rehearsal space" in which to voice and share "outlaw emotions" these authors may have laid the foundation for a subculture opposing the prevailing gender norms. Unfortunately the lifespan of this discursive space was brief, since from the outbreak of World War I onward there was a marked decline in literary production in Greater Syria, and "for women the decline was, in fact, a complete hiatus."[3] These "outlaw emotions" were only picked up in the late 1940s and early 1950s in the novels of women authors such as the Lebanese-Syrian scholar and novelist Widad Sakakini's (1913–91), *al-Hubb al-Muharram* (*Forbidden Love*, 1947), *Arwa Bint al-Khutub* (*Arwa, Daughter of Woe*, 1949) and Collette Khoury's (1937–) *Ayyam Ma'ahu* (*Days with Him*, 1959).

The Trials of Sa'iba, or Deflating the Marriage Plot

Alice al-Bustani (1870–1926), the daughter and sister of two of the *Nahda*'s leading intellectuals, Butrus al-Bustani and Salim al-Bustani, respectively, was born in Beirut and at some point immigrated to Egypt where she died in 1926. Very little is known about her life and education, except that she was a member of the first female literary society in Greater Syria, *Bakurat Suriyya* (founded by Maryam Makariyus), and wrote one novel *Riwayat al-Sa'iba* (*A Novel of Sa'iba*, 1891).[4]

Alice al-Bustani's heroine, the virtuous Sai'ba, has chosen to marry Lutfi, an upstanding young army officer, rather than her dissolute cousin, Farid. Farid first tries to break up Sai'ba's marriage by sending anonymous letters insinuating that Sai'ba and Farid have been long-time lovers; later he bribes Sai'ba's maid to take Sai'ba to a secret rendezvous. When all Farid's convoluted plots to break up the marriage fail, he resolves to kill Lufti, but instead he accidentally shoots and kills Sai'ba. Alice al-Bustani's exploration of courtship and the inner workings of a marriage in this novel are unique. She does not present an idealized view of the roles of men and women, but rather attempts to think about the meaning of marriage and its role in the emotional life of a woman. While Alice al-Bustani did make use of the marriage plot employed time and again by several earlier novelists (including her brother), her focus did not remain solely on the constitution of the marriage; rather, she tried to examine the relationship between husband and wife after their marriage. She compared the various foundations for marriage, and came out in favor of love and virtue rather than tradition (in this case cousin marriage). Her plot suggests that in her view women (and their reputations) remained vulnerable even after marriage, even in one based on love.

There are two possible sources of influence for *Riwayat al-Sa'iba*, which would have had a cultural resonance for both Muslim and Christian readers. The first, which is referred to in the text, was the medieval tale of Genovefa of Barabant; the story of a chaste wife who is falsely accused of infidelity by a rejected suitor, and repudiated by her husband for years until finally reinstated. Alice al-Bustani has Sai'ba reading the story of Genovefa in the narrative, and contemplating the meaning of the tale and discussing it with Lutfi. The second source may easily have been the well-known story in Arab culture of the false accusation of adultery made against 'A'isha bint Abi Bakr, the favorite wife of the Prophet Muhammad, in "the account of the lie" (*hadith al-ifk*). This *hadith* explains the historical context of the *Surat al-Nur* that discusses *zina* (fornication) and *qadhf* (slander). According to the hadith, 'A'isha was separated from her caravan when she set out to search for a lost necklace and was forced to wait alone until found. She was rescued by a young man named Safwan ibn Mu'attal al-Sulami, and reunited with the caravan the next day. Her overnight absence gave rise to rumors of impropriety and her wrongful accusation of adultery by three individuals. Subsequently the Prophet pronounced several verses included in *Surat al-Nur* defining the criteria of evidence for *zina* and the punishment for anyone who wrongfully accuses another of *zina* without the corroboration of four witnesses.[5] Alice al-Bustani may have adapted this theme of the false accusation of adultery of a married woman and transported it to turn-of-the-century Beirut.

In her novel, Alice al-Bustani tacitly blamed society for her ultimate frustration with the marriage plot. Despite the fact that both Sai'ba and Lutfi personify all the virtues of the "New Woman" and "New Man" and their marriage is based on love, its falls prey to the envy of the dissolute Farid, who senses that this marriage signals the end of his patriarchal prerogative to marry his cousin if he so desires.[6] Unlike male authors who placed the decision to flaunt patriarchal conventions firmly in the hands of their heroines, lauding them if they persevered or reviling them if they succumbed to parental pressure, while ignoring the physical and emotional price paid for this disobedience, Alice al-Bustani was all too aware of the "price" paid by young women who refuse to conform to societal pressure.[7] Rather than buying into the romantic myth of the marriage plot, which assumes that love can tear down the bars of the patriarchal prison, Alice al-Bustani subverted it by enabling the novel's patriarchal representative (cousin Farid) to kill the heroine and thwart the desired happy ending.

We can only speculate as to the emotional response of the readers, who were probably shocked by the sudden and abrupt deflation of the expected outcome of the traditional marriage plot.[8] Recent historical case studies of marriage formation in the period suggest that these novelists may have been far more attuned to the hidden undercurrents and power struggles between parents and guardians and their young charges.

The dearth of personal accounts (autobiographies, memoirs, diaries and letters) dealing with the emotional and sexual aspects of their authors' personae at this time and place makes the cultural historians' task of tracing such undercurrents in Greater Syria a difficult one. However, Engin Deniz Akarli and later Jens Hanssen, who found rare evidence of one such generational power struggle in the Ottoman archives, provide a glimpse into its inner workings and show how such silent, deep undercurrents may have seeped into works of fiction. The case in question is that of Najla Arslan (1869?–1935?) and Amin Majid (1868?–1943), a young Druze couple who wished to decide upon their own marital future only to find that it was not destined to be.[9]

Both Najla Arslan and Amin Majid were graduates of French missionary schools in Beirut, and it was during their studies there that the two met and fell in love. Sometime in late 1893 the two decided to inform their parents of their decision. Despite the fact that the two were cousins and shared the same faith and interests, Najla's family strongly objected to the match as they had promised (in infancy) her hand in marriage to the son of Mustafa Arslan, the clan's autocratic leader. Believing that Najla had sullied the family's reputation, her parents confined her to the home and prevented her from meeting or communicating with Amin; they also threatened to disinherit her if she did not obey them. After she escaped from her parents' home and fled to her former convent school, she was forcibly turned over to the custody of Mustafa Arslan, where the pressure to marry his son continued. In one instance, Mustafa Arslan attempted to force Najla's compliance by threatening to assassinate Amin. When she remained adamant, he staged a mock execution and then showed her the bloodied items; at this point Najla began to scream, attacked Arslan's men and had to be physically restrained. Despite the couple's earlier and separate appeals to Ottoman authorities to intervene on their behalf (which the authorities did, albeit rather hesitantly), they were unsuccessful; only when the news of Najla's deteriorating mental condition emerged and attracted the attention of Sultan Abdul Hamid II was she removed to the custody of the governor of Beirut and later sent to Istanbul to recuperate. However, Najla Arslan was never to recover from this ordeal and she spent the remainder of her life in and out of mental hospitals; she and Amin never married.

In his study of this case, Engin Deniz Akarli found that the Arslan affair generated considerable interest and gossip in Beirut and that even if one takes into account the political resentment toward Mustafa Arslan, many felt considerable sympathy for the young lovers' plight. Akarli argues that both Najla's parents and Mustafa Arslan found it difficult to perceive the two lovers as independent individuals and they constantly sought to understand who had led them into disobedience. Their insistence that the two young lovers were immature individuals with limited agency led to the disciplinary measures, which caused Najla's mental breakdown and Majid's eventual self-enforced exile.[10]

Regardless of whether this case inspired (or was inspired by) marriage-plot novels that were so popular in the period, a closer look at these two historical characters shows an uncanny resemblance to many of the fictional ones. In their mid-twenties, both Amin and Najla were well-educated and reform minded. Possibly both had expected to make use of their talents to influence and mold both family and society. While much less is known about Najla Arslan's views and activities, Amin Majid had already established a name as a talented journalist and had published a book entitled *Women and Their Influence in Society*. Following his exile to Paris he became the editor of the newspaper *Kashf al-Niqab* (*Lifting of the Veil*). In later years he would go into diplomatic service, and after retiring in 1914 he strongly favored the cause of Lebanese and Syrian independence.[11] While their contemporaries may have admired and certainly sympathized with the two, many would have viewed their unhappy fate as a cautionary tale. For all their virtue, education, and forward-looking ideas, the two were ultimately unable to dislodge the patriarchal system and in their attempt to do so the two paid a very high price, in particular Najla, who like her fictional counterparts, seems to have borne the brunt of the parental disciplinary efforts.

"Cast Off Like a Date Pit" – Niqula Haddad and the "Fallen Woman"

Born in the same year as Alice al-Bustani, journalist and novelist Niqula Haddad (1870–1954) also turned his attention to the social consequences of the plight of young lovers. Haddad was born in the village of Junih near Sidon, and after attending the American secondary school in Sidon, he began his studies at the Syrian Protestant College in Beirut. After a year he left for Egypt for three years to edit the journal *al Ra'id al-Misri* (*The Egyptian Explorer*). He returned to Beirut to complete his education in pharmacy and upon graduating returned to Egypt, but soon after left for the United States for two years. After marrying journalist Rose Antun (1882– 1955), the sister of fellow journalist Farah Antun (1874–1922), in 1909, the two returned to Egypt and both began working as editors, Niqula Haddad for the *al-Mahrusa* newspaper and Rose Antun for *Majallat al-Sayyidat wa al-Rijal* (*A Journal for Ladies and Men*).[12]

Haddad was deeply interested in a variety of social issues and socialist ideas. He wrote one of the earliest Arabic works on socialism (in 1920), and both these interests figure prominently in his novels. Haddad authored some 20 novels besides the two we discuss here, including *Asirat al-Hubb* (*Prisoner of Love, c.*1902), *al-'Ayn bil-'Ayn* (*An Eye for an Eye*, 1904), and *Adam al-Jadid* (*The New Adam*, 1924– 1925).[13] In *Kulluhu Nasib* (*All is Fate, or Kismet*, 1903), for example, Haddad considered the education of young women and their social views before and after marriage. His two main female protagonists, Mary and Eugenie, embody the good and bad aspects of "Woman." Once again, a serious, young English-educated Syrian doctor, Dawud Fadl, has to decide which of two women he should marry: the poor and orphaned but serious and responsible governess (Mary), or the superficial and flighty daughter of a wealthy man (Eugenie Khalil). After numerous (and familiar) plot twists, including attempts by Fadl's friend, Yusuf Bey, to break up Fadl's engagement with Eugenie, and the Khalil family's false accusation and dismissal of Mary (for supposedly succumbing to Fadl's desires), the two virtuous lovers marry, and Mary turns out to be Muhsin Khalil's daughter by a previous marriage.[14]

Besides a deliberation on the appropriate education for young women (and future wives), Haddad turned the readers' attention to the ambivalent and contested relationship between a governess and her employers, and the governess' vulnerable social position in a bourgeois household. As an employed middle-class woman, the governess was a constant reminder of what could happen to any middle-class woman should her family fortunes decline. Her presence in the home was also a potential threat to the family itself, both as a stranger privy to knowledge regarding its intimate affairs and as a target of the sexual desires of the men of the household. Unsurprisingly, the governess was a recurrent figure in nineteenth-century Euro-American literature; Haddad, however, was one of the first to position her in an Arabic novel.[15] While in *Kulluhu Nasib* Haddad only raised the specter of a decent, young woman threatened by an accusation of sexual seduction, in his novel *Hawwa al-Jadida aw Yvonne Monar* (*The New Eve, or Yvonne Monar*, 1906) Haddad turned his attention to the unhappy fate of a young middle-class girl with a "noble spirit" (*sharifat al-ruh*),[16] who is indeed seduced, abandoned and dishonored, ostracized and left to make her way in the world alone.

The novel tells of the pampered daughter of a respectable family, Josephine, who later assumes the name of Yvonne Monar. Since childhood Yvonne had been friends with the son of a family whom her family knew well. In their late teens the two fell in love and Yvonne notes that her mother and brother had hoped the two would marry and the two were permitted to spend time together unsupervised. Arguing that she did not know she had to be on her guard, Yvonne soon discovered she was pregnant and asked the young man to marry her. He only then tells her that his family was busy arranging his marriage to another woman and that he is afraid to approach them. Promising to marry her as soon as the baby is born, the young man removes Yvonne to a house away from her family. Only when she delivers the baby and the young man abandons her does Yvonne finally understand that he never intended to marry her at all. Finding that she is disowned by her family and despised and reviled by society as a "fallen women" (*imra'a saqita*),[17] she in despair even contemplates suicide. Determined to survive for her child's sake, she supports herself by sewing and by a small allowance from her mother, but eventually she gives up her daughter to be raised by her family. Haddad describes how Yvonne is unable to shake off her past, even though she tries to live an honest and decent life; she is forced to move from place to place and reinvent and re-establish herself repeatedly once people find out about her "sins" and ostracize her. Haddad contrasted Yvonne's fate with that of her seducer, who is still welcomed by society as a respectable gentleman.

At this point Yvonne meets a prince who asks her to give up her work and become his mistress (*mukhtassa bihi*).[18] While Haddad is rather vague on the nature of Yvonne's relationship with the prince, she does move into one of his houses. At this point Yvonne falls in love with a young man named Maurice, who had defended her from a group of men who had harassed and made sexual advances toward her; Maurice becomes infatuated with Yvonne. However, Yvonne soon receives a visit from a beautiful young woman, Mary Martal, who turns out to be Maurice's fiancée. Mary begs Yvonne to give up Maurice. Believing that Mary is "an angel sent from heaven to purify my heart and cleanse my soul," so that she may redeem her sins, Yvonne decides to give up Maurice despite his violent protestations.[19] Yvonne falls ill and on her deathbed (in the course of a grand family reconciliation) finds out that Mary is the daughter she had given up in infancy.

In the introduction to *Hawwa al-Jaddida*, Haddad claimed that he had long contemplated the question of the sexual double standard applied to fallen women (as opposed to the casual social attitude toward their seducers), but was unsure as how to present it to readers. Haddad maintained that he wrote the novel in two weeks after attending a Western play about the master of a house who had seduced (*ghawa*) his wife's maid; when rumors concerning this affair emerged, the master dismissed the maid but he himself remained a respected member of society. Haddad set his novel in Egypt and provided his characters with European names so that his readers would not speculate who they really were.[20] However, this led Haddad's critics to accuse him of Arabizing the plot of some French novel, such as Jacques-Henri Bernardin's *Paul et Virginie* (1787) Victor Hugo's *Les misérables* (1862) or Dumas fils' *La Dame aux camélias* (1848).[21]

While not dismissing either Haddad's account or that of his critics as to the origins of the plot, it is possible that another source of influence on the novel was the turn-of-the-century European debate on the "New Eve." Within Jewish and Christian traditions, Eve as the temptress and the seductress is viewed as the prototype of womanly guile. She bears the burden of responsibility both for leading Adam astray and for bringing about their expulsion from the Garden of Eden. Thus Eve is both the mother of mankind and the source of its misery. The woman who atones for Eve's sin is the Virgin Mary, the New Eve, who immaculately conceives and gives birth to Christ the redeemer.[22]

These traditional figures of Eve and the New Eve were given a new twist in the closing decade of the nineteenth century, when writers began to use both figures to comment on contemporary women and their place in society, and both were employed in numerous novels, plays and works of art.[23] Of particular importance was Jules Bois' (1868–1943) *L'Ève nouvelle* (1894–7). In this feminist work, Bois re-evaluated the Eve paradigm and deployed the figure of Eve as the symbol of women's continued subjugation; Bois recounted the history of the subjugation of women and considered the genesis of the "New Woman." In particular he rejected the binary view of women (the Eve/Mary dichotomy) and turned his sights on ordinary women "in whom dwelt something sacred."[24]

Art historian Elizabeth Menon argues that in many of these cultural texts "the invocation of Eve was merely a prelude to the 'real' problem: the place of woman in contemporary society. The woman that most obviously manifested the ills of society was, from a medical as well as a social and moral point of view, the prostitute."[25] Arab readers were quite familiar with the social and psychological debate concerning the criminal and immoral behavior of women; this included translated texts on female criminality (and madness) such as those of Caesar Lombroso (1835–1909) and Gugliemo Ferrero (1871–1942),[26] and original articles appearing in the press dealing with the loose behavior of working women.[27]

Academic studies on the theme of the "fallen woman" in modern Arabic literature have focused on the 1920s and on the connections between this theme and the national discourse.[28] This theme, however, appeared years earlier. Given the century-long fascination in nineteenth-century Euro-American literature and art with the seduction plot and the figure of the fallen woman in literature,[29] it is somewhat surprising that it took so long for it to percolate into the work of Arab authors, who were attuned to Euro-American literary genres and techniques. The growing dislocation brought about by urbanization that necessitated cautionary tales about "fallen women" may have prompted these writers to incorporate these figures into their works, or perhaps writers sensed a greater openness on the part of their readers to contemplate this issue seriously and extend their compassion to such ostracized figures.

Haddad's evocation of the figure of Eve and the "New Eve" in the novel, and his sympathetic portrayal of Yvonne as a repentant sinner, may have also been influenced by the prevailing Islamic view of Eve. Contrary to Jewish and Christian traditions, which firmly place the blame for the Fall on Eve, in the Qur'an Adam and Eve are seduced together and thus share equal blame (*Surat al-A'raf*).[30] Haddad referred directly to these meaning-laden figures in his novel. When he had Yvonne Monar contemplate the sexual double standard, she asks:

> Why is all human misery attributed to the "Ancient Eve" (*Hawwa al-qadima*)? [Is it] because she once seduced the "Ancient Adam" (*Adam al-qadim*)? Why [then] isn't this misery attributed to the "New Adam" (*Adam al-jadid*), if he is the one who seduces the "New Eve" (*Hawwa al-jadida*) every day a thousand times?[31]

Haddad stressed that Yvonne not only pays the social price for her first transgression, but that she is condemned to pay for it time and time again. Yvonne is brought tantalizingly close to the fringes of the family (during her courtships and marriage proposals) several times, but she is repeatedly cast out and condemned never to enter it. Her alliance with Mary, who is in many ways her unblemished alter ego and the future model of virtuous wifehood, is brief and the two never recognize their shared mother–daughter bond. Yvonne chooses to redeem herself and not to destroy Mary and Maurice's future but she also figures as the silent specter haunting their marriage, reminding the reader both of its fragility and of the fact that it would not have taken place had she not chosen to withdraw from the scene.

Evidence suggests that the novel, which garnered both praise (for its writing style and subject) and criticism (for his sympathetic treatment of Yvonne) generated considerable unease. Haddad himself acknowledged that "the Syrian newspapers showered criticism and praise" on the novel. To challenge his critics, the author appended the comments of four writers and his own rebuttal to the text of the novel. Authors Shibli Shumayyil and Jurji Zaydan both praised Haddad's novel, his treatment of a highly contentious subject, and the subtle rendition of the heroine's emotional world. Zaydan concurred that there were numerous social customs that needed to be reformed, and argued that fiction (plays, novels and philosophical novels) is the best medium with which to achieve this purpose. As'ad Khalil Daghir (d. 1935), a translator and intellectual, praised the originality and importance of the novel as well as the courage of the author; he noted that the novel was "widely distributed" and both the novel and its author were highly popular. Daghir expressed his astonishment that women writers and novelists abstained from this debate on the "fallen woman." Given what we know about the stricter social constraints applied to women (and women writers in particular), this hesitancy may be understandable; however, Daghir had little patience with their silence and enjoined them to engage with this issue, "which may release the tongues of rocks."[32]

The severest attack on the novel and the "outlaw emotions" it generated came from Rashid Rida (1865–1935), a leading Syrian Muslim modernist, who later founded the journal *al-Manar* (*The Lighthouse*, 1898–1935) in Egypt. Rida praised Haddad's writing and psychological insights and foresaw a great future for the author, but was uncomfortable with Haddad's sympathetic treatment of "fornicators" (*musafihat*) such as Yvonne. Rida preferred to view Haddad's novel as a cautionary tale: "You may describe their [the fallen women's] suffering so as to warn other [women] of these deeds [and] so that they don't descend into the abyss of prostitution." He also encouraged parents to read Haddad's description of Yvonne and his criticism of her family's lax supervision, which led to her seduction. Rida acknowledged the need to be compassionate towards sinners and suggested that homes be founded for "fallen women" seeking to reform themselves so that they did not resort to prostitution. Nevertheless he saw no reason to minimize the significance of their sin. Rida was particularly concerned about the immoral effect such sympathetic stories of "fallen women" could have on the behavior of "maidens" (*'adhara'*), "married housewives" (*rabbat al-buyut*) and "widows" (*ayyima*).[33]

Rida's choice of vocabulary shows that these novels and the "outlaw emotions" they aroused were of considerable concern to Haddad's contemporaries. Rida and others feared in essence that reading such texts would foster false expectations in women concerning their lot in life and might lead them to believe that such immoral behavior would be forgiven, thus leading them into ruin. Implicit in Rida's comments was the underlying fear that reading itself is a solitary and potentially subversive activity, which may create bonds among women, alienate them from the men in their lives, and empower them to form their own moral judgments.[34]

"The Eve of My Heart":[35] Khalil Jubran and the Social Origins of the Tale of Dissatisfied Love

Jubran Khalil Jubran (1883–1931), the best known of these late *Nahda* writers, was born in the village of Bsharri in Mount Lebanon. At the age of 12, after his father was imprisoned for tax evasion, Jubran's family immigrated to the United States, settling in 1895 in Boston's South End, which had a large concentration of Syrian-Lebanese immigrants. In Boston, while attending a settlement house school nearby, Jubran was introduced by one of his teachers to photographer and publisher Fred Holland Day (1864–1933), who encouraged his artistic interests. Perhaps fearing that Jubran was moving away from his Arab roots, his family decided to send the 15-year old back to Beirut to complete his education. Arriving in Beirut in late 1898, Jubran enrolled in the *Madrasat al-Hikma*, a Maronite college, to study Arab language and literature, and it was there that he met his lifelong friend, the artist Yusuf Huwayyik

(1882–1962), with whom he edited the journal *al-Manar*. Before returning to the United States in 1902 Jubran set out on an extensive tour of Greater Syria. Upon his return Jubran first directed most of his attention to painting, exhibiting his work in 1904; he also began writing for an Arabic émigré newspaper *al-Muhajir* (*The Immigrant*), where he met up with fellow *mahjar* writers Amin al-Rayhani (1876–1940) and Mikha'il Nu'ayma (1889–1988). He soon went on to publish two collections of Arabic short stories, *'Ara'is al-Muruj* (*Nymphs of the Valley*, 1906) and *al-Arwah al-Mutamarrida* (*Spirits Rebellious*, 1908). In 1908 Jubran left for Paris to study art, and it was there that he began work on his novella *al-Ajniha al-Mutakassira* (*Broken Wings*, 1912).[36]

Most of Jubran's critical and popular acclaim derives from his later works of poetry written in English (from 1918 onward). Here, however, we turn our attention to his early prose writing in Arabic, written soon after his departure from Beirut. This prose was clearly attuned to its social and moral concerns. We focus on three short stories, "Martha al-Baniya," "Warde al-Hani" and "Madja'" ("The Marriage Bed") and his novella *al-Ajniha al-Mutakassira*. The first story deals with a fallen woman's descent into prostitution and the others are focused on the fates of three loveless marriages. In these texts Jubran expressed strong anti-clerical feelings and contrasted organized religion with true spiritual beliefs, but most significantly Jubran condemned the prevailing patriarchal marriage customs of Beirut which prefer the dynastic and financial ambitions of the older generation over the desires of two young people. This preference results not only in loveless, unhappy marriages, but in deceit, infidelity and death. Jubran argued that if young people do not challenge and change such customs, they are destined to "remain the slaves of the strict laws enacted by their forefathers."[37]

In "Martha," one of his earliest short stories, Jubran explored the issue of prostitution, which was of great importance to several intellectuals both in the Ottoman Empire and in Greater Syria in the latter decades of the nineteenth century. Prostitution was a familiar social phenomenon and an important issue in Ottoman literature. Although there was no regulation of prostitution in Greater Syria during the Ottoman period, *shari'a* court evidence suggests that prostitution was tolerated and patronized by traveling merchants, *caravanserai*, soldiers and sailors. Elizabeth Thompson found that during the Mandate period, when the French regulated prostitution, a total of 764 prostitutes were registered in Mandate Syria and 242 in Lebanon (in 1922); however, local accounts suggest that actual numbers were higher, with an estimated 1,250 prostitutes active in the Beirut area alone.[38] Given these relatively low numbers of registered prostitutes (out of an estimated population of 120,000),[39] one may well wonder why the theme of prostitution was to become prevalent in Arabic literature in the coming years. One explanation is that the phenomenon was perhaps becoming more visible in the cities and with the growth of nightlife in Beirut,[40] or perhaps writers were influenced by the nonfictional works of social reformers and feminists and by fictional works (operas, plays, shorts stories and novels) written on the topic in European languages and in Turkish.[41] In any case, Haddad and Jubran were among the first to integrate the figure of the prostitute into Arabic prose fiction, to treat her with considerable sympathy, and to position her as the symptom of Arab society's sexual double standard.

"Martha," one of three short stories appearing in Jubran's first collection *'Ara'is al-Muruj*, tells the tale of a beautiful, young, orphaned village girl who is seduced and then abandoned by her wealthy lover. Written in the first person, the narrator, a young college graduate, returns in 1900 to Beirut from his countryside vacation, where an old villager tells him of Martha's disappearance. In Beirut the narrator encounters Fua'd, a young boy selling flowers, who tells him about his mother and her illness. The narrator immediately realizes that this is Martha's son and out of compassion follows him to the dying woman's hovel. There Martha tells of her seduction and how, following the birth of her son, her lover tired of her and she was passed off to her seducer's friends until illness took hold. The narrator comforts the dying Martha by accepting her version of her life story and asserting that she was the one "oppressed" while her oppressor was "a child of the palaces, great wealth and of little soul." Like Haddad in *Hawwa al-Jadida*, Jubran has his narrator reverse conventional social judgment which has rendered Martha an outcast (even in burial) while exempting her seducer from any social or moral culpability. The narrator overturns the earlier social verdict and hands down an alternative one, telling Martha (and the reader): "You are not unclean even if life has put you in the hands of the unclean. The dross of the flesh cannot reach out its hand to the pure spirit."[42]

The reversal or overturning of conventional social judgments regarding women's sexual transgressions would recur in his two other short stories published two years later, "Warda al-Hani" and "The Marriage Bed" appearing in *al-Arwah al-Mutamarrida*. In "Warda al-Hani" the story of a couple's unhappy marriage is retold, twice: first by the husband and then by the wife. The narrator, who has just returned to Beirut, goes to visit an old friend, Rashid Bey Nu'man, and is shocked by his pale and sickly appearance. Rashid Bey Nu'man tells the narrator that his wife, Warda al-Hani, whom he "delivered from penury and slavery" and showered with "fine clothes and priceless jewels and carriages and thoroughbred horses" left him to live with a young man "in the shadow of poverty."[43]

Next, the narrator sets out to meet Warda al-Hani herself and hears her version of events, which concurs with the facts of Rashid Bey Nu'man's version but not with their meaning. While Warda agrees that her husband loved her, she claims he loved her as one would love a precious possession displayed for others to admire. Warda claims that by leaving her husband she remained true to her heart rather than to the man-made customs of society. Reversing the conventional social opinion which judges her now to be an unfaithful wife, she asserts:

I was a harlot and a faithless woman in the house of Rashid Nu'man because he made me the sharer of his bed by virtue of tradition and custom rather than as a wife before Heaven, bound to him by the sacred law of love and the spirit. I was one filthy and unclean in my own eyes and before God when I took of his property, that he might take of my body. But now I am pure and clean, for the law of love has set me free. I am become faithful and good because I have ceased to trade my body for bread and my days for clothes. Yes, I was a whore whilst people thought me a virtuous wife.[44]

In this passage, which is reminiscent of Friedrich Engels' denunciation of capital-based, bourgeois marriage as a form of legalized prostitution in *The Origins of the Family, Private Property and the State* (1884), Jubran lashed out against the prevalent custom of property-based arranged marriages in turn-of-the-century Beirut. To reiterate this point, Jubran has Warda take the narrator to a window to look at various homes, each one concealing a dysfunctional and unhappy marriage maintained for financial reasons or social standing. The narrator, who has finally fathomed Warda's "immoral" behavior as well as "the secret of her protest against a society that prosecutes the rebel against its edicts before knowing the cause of his rebellion," leaves her house and wonders aloud (and to the readers) "who is the guilty and who the innocent?"[45]

In the accompanying short story "The Marriage Bed," Jubran mustered all of his authority as a writer to attest to the veracity of the events and characters, claiming that these events had taken place several years earlier in northern Lebanon and were told to him by a woman related to one of the main characters. The story tells of a bride, Layla, who regrets her decision to marry her older and wealthier suitor soon after the marriage ceremony. She begs her friend Susan to ask Salim, her beloved, to meet her in secret. The two meet and Layla begs him to run away with her, but honor-bound he refuses to break her vows and claims to love another. In a fit of rage and jealousy Layla stabs Salim; the stunned guests who come running when they hear her screams witness her suicide, but not before she launches in a scathing diatribe against all those who engineered her arranged marriage and those who would speak ill of her after her death: "You shall remember me and curse me with foul lips. But your children's children will bless me, for truth and the spirit will abide with the morrow."[46]

The heavy price of an unhappy arranged marriage is once again the theme of Jubran's next work *al-Ajniha al-Mutakassira*, and here too it is the woman who pays the heaviest price. The 18-year-old narrator, Jubran, falls in love with Salma Karama, the daughter of Faris Karama who was an old friend of his father. Salma reciprocates Jubran's feelings but the two soon learn that Bishop Bulus Ghalib wishes her to marry his dangerous and corrupt nephew, Mansur Bey. Despite Faris Karama's reluctance to accept this offer, he is forced to agree to the marriage for fear that if he does not do so Salma's "reputation would have been ruined and her name sullied by the dirt of lips and tongues."[47] Salma, while acknowledging the injustice of the situation, bows to custom:

> My father's wealth has placed me in the slave market, and this man has bought me. I neither know nor love him, but I shall learn to love him, and I shall obey him, serve him, and make him happy. I shall give him all that a weak woman can give a strong man.[48]

Jubran, the author, claimed that Salma Karama is a member of a generation that "exists between sleeping and waking," and that "in the city of Beirut, Salma Karama was the symbol of the future Eastern woman, but, like many who lie ahead of their time, she became victim to the present." Jubran compared Salma's subjugation to her husband to the subjugation of "the people of Eastern nations" to "their betrayers," "wolves and butchers who ruin their country through covetousness and crush their neighbors with an iron hand."[49]

For five years Salma endures her unhappy marriage to a man who does not care for her and spends his time "with those poor girls whom poverty has driven into the houses of ill fame; those girls who sell their bodies for bread kneaded with blood and tears." After her father's death, Salma turns to Jubran for comfort and the two begin to meet in secret at the temple of Astarte on the outskirts of Beirut. Jubran describes their encounters as a meeting of mind and soul and notes that "during the course of conversation Salma spoke of woman's place in society, the imprint that the past generation had left on her character, the relationship between husband and wife, and the spiritual diseases and corruption which threatened married life."[50]

Fearing that the bishop has got wind of her meetings with Jubran, Salma breaks off their meetings despite Jubran's pleas to run off together. Soon and to her great joy Salma is pregnant, but the baby dies at birth and she soon follows. Jubran, the mournful true lover, contrasts his hidden feelings when attending Salma's and her baby's funerals with that of her legal and "pitiless husband" to whom people pay their respects and offer "sweet words of sympathy." The text makes this clear through the attendees' comments on the husband's demeanor:

A third one said "Look at Mansour Bey: he is gazing at the sky as if his eyes were made of glass. He does not look like he has lost his wife and child in one day." A fourth one added, "His uncle, the Bishop, will marry him again tomorrow to a wealthier and stronger woman."[51]

In *al-Ajniha al-Mutakassira* Jubran's criticism of the marriage customs of the Beirut bourgeoisie reached its peak. He emphasized the characters' inability to withstand patriarchal social pressure. Faris Karama, Salma's father, does not favor his daughter's marriage to a dissolute man interested only in her fortune, but he is unable to oppose the bishop's power and influence. The well-bred and well-educated Salma, who is Jubran's prototype of the "New Woman," resigns herself to her duties as a daughter and obeys her father's reluctant request even though her heart lies elsewhere.

Soon after the publication of *al-Ajniha al-Mutakassira*, Jubran noted that there was considerable critical attention in the Arab and Arab-American press. As in Haddad's case the critics were divided; while most admired the author's dexterous style, others were far less taken with his views.[52] Readers were highly affected by these stories, a fact that greatly concerned more conservative critics. Jubran's friend Mary Elizabeth Haskell (1873–1964) recalled that this concern over the impact of Jubran's fiction on his readers was expressed soon after the publication of his earlier short story collections. She noted that initially Jubran's second collection of short stories, *al-Arwah al-Mutamarrida*, "was suppressed by the Syrian government" and only

200 copies were smuggled into the country. Even these few copies aroused great consternation, and on one occasion Jubran was asked by two representatives of the Maronite Patriarch to withdraw the book from the market or face excommunication. Jubran declined and announced instead that soon he would be publishing *al-Ajniha al-Mutakassira*.[53] Many years later, literary scholar Matti Moosa eloquently attested to the great emotional impact this novella had on him when he read it as a boy:

> I still recall that when I read it at the age of thirteen, I could not help crying over the fate of the lovers. The story had such a tremendous sentimental appeal that it is no exaggeration to say almost every adolescent in the Arab countries has read it.

Moosa concluded that "whether it was considered a well-crafted work of fiction or a factual narrative, *al-Ajniha al-Mutakassira* created a stir in the Arab world for both its sentimental content and its style."[54]

***

This set of late *Nahda* novels, novellas and short stories written by novelists who questioned and challenged the prevailing societal and sexual norms did so by drawing their readers into an intimacy with the fictional characters. By arousing the readers' sympathy toward the "good" characters and their ire against the "bad" ones, Alice al-Bustani, Niqula Haddad and Jubran Khalil Jubran encouraged their readers to reconsider societal norms and to find them wanting; in effect, they formulated an alternative set of values. To all intents and purposes they created a discursive space, a "rehearsal space," in which to voice and share "outlaw emotions."

Perhaps by arousing and appealing to the readers' emotions through a work of fiction these authors felt they could ensure that this alternative set of values would be favorably considered, or that they could circumvent the possible de-legitimization of a non-fictional essay or treatise. In doing so the authors were able to raise serious questions for the readers' contemplation well after they had completed reading the fictional texts; these issues may then have been shared with others in literary salons, letters, and book reviews. The novelists expanded the parameters of the traditional marriage-plot novel in order to consider the present and to envision future political and social avenues. They in essence created an intellectual "rehearsal space," in which readers could practice and mull over alternative outcomes, but they veiled this space behind tales of thwarted love. Their critics' responses show that the ruse was uncovered. Yet despite critics' attempts to draw the readers' attention to the dissimulation, they were unsuccessful, and the stories retained their emotional power.

Jens Hanssen suggested that during the second half of the nineteenth century Beirut society "silenced critiques of existing norms and habits by 'emasculating' their articulators" and by delegitimizing the emerging middle-class intellectuals as Westernizers.[55] This ideological de-legitimization of middle-class intellectuals and their literary products became far easier with the disintegration of the Ottoman Empire during World War I and the beginning of the French Mandate in Syria and Lebanon, with the creation of an "unholy alliance" between local religious and conservative elements and/or national movements, on the one hand, and French Mandate authorities, on the other. Elizabeth Thompson pointed out that "gender hierarchy was a pillar of colonial paternalism, wherein the French and indigenous elites bargained to maintain hierarchies of privilege in colonial society."[56] By establishing "gender as a site of conflict and compromise among men," not only was women's political bargaining power weakened,[57] but women as a literary subject suffered as well. As the nationalist question grew to become the focal point of Arab intellectual activity, other intellectual and philosophical concerns (including discussions on gender) were subordinated to it.[58]

This shift in focus had a significant impact on discussions about gender roles and women's lives in journal articles and the novels. In journals this rapid thematic shift can be easily discerned when comparing *al-Fatat* (1892–4), the first women's journal founded by Hind Nawfal, and the later *Anis al-Jalis* (1898–1908), founded by Alexandra Khuri Averino. *Al-Fatat* focused on bourgeois women both as readers and as subject matter whereas, *Anis al-Jalis* retained its target audience of bourgeois women readers, but its main subject matter became peasant women. A parallel trend can be found in novels. In many Egyptian novels such as in Mahmud Khayrat's *al-Fatat al-Rifiyya* (*The Young Countrywoman*, 1906), Mahmud Tahir Haqqi's '*Adhra' Dinshaway* (*The Maid of Dinshaway*, 1906) and especially Muhammad Husayn Haykal's novel *Zaynab* (1914), women – and in particular peasant women – came to stand for the nation. Literary production in Greater Syria (and later Lebanon and Syria) declined sharply from the outbreak of World War I onward, and the lives and concerns of women (not just bourgeois women) all but disappeared from sight.

EPILOGUE

DID WOMEN HAVE A *NAHDA*?

Throughout the nineteenth century and up to the end of World War I there was an intense engagement with modernity in Greater Syria. Modern ideas, lifestyles, social and economic activities and consumer practices were not viewed as inimical to Arab cultural and even political identity. Thus, the abruptness with which the cultural facet of the Nahda came to a halt comes as a shock. Some scholars have argued that the *Nahda* was a "failure," and others even refer to the recent "Arab Spring" as proof of its inability to bring about lasting political, cultural and gender changes. But did the *Nahda* fail? Or was this "failure" more on the lines of an interruption or a disruption?

Hisham Sharabi's thesis on "neopatriarchy" suggests that the socio-intellectual project of the *Nahda* may have been doomed from the start. Sharabi argued that

> the Arab Awakening or renaissance (*Nahda*) of the nineteenth century not only failed to break down the inner relations and forms of patriarchy but, by initiating what it called the modern awakening, also provided the ground for producing a new, hybrid sort of society/culture – the neopatriarchal society/culture we see before us today.

Sharabi claimed that despite the best intentions and efforts of Arab intellectuals, the *Nahda* "did not constitute a general cultural break" on the lines of the European Renaissance or Enlightenment and that the *Nahda* both failed to "achieve genuine transcendence of inherited structures of thought and social (including economic and political) organization, and on the other it failed to grasp the true nature of modernity."[1]

Although Sharabi offered a persuasive analysis of neopatriarchy from the 1920s onward, he seemed unaware of the historical importance of the *Nahda* in Greater Syria and did not grasp the full extent of the intense debate on modernity, gender and the re-formation of the nuclear family (and the women within it), which was an integral part of any social and intellectual debate before 1914. Stephan Sheehi argues that Sharabi's dismissal of the *Nahda*, along with its accompanying innovative linguistic and literary changes as "superficial and uncritical gestures" or as "expressions of 'minor' literature" blinded him to its significance and key function in the shaping of a modern Arab subjectivity.[2] By distinguishing between "Christian Arabs" and "Muslim Arabs" and viewing the former as inherently estranged from the Arab world, and the Muslim Ottoman state in particular, and claiming that they possessed a natural disposition for capitalism and modernity,[3] Sharabi positioned them as "the perennial Other" who colluded with the West.[4]

Several feminist scholars, such as Chandra Talpade Mohanty, Kumari Jayawardena, Uma Narayan and Alison Jaggar, have cautioned against taking such a "cultural essentialist" position concerning the articulation of an entire range of political demands for individual rights, equality or democracy. The contestation of local norms and practices, whether in the form of democracy or feminism, cannot be written off discursively as "cultural treason" or "mindless westernization."[5] Nayaran suggests that one of the ways feminist scholars may counter such essentializing impulses is by cultivating a "cultural stance that 'restores history and politics'" and demonstrating that "cultures are not pre-discursively individuated entities" but rather "entities whose individuation depends on complex discursive processes linked to political agendas."[6] This view was one of our main reasons for integrating the study of the cultural aspects of the *Nahda* period with the social and economic changes accompanying it and suggesting how they inflected each other.

Our analysis clearly shows that the *Nahda*, both as a period and as an intellectual movement, accompanied the rise of an urban bourgeoisie in Greater Syria. We have depicted the vibrancy of the *Nahda*, and the ways in which it drew growing numbers of people into its intellectual and cultural orbit throughout the region. It was both an inclusive movement (men and women, Christians, Muslims, Druze and Jews) and a comprehensive socio-cultural one, intent on transforming almost every aspect of people's lives. From the structure of the family and the design of the home, consumer patterns and leisure practices, to the question of women's participation in social and political life and the establishment of the nation state, not a single facet of cultural, social, economic or political life escaped the attention of the *Nahda* intellectuals. The modern forms of Arab culture and society cannot be considered accurately without appreciating the ways in which the *Nahda* and its intellectuals remolded their society.

The *Nahda* intellectuals believed that modernization included much more than the adoption of more advanced science and technology, or a slavish adoption of Western mannerisms; modernization was also a commitment to a set of values and behaviors. The *Nahda* was a period of active negotiation and intellectual "sorting out" of ideas, literary genres, values and lifestyles. Some would be retained, whereas others were disposed of over the course of time.

Arab women in Greater Syria used this historical moment to insert themselves and their rights into the discourse on modernity. Feminist philosopher Alison Jaggar highlighted the important role language (both in the linguistic and literary sense) plays as a conceptual framework in the articulation of the needs and aspirations of a rising group. She suggested that in order to overcome their silence, subaltern women need to collaborate with "other subaltern women in developing a public language for their shared experiences, to claim a collective identity and break through the barriers inhibiting their speech." However the articulation of such a public language "requires a community;"[7] an intimate, moral and political community united by shared assumptions, which provides the "intellectual space in which members are freed from pressure to continually defend their premises and explain their technical vocabulary."[8] The *Nahda* intellectuals and writers as well as their bourgeois readers constituted just such a community, and this was one of the reasons why a modern, Arab feminist discourse was able to blossom in this period. Women and men could very publically debate and even disagree with each other within this ever-expanding small community of shared values, and thus in this respect women did indeed experience a *Nahda*.

While it was and remains possible for those who wish to contain the changes within Arab society to brand and delegitimize such intellectuals, readers, writers, and feminists as "Westernizers" or "inauthentic" members of Arab society, we as feminist historians cannot endorse such a project which deracinates cultural periods or intellectual movements. The often-voiced perception concerning the *Nahda*'s "failure" is possible mainly because of the very abrupt way in which *Nahda* came to a close. Although it is tempting to speculate on the impact of the *Nahda* had it been able to run its course within an Ottoman Empire or an independent Arab state, the fact remains that it did not. When the sequence of events that preceded the emergence of the neopatriarchy in the 1920s is re-examined and re-assessed, it becomes clear that it was not the "failure" of the *Nahda* and its ideals that brought about "neopartiarchy"; rather it was the abrupt cessation of much of the cultural and social activity associated with the *Nahda*, due to the imposition of colonial Mandate rule, and more importantly the "patriarchal bargain" struck between local elites and the ruling colonial power that tainted the socio-political legacy of the *Nahda*.

In some ways the lasting legacy of the *Nahda* for modern Arab culture can be compared to archeological treasures concealed by shifting sands. The sand may remain undisturbed until sudden gusts of wind blow the dunes away and reveal former splendor, forever reminding the viewer of the vivacity and lessons of another era.

APPENDIX 1

ILLUSTRATIONS FROM THE NOVEL *ASMA*

This appendix contains 11 illustrations out of a total of 22 that appeared in the novel *Asma*, published in 1873 by Salim al-Bustani in his periodical *al-Jinan*, and are some of the earliest illustrations appearing in Arabic novels. They include images of men and women and reflect some of the characters' engagement with modernization and Westernization. The illustrations were intended to reflect both the characters' dress and personality.

The illustrator is unknown.

A. Male characters

Figure 5   Badi' is the villain of the novel. He is vain, self-centered, and immoral. Although he is interested in marrying Asma, she is repulsed by his personality. His posture reflects his character.
Source: Salim al-Bustani, "Asma," *al-Jinan* 4 (1873), p. 127.

Figure 6   Karim al-Baghdadi is the hero of the novel. He is a well-educated, generous, and upstanding young merchant, and at the end of the novel he marries Asma.
Source: Salim al-Bustani, "Asma," *al-Jinan* 4 (1873), p. 101.

جليل

Figure 7 Jalil is Asma's brother (and her male counterpart). Jalil courts Badiʻa but eventually marries Saʻada, since she embodies the feminine qualities promoted by the novel.
Source: Salim al-Bustani, "Asma," *al-Jinan* 4 (1873), p. 173.

فريد

Figure 8 Farid is another scoundrel. He courts several young women over the course of the novel but eventually ends up with Badiʻa.
Source: Salim al-Bustani, "Asma," *al-Jinan* 4 (1873), p. 281.

قريد والعجوز

Figure 9   Farid scheming with his servant. His bearing indicates laziness and immorality.
Source: Salim al-Bustani, "Asma," *al-Jinan* 4 (1873), p. 381.

B. Female characters

سعدى

Figure 10   Sa'da is the young woman who eventually marries Jalil. She symbolizes innocence, kindness and orderliness.
Source: Salim al-Bustani, "Asma," *al-Jinan* 4 (1873), p. 209.

نبيهة

Figure 11   Nabiha is one of the minor female characters in the novel. She is mesmerized by everything Western but understands the merits of her own culture.
Source: Salim Al-Bustani, "Asma," *al-Jinan* 4 (1873), p. 245.

لو لبستها أفرنجية للبرق لها

Figure 12   "Do I look Euxopean?" – Nabiha showing off her new dress and shoes to her European fiancé (Richard). Nabiha is so eager to flaunt her new matching shoes that she does not notice she has lifted her skirt so much that the dress is now immodestly short.
Source: Salim al-Bustani, "Asma," *al-Jinan* 4 (1873), p. 281.

Figure 13   Karim and Asma. In this image they are contrasted with Nabiha and Richard.
Source: Salim al-Bustani, "Asma," *al-Jinan* 4 (1873), p. 713.

اسمع ما قال هذا الرجل

Figure 14 Nabiha and Richard taking a stroll to impress onlookers. Nabiha was so impressed by Richard's beret that she asked him to wear it at home as well.

Source: Salim al-Bustani, "Asma," *al-Jinan* 4 (1873), p. 677.

APPENDIX 2

ANONYMOUS LETTER ON WOMEN'S RIGHTS AND ELECTIONS

حقوق النساء والانتخاب

حضرة الدكتور عن منشئي المقتطف الفاضلين

قرأت مسرورة ما نشرتموه في الجزء الثاني من المقتطف بقلم حضرة الاديب ودیع افندي
ابي رزق نزیل استرالیا عن حقوق النساء وقيامهن في استرالیا يطالبن بمشاركة الرجال في
انتخاب النواب عنهنّ وعن عيالهنّ وما فاهت به احداهنّ من الكلام الجزل الآخذ بمجامع
القلوب حيث قالت " ونحن اقرب منكم الى العدل وانصاف المظلوم من الظالم " لله درّها
ما اقوى حجتها واوضح بيانها ولقد اصابت حيث قالت " ان المرأة تضاهي الرجل في تدبير
شؤون الاحكام وهي اقدر منهُ على ابطال الاسراف وترع الفساد و بث الاستقامة في البلاد .
ولو كانت النساء قابضات على زمام الاحكام لابطان الحانات او لـعين في تقليلها على الاقل
ان لم يتيسر لهنّ ابطالها لانها بينبوع كل شقاه وفساد . وكنّ وضعن على الخمور الضرائب
الفاحشة فترتفع اسعارها ويقلّ شربُها فيقل التعدي ويجو الفقير من مجالس الفقر " الى غير
ذلك من الاقوال التي يُسمع صداها من قلب كل من لم يعدم روح الغرض . وبما يليق ان
يضاف إلى ذلك ما أتينا على ذكره مرةً في المقتطف نقلاً عن فلامريون الفلكي الفرنسوي
الشهير على سبيل الرواية وهو ان النساء ستتمكنّ اخيراً من ابطال الحروب لانهن سيرفضن
التزوج بكل مَن يحمل سلاحاً ويستعدّ لقتال ابناء نوعه فيضطرّ الرجال ان يبطلوا هذه
الخلة القبيحة اللتي تدنين نوع الانسان وتلقي على الملك عبئاً ثقيلاً تئنّ تحتهُ وتضطر ان تضرب
الضرائب الفادحة على رعاياها بسببه

ولم استغرب من حضرة الكاتب رفضهُ مطالب النساء لانهُ يعزّ على الرجال ان يتنازلوا
عن الاستئثار بحقوق النساء المهضومة . وهل رأيتَ مالكاً تنازل عن ملكه عنواً . ولكني
استغربت الدليل الذي اقامهُ على ذلك وهو انهُ " لا حق لمرأة بالتصويت والانتخاب
والاشتغال بالسياسة عموماً ما زالت خاضعة لناموس الطبيعة غير المغيّر " . وهو استدلال فاسد .
فما دليلهُ على ان الخضوع لناموس الطبيعة يمنع من قضاه عمل يُعَدّ عندنا من اخف الاعمال
اللتي تعملها المرأة كل يوم . واي امرأة لا تستطيع ان تكتب اسمها على ورقة وتلقيها في
صندوق الانتخاب مرةً كل سنتين او ثلاث . واي امرأة لا تستطيع ان تجلس على كرمي
الوالي وتفهم ما يعرض عليها من الاوراق . وهل هذه الاعمال اصعب من اعمالها البيتية . هذه
ملكة الانكليز وسلطانة الهند خاضعة لنواميس الطبيعة مثل كل النساء بل اكثر من اكثر

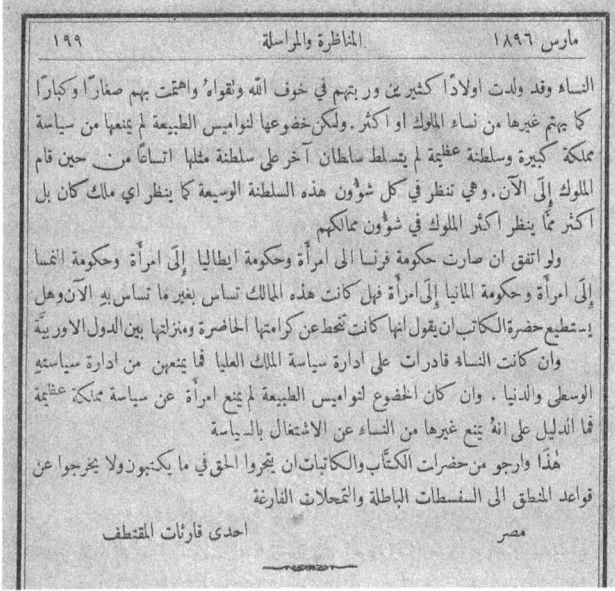

النساء وقد ولدت أولاداً كثيراً ورّبتهم في خوف الله وتقواه واهتمّت بهم صغاراً وكباراً

كما يهتم غيرها من نساء الملوك أو أكثر. ولكن خضوعها لنواميس الطبيعة لم يمنعها من سياسة

مملكة كبيرة وسلطنة عظيمة لم يبسط سلطان آخر على سلطنة مثلها اتساعاً من حين قام

الملوك إلى الآن. وهي تنظر في كل شؤون هذه السلطنة الوسيعة كما ينظر أي ملك كان بل

أكثر مما ينظر أكثر الملوك في شؤون ممالكهم

ولو اتفق ان صارت حكومة فرنسا الى امرأة وحكومة ايطاليا إلى امرأة وحكومة النمسا

إلى امرأة وحكومة ألمانيا إلى امرأة فهل كانت هذه الممالك تساس بغير ما تساس به الآن وهل

إ ـ تطيع حضرة الكاتب ان يقول انها كانت تحط عن كرامتها الحاضرة ومنزلتها بين الدول الاوربيّة

وان كانت النساء قادرات على ادارة سياسة الملك العليا فما يمنعهن من ادارة سياستهم

الوسطى والدنيا . وان كان الخضوع لنواميس الطبيعة لم يمنع امرأة عن سياسة مملكة عظيمة

فما الدليل على انه يمنع غيرها من النساء عن الاشتغال بالسياسة

هذا وارجو من حضرات الكتّاب والكاتبات ان يجروا الحق في ما يكتبون ولا يخرجوا عن

قواعد المنطق الى السفسطات الباطلة والتحلات الفارغة

احدى قارئات المقتطف   مصر

Figure 15   Letter from *al-Muqtataf* Vol. 20 (1896), pp. 198–9. Published in the section: *al-Munazara wal-Murasala* – A Public Debate and Exchange of Letters. The translation appears below.

Women's Rights and Voting (Huquq al-Nisa' wal-Intikhab)

To the respected doctors, founders of *al-Muqtataf*,

I was pleased to read [the column] you published in the second section of *al-Muqtataf*, by the honorable writer Wadi' Effendi Abi Rizq, a resident (*nazil*) of Australia, who wrote about women's rights in Australia, and their demand to participate in the election of delegates both on their behalf and on behalf of their daughters: [I was also pleased to read] the words of one of [those women] – valuable, powerful, and captivating words. She said: "we [women] have a greater affinity to justice than you [men] do, and we are better able to demand the rights of the oppressed from the oppressor (*insaf al-mazlum min al-zalim*)." Good for her. She makes a strong case, and her statements are very clear. She was right when she said:

Woman is equal to man in managing governmental affairs, and she is even more capable than him when putting an end to wastefulness, rooting out corruption, and spreading integrity throughout the land. If women were to hold the reins of power, they would close the taverns, or at the very least try to limit their number, if they could not entirely close them, since these are the source of much suffering and corruption. They would levy heavy taxes on wines, raising the prices and making the number of drinkers go down, and as a result so would oppression be lessened and the pauper rescued from the clutches of poverty.

[These words combine] with other statements that echo from the depth of the heart of anyone who hasn't been seized by greed. Furthermore, it is worth noting something you published in the past in *al-Muqtataf*. [I am referring to] a quote from the famous French astronomer [Nicolas Camille] Flammarion, in which he says that in the end women will be able to put an end to wars by refusing to marry anyone who bears arms and is willing to fight his own kind, and as a result the men will have to cease this ugly habit, which mars the human species and places a heavy yoke on the kingdom and makes [the kingdoms] impose heavy taxes on their subjects.

I was not surprised that the respectable writer [Abi Rizq] rejected the demands of the women, since men are incapable of relinquishing the rights denied women and which they keep for themselves. Have you ever seen a property owner give up his property so casually? I was, however, surprised by the logic that led him to this, namely that "women cannot have a right to vote (*taswit*), to be elected (*intikhab*), or to be involved in politics (*ishtighal bil-siyasa*) at all, so long as they are subject to the unchangeable laws of nature." This is faulty reasoning. But what evidence does he have that subjugation to the laws of nature prevents men from doing work that is commonly considered easier than the jobs that women do every day?

What woman cannot write her name on a note and place it in a ballot box every two or three years? What woman is not capable of sitting on a governor's seat and signing papers that are placed before her? Are these jobs more difficult than her housework? The Queen of England and Empress of India is subject to the laws of nature like all women, and even more than most women. She gave birth to children, reared them to fear God, and cared for them when they were small and as they grew, just as women who are not the wives of kings do, and even more. And yet, her subjugation to the laws of nature did not prevent her from steering a great kingdom or a powerful sultanate of a scale that no other sultan, from the beginning of the days of empire and to this day, has been able to manage. She oversees all the matters of this vast sultanate, just as any king examines them, and in fact more than the greatest of kings examine the matters of their kingdoms.

If it were agreed to place the government of France in the hands of a woman, and the government of Italy in the hands of a woman, and the government of Austria in the hands of a woman, and the government of Germany in the hands of a woman – would these kingdoms be governed differently than they are today? Would the respected writer state that their esteem and status among the European states would lessen?

If women are capable of dealing with the highest matters of the kingdom, what keeps them from [also] handling the run of the mill and mundane matters of the kingdom? If subjugation to the laws of nature does not keep a woman from running a powerful kingdom, then what is the justification for preventing other women from dealing in politics?

Furthermore, I ask the honorable writers, men and women, to be fair with regard to what they write and not to stray from the rules of logic towards vain philosophizing and empty tricks.

Egypt
From one of the readers of *al-Muqtataf*

NOTES

Introduction

1. Butrus al-Bustani, "Khitab fi Ta'lim al-Nisa'," in Yusuf Qizma al-Khuri (ed.), *al-Jam'iyya al-Suriyya lil-'Ulum wal-Funun 1847–1852* (Beirut: Dar al-Huda', 1990), pp. 45–53. This lecture was published in 1852 as part of series delivered at the society, and again in 1882 in al-Bustani's periodical *al-Jinan*.
2. Al-Bustani, "Khitab fi Ta'lim al-Nisa'," p. 47. We would like to thank Tarek Abboud, who translated al-Bustani's lecture, and also Adel Beshara, who drew our attention to this translation.
3. Al-Bustani, "Khitab fi Ta'lim al-Nisa'," p. 45.
4. Ibid., pp. 45–46. At the time pouring oil or wine onto a wound was considered a popular home remedy.
5. Ibid., p. 52.
6. Butrus al-Bustani, "Khutba fi Adab al-'Arab," in *al-Jam'iyya al-Suriyya lil-'Ulum wal-Funun 1847–1852*, p. 117.
7. Ibid.
8. The early days of the *Nahda* in Greater Syria, in the 1840s, have not been examined in detail until recently. However, the *Nahda* was clearly a multi-causal sociocultural phenomenon, which lay at the confluence of diverse processes, such as the rise of the middle class (especially in Beirut and the other large cities), the expansion of educational opportunities, the emergence of an intelligentsia, and the encounter with Western culture, ideas, and technology.
9. Patel Abdulrazzak, *The Arab Nahda: The Making of the Intellectual and Humanist Movement* (London: Edinburgh University Press, 2013).
10. Stating that the *Tanzimat* reforms were inspired by the Westernizing reformers by no means suggests that we are ascribing to a view of the Ottoman Empire as "static" until this point and the reforms as a mimetic reaction; rather we argue that the pace of change accelerated. For earlier legal reforms and changes in

gender discourse, see for example Dror Ze'evi, "Changes in the Legal-Sexual Discourses: Sex Crimes in the Ottoman Empire," *Continuity and Change* 16:2 (2001), pp. 219–242 and Marc Baer, "Islamic Conversion Narratives of Women: Social Changes and Gendered Religious Hierarchy in Early Modern Ottoman Istanbul," *Gender and History* 16:2 (2004), pp. 425–458.

11. Roderic H. Davidson, *Reform in the Ottoman Empire, 1856–1876* (Princeton: Princeton University Press, 1963), pp. 81–113; Butrus Abu-Manneh, *Studies on Islam and the Ottoman Empire in the 19ᵗʰ Century, 1826–1876* (Istanbul: Isis Press, 2001), pp. 115–124; Fatma M. Göçek, "Ethnic Segmentation, Western Education, and Political Outcomes: Nineteenth-Century Ottoman Society," *Poetics Today* 14 : 3 (1993), pp. 507–538, and Fatma M. Göçek, *Rise of the Bourgeoisie, Demise of Empire: Ottoman Westernization and Social Change* (Oxford and New York: Oxford University Press, 1996); for its impact in Greater Syria, see Moshe Maoz, "Syrian Urban Politics in the Tanzimat Period between 1840 and 1861," *Bulletin of the School of Oriental and African Studies* 29:2 (1960), pp. 277–301.

12. Ehud Toledano, "Lishkoach et Heavar Haosmani shel Mitsrayim (in Hebrew)" *Jama'a* 1 (1997), pp. 67–87; Jens Hanssen, "'Your Beirut is on My Desk': Ottomanizing Beirut under Sultan Abdülhamid II," in Peter Rowe and Hashim Sarkis (eds.), *Projecting Beirut: Episodes in the Construction and Reconstruction of a Modern City* (Munich: Prestel, 1998), pp. 41–67; see also Fruma Zachs, *The Making of a Syrian Identity: Intellectuals and Merchants in Nineteenth-Century Beirut* (Leiden and Boston: E. J. Brill, 2005) and Ussama Makdisi, "Ottoman Orientalism," *American Historical Review* 107 : 3 (2002), pp. 768–796.

13. For example, see one of the latest works on this subject, Tarek El-Ariss, *Trails of Arab Modernity: Literary Affects and the New Political Identity* (New York: Fordham University Press, 2013), pp. 1–18.

14. For more on Muhammad 'Abduh, Tahir al-Jaza'iri and Rashid Rida, see Elie Kedouri, *Afgahni and 'Abduh: An Essay on Religion Unbelief and Political Activism in Modern Islam* (London: Frank Cass, 1966); Albert Hourani, *Arabic Thought in the Liberal Age, 1798–1939* (London: Oxford University Press, 1962; 1970 ed.), pp. 130–244; Malcolm Kerr, *Islamic Reform: The Political and Legal Theories of Muhammad 'Abduh and Rashid Rida* (Berkeley: University of California Press, 1966); David D. Commins, *Islamic Reform: Politics and Social Change in Late Ottoman Syria* (New York: Oxford University Press, 1990); Joseph S. Escovitz, "'He Was the Muhammad 'Abduh of Syria': A Study of Tahir al-Jaza'iri and his Influence," *International Journal of Middle East Studies* 80:3 (1986), pp. 293–310; Eliezer Tauber, "Rashid Rida as Pan-Arabist: Before World War I," *The Muslim World* 79:2 (1989), pp. 102–112, and Eliezer Tauber, "Three Approaches, One Idea: Religion and State in the Thought of 'Abd al-Rahman al-Kawkabi, Najib 'Azuri and Rashid Rida," *British Journal of Middle Eastern Studies* 21:2 (1994), pp. 190–198.

15. Both Ya'qub Sanu' and Shim'on Moyal were friendly with Muhammad 'Abduh and other members of his circle. For more on the activities of these men and

other Jewish intellectuals in the Nahda, see Ammiel Alcalay, *After Jews and Arabs: Remaking Levantine Culture* (Minneapolis: University of Minnesota Press, 1993) and Lisa L. Levy, "Jewish Writers in the Arab East: Literature, History, and the Politics of Enlightenment, 1863–1914" (Ph.D. dissertation, University of California-Berkeley, 2007).

16. Deniz Kandiyoti, "Paradoxes of Masculinity: Some Thoughts on Segregated Societies," in Andrea Cornwall and Nancy Lindisfarne (eds.), *Dislocating Masculinity: Comparative Ethnographies* (London and New York: Routledge, 1994), pp. 197–213; Hisham Sharabi, *Neopatriarchy: A Theory of Distorted Change in Arab Society* (New York, NY, and Oxford: Oxford University Press, 1988), p. 4.

17. Timothy Mitchell, "The Stage of Modernity," in Timothy Mitchell (ed.), *Questions of Modernity* (Minneapolis: University of Minnesota Press, 2000), p. 26. For more on the debate, see Arjun Appadurai, "Disjuncture and Difference in the Global Cultural Economy," *Theory, Culture and Society* 7 (1990), pp. 295–310; Shmuel. N. Eisenstadt, "Multiple Modernities," *Daedalus* 129:1 (2000), pp. 1–29; Jan N. Pieterse, "Globalization as Hybridization," in Mike Featherstone, Scott Lash and Roland Robertson (eds.), *Global Modernities* (London: Sage Publications, 1995), pp. 45–68.

18. Ami Ayalon argues that the first region in the province to experience this cultural revitalization was Lebanon, with Palestine and Jordan undergoing these changes only well into the twentieth century. Thus Palestine and Jordan are beyond the scope of this study. See Ami Ayalon, *Reading Palestine: Printing and Literacy, 1900–1948* (Austin: University of Texas: 2004), p. 2.

19. For more information on Damascus, see James A. Reilly, "Inter-Confessional Relations in Nineteenth-Century Syria: Damascus, Homs and Hama Compared," *Islam and Christian-Muslim Relations* 7:2 (1996), pp. 213–224 and Linda S. Schilcher, *Families in Politics: Damascene Families and Estates of the 18th and 19th Centuries* (Stuttgart: Franz Steiner Verlag Wiesbaden GMBH, 1985).

20. For more information on Aleppo, see Kamil al-Ghazzi, *Kitab Nahr al-Dhahab fi Ta'rikh Halab*, vol. 2, 2nd ed. (Aleppo: Dar al-Qalam al-'Arabi, 1991–1993), p. 397. Eds. Shawqi Sha'th and Mahmud Fakhuri; Margaret Meriwether, "Women and Economic Change in Nineteenth Century Syria: The Case of Aleppo," in Judith E. Tucker (ed.), *Arab Women: Old Boundaries, New Frontiers* (Bloomington: Indiana University Press, 1993), pp. 65–83 and Margaret Meriwether "Urban Notables and Rural Resources in Aleppo, 1770–1830," *International Journal of Turkish Studies* 4 (1987), pp. 55–73; Keith D. Watenpaugh, *Being Modern in the Middle East: Revolution, Nationalism, Colonialism and the Arab Middle Class* (Princeton: Princeton University Press, 2006), especially Chapter 1; see also Bruce Masters, "Aleppo: The Ottoman Empire's Caravan City," in Edhem Eldem, Daniel Goffman, and Bruce Masters (eds.), *The Ottoman City between East and West: Aleppo, Izmir, and Istanbul* (Cambridge: Cambridge University Press, 1999), pp. 17–78; Bruce Masters,

"The Political Economy of Aleppo in an Age of Ottoman Reform," *Journal of the Economic and Social History of the Orient* 53 (2010), pp. 290–316.

21. One of the rare serious historical studies of Tripoli is by Khalid Ziyada, *al-Sura al-Taqlidiyya lil-Mujtama' al-Madani: Qira'a Manhajiyya fi Sijillat Mahkamat Tarablus al-Shar'iyya fil-Qarn al-Sabi' 'Ashar wa-Bidayat al-Qarn al-Thamin 'Ashar* (Tripoli: Manshurat Ma'had al-'Ulum al-Ijtima'iyya, 1983).

22. Philip S. Khoury, "Continuity and Change in Syrian Political Life: The Nineteenth and Twentieth Centuries," *American Historical Review* 96:5 (1991), p. 1382.

23. Rashid Khalidi, "Ottomanism and Arabism in Syria before 1914: A Reassessment," in Rashid Khalidi (ed.), *The Origins of Arab Nationalism* (New York: Columbia University Press, 1991), p. 56; Leila T. Fawwaz, *Merchants and Migrants in Nineteenth-Century Beirut* (Cambridge, MA: Harvard University Press, 1983), p. 1, 31.

24. Ami Ayalon, "Private Publishing in the Nahda," *International Journal of Middle East Studies* 40 (2008), pp. 561–577; Dagmar Glas, *Der Muqtataf und seine Öffentlichkeit: Aufklärung, Räsonnement und Meinungsstreit in der Frühen Arabisschen Zeitschriftenkommunikation*, 2 vols. (Würtzburg, Germany: Ergon Verlag, 2004); Fruma Zachs, *The Making of a Syrian Identity*.

25. Leila T. Fawaz, *Merchants and Migrants in Nineteenth Century Beirut*; Margaret L. Meriwether, *The Kin Who Count: Family and Society in Ottoman Aleppo, 1770–1840* (Austin: University of Texas Press, 1999); James A. Reilly, "Damascus Merchants and Trade in the Transition to Capitalism," *Canadian Journal of History* 27 (1992), pp. 1–27.

26. For studies on the Greater Syrian middle class in a later period, see Keith D. Watenpaugh, "Being Middle Class and Being Arab: Sectarian Dilemmas and Middle Class Modernity in the Arab Middle East, 1908–1936," in A. Ricardo Lopez and Barbara Weinstein (eds.), *The Making of the Middle Class: Toward a Transnational History* (Durham: Duke University Press, 2012), pp. 267–287.

27. Shereen Khairallah, *The Sisters of Men: Lebanese Women in History* (Beirut: American University of Beirut, 1996), p. 182. The salon is an excellent example of the ways in which the Arab middle classes merged Arab and European traditions; Boutheina Khalidi, for example, argues that while they drew upon the model of the eighteenth-century French salon they also drew on a "solid tradition of Arabic chancery art that reached its peak in between the tenth and fifteenth centuries." Boutheina Khalidi, ""Epistolarity in the Nahda Climate: The Role of Mayy Ziyadah's Letter Writing," *Journal of Arabic Literature* 49 (2009), p. 1.

28. Marilyn Booth, *May Her Likes Be Multiplied: Biography and Gender Politics in Egypt* (Berkeley: University of California Press, 2001); Margot Badran, "The Feminist Vision in the Writings of Three Turn-of-the-Century Egyptian Women," *Bulletin of the British Society for Middle Eastern Studies* 15:1/2 (1988), pp. 11–20; Fruma Zachs and Sharon Halevi, "From *Difa' al-Nisa'* to *Mas'alat al-Nisa'* in Greater Syria: Readers and Writers Debate Women and their Rights, 1858–1900," *International Journal of Middle East Studies* 41 (2009), pp. 615–634; Juan R. Cole,

"Feminism, Class, and Islam in Turn-of-the-Century Egypt," *International Journal of Middle East Studies* 13 (1981), pp. 387–407.

29. See for example Khalil al-Khuri, "Talab al-Samah," *Hadiqat al-Akhbar* no. 31 (Aug. 1858), p. 3; Adelaide (Idlid) al-Bustani, "Hanri wa-Imilya (Henry and Amelia)," *al-Jinan* 1 (1870), pp. 366–367, 406–407; Jibra'il Sadqah, "Fi Huquq al-Nisa'," *al-Jinan* 1 (1870), pp. 401–402; Labiba Hanifa, "Letter to the editor," *al-Fatat*, January 15, 1893, p. 153; Wadi' al-Khuri, "Huquq al-Mar'a," *al-Muqtataf* 7 (1882), p. 21; Nu'man 'Abduh al-Qasatli, "Riwayat Murshid wa-Fitna," *al-Jinan* 11 (1880), p. 665. Our findings contradict those of Afsaneh Najmabadi and Joseph Massad, who claim that this new meaning of the word in Persian and in Arabic emerged only in the early twentieth century. Afsaneh Najmabadi, "Beyond the Americas: Are Gender and Sexuality Useful Categories of Historical Analysis?" *Journal of Women's History* 18:1 (2006), p. 13; Joseph A. Massad, *Desiring Arabs* (Chicago: University of Chicago Press, 2007), p. 171.

30. Here, *janasat* is a verb in the third person singular feminine form, meaning "belonging to the same species."

31. Butrus al-Bustani, *Muhit al-Muhit*, vol.1 (Beirut: n.p., 1870), pp. 128–129; the quotation is found on page 129.

32. See Ami Ayalon, *The Press in the Arab Middle East: A History* (New York and Oxford: Oxford University Press, 1995); Ami Ayalon, "Private Publishing in the Nahda," *International Journal of Middle East Studies* 40 (2008), pp. 561–577; Nadia Farag, "The Lewis Affair and the Fortunes of al-Muqtataf," *Middle Eastern Studies* 8 (1972), pp. 73–83; Elizabeth M. Holt, "Narrative and the Reading Public in 1870s Beirut," *Journal of Arabic Literature* 40 (2009), pp. 37–70; Samah Selim, "The Nahda, Popular Fiction and the Politics of Translations," *The MIT Electronic Journal of Middle East Studies* 4 (2004), pp. 75–89; see also Mahmoud Haddad, "Ottoman Economic Nationalism in the Press of Beirut and Tripoli (Syria) at the End of the Nineteenth Century," in Gisela Procházka Eisl and Martin Strohmeier (eds.), *The Economy as an Issue in the Middle Eastern Press* (Vienna and Berlin: LIT Verlag GmbH, 2008), pp. 75–84, and Ilham Khuri-Makdisi, *The Eastern Mediterranean and the Making of Global Radicalism, 1860–1914* (Berkeley and Los Angeles, University of California Press, 2010), pp. 35–59 for an examination of the role of the periodical press in disseminating radical reformist ideas.

33. See Byron D. Cannon, "Nineteenth-Century Arabic Writings on Women and Society: The Interim Role of the Masonic Press in Cairo (*al- Lata'if*, 1885–1895)," *International Journal of Middle East Studies* 17 (1985), pp. 462–484; Jurj Kallas, *al-Haraka al-Fikriyya al-Nasawiyya fi 'Asr al-Nahda, 1849–1923* (Beirut: Dar al-Jil, 1996); Jurj Kallas, *Ta'rikh al-Sihafa al-Nasawiyya, Nash'atuha wa-Tatawwuruha 1892–1932* (Beirut: Dar al-Jil, 1996); Mervat F. Hatem, *Literature, Gender, and Nation-Building in Nineteenth-Century Egypt: The Life and Works of 'A'isha Taymur* (New York: Palgrave Macmillan, 2011).

34. Laura Bier, "Modernity and the Other Woman: Gender and National Identity in the Egyptian Women's Press, 1952–1967," *Gender and History* 16 (2004),

pp. 99–112; Marilyn Booth, "*Women in Islam*: Men and the 'Women's Press' in the Turn-of-the-20th-Century Press," *International Journal of Middle East Studies* 33 (2001), pp. 171–201; Basilius Bawardi and Fruma Zachs, "Between Adab al-Rihlat and "Geo-Literature": The Constructive Narrative Fiction of Salim al-Bustani," *Middle Eastern Literatures* 10 (2007), pp. 203–217; Sharon Halevi and Fruma Zachs, "Asma (1873): The Early Arabic Novel as a Social Compass," *Studies in the Novel* 39 (2007), pp. 416–430; Fruma Zachs and Sharon Halevi, "From Difa' al-Nisa' to Mas'alat al-Nisa' in Greater Syria."

35. See also Roger Allen, *The Arabic Novel: An Historical and Critical Introduction* (Syracuse: Syracuse University Press, 1982); Sabry Hafez, *The Genesis of Arabic Narrative Discourse: A Study in the Sociology of Modern Arabic Literature* (London: Saqi Books, 1993); Matti Moosa, *The Origins of Modern Arabic Fiction*, 2nd ed. (Boulder and London: Lynne Rienner Publishers1997); Muhammad Y. Najm, *al-Qissa fil-Adab al-'Arabi al-Hadith*. 3rd ed. (Beirut: Dar al-Thaqafa,1961); Sharifa al-Qiyadi, *Isham al-Katiba al-'Arabiyya fi 'Asr al-Nahda hata 1914* (Malta: Sharikat Elga, 1999); Ibrahim al-Sa'afin, *Tatawwur al-Riwaya al-'Arabiyya al-Haditha fi Bilad al-Sham* (Baghdad: Dar al-Rashid lil-Nashr, 1980); Hamdi al-Sakkut, *The Arabic Novel: Bibliography and Critical Introduction, 1865–1995*, 6 vols. (Cairo: The American University in Cairo Press, 2000); Samah Selim, "The Nahda, Popular Fiction and the Politics of Translations," pp. 75–89; Samah Selim, *The Novel and the Rural Imaginary in Egypt 1880–1995* (New York: Routledge Curzon, 2004); Buthayna Sha'ban, *100 'Am min al-Riwaya al-Nisa'iyya al-'Arabiyya 1899–1999* (Beirut: Dar al-Adab lil-Nashr wal-Tawzi', 1999); Joseph T. Zeidan, *Arab Women Novelists: The Formative Years* (Albany: SUNY Press, 2005).

36. Jane Tompkins, *Sensational Designs: The Cultural Work of American Fiction 1760–1860*, (New York: Oxford University Press, 1985), p. xi; Nancy Armstrong, *Desire and Domestic Fiction: A Political History of the Novel* (New York: Oxford University Press, 1987), p. 895.

37. Several important studies include Robert Darnton, *The Great Cat Massacre and Other Episodes in French Cultural History* (New York: Basic Books, 1984); Rita Felski, *The Gender of Modernity* (Cambridge, MA: Harvard University Press, 1995); Lynn Hunt, *The Family Romance of the French Revolution* (Berkeley and Los Angeles: University of California Press, 1992); Natalie Z. Davis, *Fiction in the Archives: Pardon Tales and their Tellers in Sixteenth-Century France* (Cambridge: Polity Press, 1988).

38. Afsaneh Najmabadi, *Women with Mustaches and Men without Beards: Gender and Sexual Anxieties of Iranian Modernity* (Berkeley and Los Angeles: University of California Press, 2005); Dror Ze'evi, *Producing Desire: Changing Sexual Discourse in the Ottoman Middle East, 1500–1900* (Berkeley and Los Angeles: University of California Press, 2006).

39. Laurel Brake, "Writing, Cultural Production, and the Periodical Press in the Nineteenth Century," in J. B. Bullen (ed.), *Writing and Victorianism* (London and New York: Longman, 1997), p. 62; Lynn Pykett, "Reading the Periodical Press:

Text and Context," *Victorian Periodicals Review* 22:3 (1989), p. 101; Margaret Beetham, "Towards a Theory of the Periodical as a Publishing Genre," in Laurel Brake, Aled Jones and Lionel Madden (eds.), *Investigating Victorian Journalism* (London: Macmillan, 1990), pp. 19–32; see also Laurel Brake and Anne Humphreys, "Critical Theory and Periodical Research," *Victorian Periodicals Review* 22:3 (1989), pp. 94–95.

40. Yumna al-'Id, "Lebanon," in Rawda Ashour, Ferial Jabouri Ghazoul, Hasna Reda-Mekdashi (eds.), *Arab Women Writers: A Critical Reference Guide, 1873–1999*. Translated by Mandy McClure (Cairo: The American University Press, 2009), p. 21.

Chapter 1   From *Difa' al-Nisa'* to *Mas'alat al-Nisa'* in Greater Syria: Readers and Writers Debate Women and Their Rights, 1858–1900

1. Anonymous, "Ikhtira' Tilighraf Jadid," *Hadiqat al-Akhbar* issue 30 (1858), p. 4.
2. Fruma Zachs, "Building a Cultural Identity: The Case of Khalil al-Khuri," in Thomas Philipp and Christoph Schumann (eds.), *From the Syrian Land to the States of Syria and Lebanon* (Beirut: Beiruter Texte und Studien, 2004), p. 30.
3. Khalil al-Khuri, "Talab al-Samah," *Hadiqat al-Akhbar* issue 31 (1858), p. 3.
4. Ibid.
5. Joan Kelly, "Early Feminist Theory and the 'Querelle des Femmes', 1400–1789," *Signs* 8 (1982), pp. 4–28.
6. While *Waqa'i' al-Misriyya* (*Egyptian Events*), founded by Muhammad 'Ali, had appeared since 1828 in Egypt, it was official in nature and did not include items with a broad public appeal.
7. Beth Baron, *The Women's Awakening in Egypt: Culture, Society and the Press* (New Haven and London: Yale University Press, 1994); Booth, *May Her Likes Be Multiplied*; Elizabeth Thompson, *Colonial Citizens: Republican Rights, Paternal Privilege and Gender in French Syria and Lebanon* (New York: Columbia University Press, 2000); Judith E. Tucker, *Women in Nineteenth Century Egypt* (Cambridge: Cambridge University Press, 1985); Laura Bier, "Modernity and the Other Woman," pp. 99–112; Hoda Elsadda, "Gendered Citizenship: Discourses on Domesticity in the Second Half of the Nineteenth Century," *Hawwa: Journal of Women of the Middle East and the Islamic World* 4 (2006), pp. 1–28.
8. Badran, "The Feminist Vision in the Writings of Three Turn-of-the-Century Egyptian Women," pp. 11–20; Margot Badran, *Feminists, Islam, and Nation: Gender and the Making of Modern Egypt* (Princeton: Princeton University Press, 1995); Cannon, "Nineteenth-Century Arabic Writings on Women and Society," pp. 462–484; Cole, "Feminism, Class, and Islam in Turn-of-the-Century Egypt," pp. 387–407.

9. Glass, *Der Muqtataf und Seine Öffentlichkeit*; Fruma Zachs, *The Making of a Syrian Identity*; Booth, *May Her Likes Be Multiplied*. Booth does devote attention to such a debate in a twentieth century journal, see "Women in Islam: Men and the 'Women's Press' in the Turn-of-the-20th-Century Press," pp. 171–201. For a more recent study, see Ayalon, "Private Publishing in the Nahda," pp. 561–577.

10. Akram F. Khater, *Inventing Home: Emigration, Gender, and the Middle Class in Lebanon, 1870–1920* (Berkeley: University of California Press, 2001), p. 148.

11. Zeidan, *Arab Women Novelists*, p. 13. A modified view is expressed by Leila Ahmed in *Women and Gender in Islam* (New Haven: Yale University Press, 1992), p. 128.

12. Ayalon, *The Press in the Arab Middle East*, pp. 28–72; Thomas Philipp, *The Syrians in Egypt* (Stuttgart: F. Steiner, 1985); Anjte Ziegler, "Arab Literary Salons at the Turn of the 20th Century," in Beatrice Gruendler and Verena Klemm (eds.), *Understanding Near Eastern Literatures: A Spectrum of Interdisciplinary Approaches* (Weisbaden: Reichart Verlag, 2000), pp. 241–253; Robin Ostle, "The Printing Press and the Renaissance of Modern Arabic Literature," *Culture and History* 16:1 (1997), pp. 145–157.

13. Dominick LaCapra, *Rethinking Intellectual History: Texts, Contexts, Language* (Ithaca: N.Y.: Cornell University Press, 1983), pp. 48–52; see also, Barbara J. Wejnert, "Integrating Models of Diffusion of Innovations: A Conceptual Framework," *Annual Reviews in Sociology* 28 (2002), pp. 297–326.

14. Beth Baron, "Readers and the Women's Press in Egypt," *Poetics Today* 15:2 (1994), p. 226.

15. We excluded later, shorter-lived newspapers, published in Egypt (e.g. *al-Fatat*, 1892–1894, and *al-Ustadh*, 1892–1893) which have been examined by other scholars, as well as *al-Jawa'ib* (1860–1883), published in Istanbul. *Hadiqat al-Akhbar* appeared until about 1911 (the exact date remains unknown). The issues from 1868–1881 and 1888–1911 have been lost; thus we are unable to establish a clear pattern of the development of themes in this journal. *Al-Muqtataf* continued until 1952, *Thamarat al-Funun* to 1908, and *al-Hilal* continues to this day. For information regarding the circulation numbers of these journals, see Hafez, *The Genesis of Arabic Narrative Discourse*, p. 279, fn. 75.

16. These themes reverberate through the fiction published in these periodicals; however, an in-depth study of them lies beyond the scope of this chapter. See Halevi and Zachs, "*Asma* (1873): The Early Arabic Novel as a Social Compass," pp. 416–430.

17. Thompson, *Colonial Citizens: Republican Rights*, p. 93; Kallas, *al-Haraka al-Fikriyya al-Nasawiyya fi 'Asr al-Nanda*, pp. 198–217.

18. Booth, *May Her Likes Be Multiplied*, p. 135; Zachs, *The Making of a Syrian Identity*, pp. 223–224; Anonymous, *al-Fatat* 1 (1894), p. 521.

19. Jurji N. Baz, *al-Nisa'iyyat: Kitab Adabi Akhlaqi Ijtima'i* (Beirut: al-Matba'a al-'Abasiyya, 1919), p. 89.

20. Al-Bustani, "Khitab fi Ta'lim al-Nisa'," pp. 45–53. Al-Bustani collated eighteen such addresses in *A'mal al-Jam'iyya al-Suriyya* (Beirut, 1852). A summary of this lecture was reprinted in 1882 in al-Bustani's periodical *al-Jinan*.

21. Assad Y. Kyat, *Voice from Lebanon with the Life and Travels* (London: Madden & Co., 1847), p. 179.

22. In this period female education in Greater Syria expanded considerably. See Kallas, *al-Haraka al-Fikriyya al-Nasawiyya fi 'Asr al-Nanda*, pp. 61–98. See also Anisa Saba', "Thiyudura Haddad," *al-Muqtataf* 14 (1889), pp. 254–265.

23. For more on the adaption and translation foreign texts into Arabic, see Halevi and Zachs, "Asma (1873): The Early Arabic Novel as a Social Compass," p. 419.

24. Khalil al-Khuri, "al-Kitab al-Faransawi al-Musamma bil-Nisa'," *Hadiqat al-Akhbar* issue 77 (1859), p. 4. See also Basilius Bawardi, "*Hadiqat al-Akhbar* Newspaper and its Pioneering Role in the Arabic Narrative Fiction," *Die Welt der Islam* 48 (2008), pp. 170–195.

25. Henry H. Jessup, *The Women of the Arabs* (New York: Dodd & Mead, Pub. 1873, reprinted 1982), p. 136.

26. Mayy Ziyada, "Warda al-Yaziji," *al-Muqtataf* 65 (1924), p. 3.

27. Idlid (Adelaide) al-Bustani, "Hanri wa-Imilya," *al-Jinan* 1 (1870), pp. 366–367, 406–407.

28. Jibra'il Sadqah, "Fi Huquq al-Nisa'," *al-Jinan* 1 (1870), pp. 401–402.

29. Salim al-Bustani, "Asma," *al-Jinan* 4 (1873), pp. 826–827.

30. Wastin Masarra, "al-Tarbiya," *al-Jinan* 2 (1871), pp. 54–56.

31. Kallas, *al-Haraka al-Fikriyya al-Nasawiyya fi 'Asr al-Nanda*, pp. 234–35; Maryana Marrash, "Shamat al-Jinan," *al-Jinan* 1 (1870), pp. 467–468.

32. "Fransis Fathallah Marrash [Obituary]," *al-Hilal* 5 (1897), pp. 742–744.

33. Fransis Marrash, "al-Mar'a bayna al-Khushuna wal-Tamaddun," *al-Jinan* 3 (1872), p. 588.

34. Fransis Marrash, "Fi Ta'lim al-Mar'a," *al-Jinan* 3 (1872), p. 769.

35. Farida Shakur, "Fil-Nisa," *al-Jinan* v (1874), p. 279. Not much is known about her; in the article itself she is only identified as the wife of the late Mansur Shakur.

36. Salim Kassab, "Ta'thir al-Walida," *al-Jinan* 16 (1885), p. 140. Al-Bustani voiced similar views regarding women and the nation in his historical novels, especially in *Zanubya* (1871). Wadi' al-Khuri, "al-Nisa'," *al-Jinan* 16 (1885), pp. 178–181; 210–214.

37. Salim Kassab was an educator and father of Marie Kassab, who later founded *Madrasat al-Banat al-Ahliya*, a girls' elementary school in Beirut (1916). Kallas, *al-Haraka al-Fikriyya al-Nasawiyya fi 'Asr al-Nanda*, p. 66; Wadad Makdisi Cortas, *A World I Loved: The Story of an Arab Woman* (New York: Nation Book, 2009), p. xi.

38. Kassab, "Ta'thir al-Walida," p. 138.

39. Ibid., p. 140.

40. Nadia Farag, "The Lewis Affair and the Fortunes of al-Muqtataf," *Middle Eastern Studies* 8 (1972), pp. 73–83, and Marwa Elshakry, "The Gospel of Science and American Evangelicalism in Late Ottoman Beirut," *Past and Present* 196 (2007), pp. 173–214.

41. Flavia Alaya, "Victorian Science and the 'Genius' of Woman," *Journal of the History of Ideas* 38 (1977), pp. 261–280; Elizabeth Fee, "The Sexual Politics of Victorian Social Anthropology," *Feminist Studies* 1:3/4 (1973), pp. 22–39; Linda K. Kerber, "The Republican Mother: Women and the Enlightenment – An American Perspective," *American Quarterly*, 28 (1976), pp. 187–205.

42. Shams Shahada, "al-Haqq Awla an Yuqal," *al-Muqtataf* 8 (1883), pp. 203–207. The item appeared in a regular column entitled "Arranging the Home" (*Tadbir al-Manzil*), which dealt with a variety of domestic matters (e.g. hygiene, dress, and children's education), was commented on by women intellectuals as well as ordinary readers. See Hannih Yanni, "Madarr al-Tamaddun al-Urubi wa-Manafi'uhu," *al-Muqtataf* 10 (1885), pp. 36–37; Amin Abu Khatir, "Huquq al-Nisa'," *al-Muqtataf* 10 (1886), pp. 621–623.

43. Shahada, "al-Haqq Awla an Yuqal," p. 205.

44. Khalid was *al-Fatat*'s distributor in Mount Lebanon and frequently contributed poems as well as articles advocating women's higher education; e.g. Maryam Khalid "Iqtirah Hasna' ba'd Wajibat al-Mar'a," *al-Fatat* 1:7 (June 1893), pp. 295–300.

45. Maryam Makariyus, "al-Khansa'," *al-Muqtataf* 9 (1885), pp. 622–626.

46. Abu Khatir, "Huquq al-Nisa'," pp. 621–623.

47. Wadi' al-Khuri, "Huquq al-Nisa'," *al-Muqtataf* 11 (1886), pp. 170–175; Najib Antunyus, "Huquq al-Nisa'," *al-Muqtataf* 11 (1886), pp. 232–237; Carroll Smith-Rosenberg and Charles Rosenberg, "The Female Animal: Medical and Biological Views of Women and their Role in Nineteenth-Century America," *Journal of American History* 60 (1973), pp. 332–356.

48. Anonymous, "Shibli Shumayyil, Tarjamatuhu," *al-Muqtataf* 50 (1917), pp. 105–112. Shumayyil was born in Kfarshima, Lebanon, studied at the Syrian Protestant College and later studied medicine in Paris; a strong proponent of Darwinian theories, he translated some of Herbert Spencer's and Ludwig Büchner's works into Arabic.

49. Shibli Shumayyil, "al-Mar'a wal-Rajul wa-hal Yatasawayan," *al-Muqtataf* 11 (1887), pp. 355–360; 401–405; quotation is on p. 405. Shumayyil collated his articles into a two-volume collection, see Shibli Shumayyil, *Kitab Falsafat al-Nushu' wal-Irtiqa' Majmu'at al-Duktur Shibli Shumayyil*, 2 vols. (Cairo: Matba'at al-Muqtataf, 1910).

50. M. A. Y., "Difa' al-Nisa' 'an al-Nisa'," *al-Muqtataf* 11 (1887), pp. 685–686.

51. Rahil Hajjar, "Difa' al-Nisa' 'an al-Nisa'," *al-Muqtataf* 11 (1887), pp. 686–687.

52. Maryam Makariyus, "Difa' al-Nisa' 'an al-Nisa'," *al-Muqtataf* 11 (1887), pp. 688–689. Makariyus, born in Hasbayya, Lebanon, studied in a missionary school in Beirut until 1885 when she left for Egypt. She married Shahin Makariyus (one of the editors of *al-Muqtataf*) and hosted a cultural salon attended by men and women. In 1880, with a group of women friends, she founded a cultural society, *Bakurat Suriyya*, and one for promoting education among poor women; she was interested and wrote about women's biographies and scientific matters. Shibli Shumayyil was one of her doctors and attended her bedside when she died.

53. Maryam Matar, "Difa' al-Nisa' 'an al-Nisa'," *al-Muqtataf* 11 (1887), pp. 745–747.

54. Khalil Sa'd, "al-Mar'a wal-Rajul wa-hal Yatasawayan," *al-Muqtataf* 11 (1887), pp. 749–750.

55. Shibli Shumayyil, "al-Mar'a wal-Rajul wa-hal Yatasawayan – Radd," *al-Muqtataf* 12 (1887), pp. 50–59.

56. The debate also took place in other short-lived journals, see Cannon, "Nineteenth-Century Arabic Writings on Women and Society," pp. 463–484.

57. Two other Syrian émigrés also established journals in Egypt; Rashid Rida (1865–1935), a Muslim intellectual from the Tripoli area, founded *al-Manar* (*The Lighthouse*; 1898–1935) and Ibrahim al-Yaziji (brother of poets Khalil and Warda al-Yaziji) founded *al-Diya'* (1898–1906).

58. Zaki M., "Hal lil-Nisa' an Yatlubna Kull Hquq al-Rijal," *al-Hilal* 2 (1894), pp. 304–306.

59. Al-Azhari later translated from Dumas in *al-Fatat*, see Booth, *May Her Likes Be Multiplied*, p. 45.

60. Amin al-Khuri, "Hal lil-Nisa' an Yatlubna Kull Huquq al-Rijal," *al-Hilal* 2 (1893), pp. 366–369; Amin al-Khuri, *al-Hilal* 2 (1894), pp. 463–470; Amin al-Khuri, *al-Hilal* 2 (1894), pp. 532–535; Amin al-Khuri, *al-Hilal* 2 (1894), pp. 563–567; Amin al-Khuri, *al-Hilal* 2 (1894), pp. 622–629.

61. Jurjus Iliyas al-Khuri, "Hal lil-Nisa' an Yatlubna Kull Huquq al-Rijal," *al-Hilal* 2 (1894), pp. 435–438; Bahiyya, "Hal lil-Nisa' an Yatlubna Kull Huquq al-Rijal," *al-Hilal* 2 (1894), pp. 590–593; Maram Antaki, "al-Haqq Ahaqq an Yutba'," *al-Fatat* 1:12 (March 1894), pp. 560–567; Istir al-Azhari, "Hal lil-Nisa' an Yatlubna Kull Huquq al-Rijal," *al-Hilal* 2 (1894), pp. 438–440; Istir al-Azhari, *al-Hilal* 2 (1894), pp. 561–563; Jabir Dumit, "Hal lil-Nisa' an Yatlubna Kull Huquq al-Rijal," *al-Hilal* 2 (1894), pp. 526–532; Anonymous ("The Moderate"), "Hal lil-Nisa' an Yatlubna Kull Huquq al-Rijal," *al-Hilal* 2 (1894), pp. 491–493; Anonymous, "Hal lil-Nisa' an Yatlubna Kull Huquq al-Rijal," *al-Hilal* 2 (1894), pp. 567–569.

62. Yaqut Sarruf, "al-Sayyida Nasra Ilyas," *al-Muqtataf* 13 (1888), pp. 549–550.

63. 'Anbara Salam al-Khalidi, *Jawla fil-Dhikrayat bayna Lubnan wa-Filastin* (Beirut: Dar al-Nahar lil-Nashr, 1978), p. 32. For more on the literary salons led by women, see Zeidan, *Arab Women Novelists*, pp. 50–55.

64. Khater, *Inventing Home: Emigration, Gender, and the Middle Class in Lebanon*, p. 149.

65. Ibn al-Hakim, "al-Zawaj," *Lisan al-Hal* issue 1639 6 (July 1894), p. 3.

66. Dawud al-Naqqash, "Ahlan bi Sahib al-Ra'y al-Jadid," *Lisan al-Hal* issue 1655 (25 July 1894), p. 3.

67. Aisha Ismat al-Taimuriya, "Introduction to The Results of Circumstances in Words and Deeds, 1887/8," in Margot Badran and Mariam Cooke (eds.), *Opening the Gates: A Century of Arab Feminist Writing* (Bloominton and Indianapolis: Indiana Unversity Press, 1990), pp. 126–133; Anonymous, "Maqdirat al-Mar'a," *al-Muqtataf* 21 (1897), pp. 59–60; Anonymous, "Hadaya wa-Tatriz," *al-Muqtataf* 16 (1892), p. 708.

68. Yaqut Sarruf, "Mu'tamar al-Nisa' al-'Amm," *al-Muqtataf* 23 (1899), pp. 564–568. Sarruf was preceded in the ICW by writer and author Hanna Kasbani Kurani (1870–1898) who attended the ICW Chicago meeing in 1893, see also Booth, *May Her Likes Be Multiplied*, p. 69.

69. Amir 'Ali, "al-Nisa' fil-Islam," *al-Muqtataf* 23 (1899), pp. 427–433; 489–497. See Martin Forward, *The Failure of Islamic Modernism? Syed Ameer Ali's Interpretation of Islam* (Bern: Peter Lang, 1999), p. 152.

70. Ayalon, *The Press in the Arab Middle East*, 36–37. See also, Booth, *"Woman in Islam*: Men and the 'Women's Press,' in Turn-of-the-20th-Century Egypt," pp. 171–201.

71. Maryam ibnat Jibra'il Nasr'allah al-Nahhas al-Tarabulusiyya al-Suriyya, *Mithal li-Kitab Ma'rid al-Hasna' fi Tarajim Mashahir al-Nisa'* (Alexandria: Mataba'at Jaridat Misr, 1879). Nahhas' husband, journalist Nasim Nawfal, was highly supportive of his wife's literary endeavors. Nahhas and Nawfal's daughter, author Hind Nawfal (1875–1957), was the founder of the women's journal *al-Fatat* (*The Young Woman*, 1892–1894).

72. Maryam Nahhas, "I'lan," *Thamarat al-Funun* issue 32 (1875). As only fragments of the two volumes (500 pages each) have survived, this notice sheds some light on its contents. This 1875 announcement of her forthcoming book precedes the later one (1879 in *Misr*) most often referred to in the literature, see Booth, *May Her Likes Be Multiplied*, p. 2.

73. Turkish author and philosopher Fatma Aliye (1862–1939) also published a notice for her book *Muslim Women* in 1893; Fatma Aliye, "Nisa' al-Muslimin," *Thamarat al-Funun* issue 916 (1893). See Serpil Çakur, "Fatma Aliye," in Francisca de Haan, Krasimira Daskalova, and Anna Loutfi (eds), *Biographical Dictionary of Women's Movements and Feminisms: Central, Eastern, and Southeastern Europe, 19th and 20th Centuries* (Budapest: Central European University Press, 2006), pp. 21–24.

74. Anonymous, "al-Zawaj wa-Mu'asharat al-'Iyal fi Uruba," *Thamarat al-Funun* issue 930 (1893).

75. *Kawkab Amrika* (*Star of America*; 1892–1907) was the first Arabic newspaper published in the US; see, Alixa Naff, "The Arabic-Language Press," in Sally M. Miller (ed.), *The Ethnic Press in the United States: A Historical Analysis and Handbook* (New York: Greenwood Press, 1987), pp. 1–14.

76. Anonymous, "Malabis al-Nisa'," *Thamarat al-Funun* issue 936 (1893); Anonymous, "Malabis al-Nisa'," *Thamarat al-Funun* issue 1001 (1894). See also Amy Kesselman, "The 'Freedom Suit': Feminism and Dress Reform in the United States, 1848–1875," *Gender and Society* 5 (1991), pp. 494–510.

77. Anonymous, "al-Mishadd," *al-Hilal* 5 (1896), pp. 134–137.

78. Karen Offen, "Ernst Legouvé and the Doctrine of 'Equality in Difference' for Women: A Case Study of Male Feminism in Nineteenth-Century French Thought," *Journal of Modern History* 58 (1985), pp. 452–484; quotation is on p. 468.

79. 'Abd al-Basit Fathallah, "Mas'alat al-Nisa'," *Thamarat al-Funun* issues 1258, 1259, 1260 (1899); nos.1280, 1282, 1293, 1296, 1301, 1306, 1307, 1323 (1899).

80. 'Abd al-Basit Fathallah, "Mas'alat al-Nisa'," *Thamarat al-Funun* issues 1260 (1899).

81. Ibid., "Mas'alat al-Nisa'," *Thamarat al-Funun* issues 1258, 1259 (1899). For more on the model modern Muslim wife, see Mervat F. Hatem, "The Nineteenth Century Discursive Roots of the Continuing Debate on the Social-Sexual Contract in Today's Egypt," *Hawwa* 2 (2004), pp. 70–78.

82. Anonymous, "al-Fatat al-Sharqiyya fi Akhir al-Qarn al-Tasi' 'Ashr," *al-Hilal* 6 (1897), pp. 169–174.

83. Wadi' Abu Rizq, "Huquq al-Nisa'," *al-Muqtataf* 20 (1896), pp. 130–132.

84. Anonymous, "Huquq al-Nisa'," *al-Muqtataf* 20 (1896), pp. 198–199.

85. Cole, "Feminism, Class, and Islam in Turn-of-the-Century Egypt," p. 392.

Chapter 2   Love, Marriage and Social Reform in the Early Arabic Novel

1. Moosa, *The Origins of Modern Arabic Fiction*, p. 183.

2. There were a handful of works, including embryonic attempts at writing a novel, which appeared before al-Bustani's novels, amongst them Khalil al-Khuri's *Way...Idhan Lastu bi Ifranji (Alas!...I'm not a European*, 1859–1861), which is a novella, and Fransis Marrash's *Ghabat al-Haqq (The Forest of Truth*, 1865), a novel-length allegorical and philosophical narrative. See also Fransis Marrash, *Ghabat al-Haqq* (Beirut: Dar al-Hamra', 1990); arguments abound as to whether these works can be defined as novels, see Hourani, *Arabic Thought in the Liberal Age*, pp. 247–8. Later attempts include the fictional narrative written by the Egyptian author Muhammad Ibrahim al-Muwaylihi's (1858–1930), *Hadith Isa ibn Hisham aw Fatra min al-Zaman (The Narrative of Isa son of Hisham, or a Period*, 1898–1900), which is a modified *maqama*. A review of the significant and ongoing controversies regarding the "rise" of the Arabic novel can be found in Hamdi al-Sakkut, *al-Riwaya al-'Arabiyya: Bibliyugrafiya wa-Madkhal Naqdi, 1865–1995*. 6 vols. (Cairo: The American University in Cairo Press, 2000), pp. 13–17; and in Moosa, *The Origins of Modern Arabic Fiction*, pp. 157–160.

3. Salim al-Bustani, "Asma," *al-Jinan*, 4 (1873); Salim al-Bustani, "Bint al-'Asr," *al-Jinan* 6 (1875); Salim al-Bustani, "Fatina," *al-Jinan* 8 (1877); Salim al-Bustani, "Salma," *al-Jinan* 9 and 10 (1878–79); Salim al-Bustani, "Samya," *al-Jinan* 13 (1882).

4. Reuven Snir, *Modern Arabic Literature: A Functional Dynamic Model* (Toronto: York Press, 2001), pp. 68–9.

5. As in the studies of Roger Allen, *The Arabic Novel: An Historical and Critical Introduction* (Syracuse: N.Y: Syracuse University Press 1982), and Rasheed el-Enany, *Arab Representations of the Occident: East-West Encounters in Arabic Fiction* (London and New York: Routledge, 2006).

6. Hafez, *The Genesis of Arabic Narrative Discourse: A Study in the Sociology of Modern Arabic Literature*, p. 111.

7. For instance see Najm, *al-Qissa fil-Adab al-'Arabi al-Hadith*, pp. 41–71; Ibrahim al-Sa'afim, *Tatawwur al-Riwaya al-'Arabiyya al-Haditha fi Bilad al-Sham, 1870–1967* (Baghdad: Dar al-Rashid lil-Nashr, 1980), pp. 13–126; 'Abd al-Rahman Yaghi, *Fil-Juhud al-Riwa'iyya Ma Bayna Salim Bustani wa Najib Mahfuz*, 2nd ed. (Beirut: Dar al-Farabi, 1981), pp. 23–24.

8. Bawardi and Zachs, "Between Adab al-Rihlat to "Geo-Literature": The Constructive Narrative Literature of Salim al-Bustani," pp. 203–17; Moosa, *The Origins of Modern Arabic Fiction*, pp. 157–183; Stephen Sheehi, *Foundations of Modern Arab Identity* (Gainesville, Fl.: University Press of Florida, 2004), pp. 79–106; Zachs, *The Making of a Syrian Identity*, pp. 186–190.

9. Samira Aghacy, "Contemporary Lebanese Fiction: Modernization without Modernity," *International Journal of Middle Eastern Studies* 38 (2006), pp. 561–580.

10. Jessup, *The Women of the Arabs*, p. 136.

11. Ami Ayalon, "Modern Texts and Their Readers in Late Ottoman Palestine," *Middle Eastern Studies* 38 (2002), pp. 17–40; Hafez, *The Genesis of Arabic Narrative Discourse*, p. 111, Moosa, *The Origins of Modern Arabic Fiction*, pp. 97–98.

12. Booth, *May Her Likes be Multiplied*, pp. 135–136; Marilyn Booth, "'She Herself Was the Ultimate Rule': Arabic Biographies of Missionary Teachers and their Pupils," *Islam and Muslin-Christian Relations* 13 (2002), pp. 433–38; Jessup, *The Women of the Arabs*, p. 137; Zachs, *The Making of a Syrian Identity*, pp. 223–24.

13. See also, Leon Zolondek, "Socio-Political Views of Salim al-Bustani (1848–1884)," *Middle Eastern Studies* 2:2 (1966), pp. 144–156.

14. Jessup, *The Women of the Arabs*, pp. 159–60; Zachs, *The Making of a Syrian Identity*, pp. 40–44.

15. Pierre Cachia, "Translations and Adaptation, 1834–1914," in M. M. Badawi (ed.), *The Cambridge History of Arabic Literature: The Modern Arabic Literature,* (Cambridge: Cambridge University Press, 1992), pp. 22–35; Moosa, *The Origins of Modern Arabic Fiction*, pp. 91–107; Selim, "The Nahda, Popular Fiction and the Politics of Translations," pp. 75–89.

16. Hans R. Jauss, "Literary History as a Challenge to Literary Theory." *New Literary History* 2 (1970), p. 8.

17. Badawi, "Introduction," in *the Cambridge History of Arabic Literature*, p. 17.

18. Selim, "The Nahda, Popular Fiction and the Politics of Translations," p. 77.

19. Badawi, "Introduction," in *The Cambridge History of Arabic Literature*, p. 3.

20. J. Paul Hunter, *Before Novels: The Cultural Contexts of Eighteenth-Century English Fiction* (New York and London: W.W. Norton, 1990), p. 225.

21. Hans R. Jauss, *Toward an Aesthetic of Reception*, trans. Timothy Bahti and introduced by Paul de Man (Minneapolis: Univ. of Minnesota Press, 1982), p. 23.
22. Ibid.
23. Hafez, *The Genesis of Arabic Narrative Discourse*, p. 98.
24. Al-Bustani, "Asma": p. 30, Al-Bustani, "Samya": p. 507.
25. There is a strong resemblance between *Asma*'s plot (as well as those of al-Bustani's later novels) and those found in the Greek new comedy and the Alexandrian romance, see Joseph A. Boone, *Tradition and Counter Tradition: Love and the Form of Fiction* (Chicago and London: University of Chicago Press, 1987), pp. 80–82. See also John Mullan, "Sentimental Novels." in John Richetti (ed.), *The Cambridge Companion to the Eighteenth-Century Novel* (Cambridge: Cambridge University Press, 1996), pp. 236–254.
26. Al-Bustani, "Khutba fi Adab al-'Arab," pp. 113–117.
27. Zachs, *The Making of a Syrian Identity*, pp. 72–73.
28. The terms modernization and Westernization are used as glosses for al-Bustani's definition of the terms *tamaddun dakhili* (lit. civilized from within) and *tamaddun khariji* (lit. superficially civilized). Other intellectuals of the *Nahda* period also used the term *tafarnuj* for Westernization.
29. Al-Bustani, "Asma," p. 66.
30. Ibid., p. 139.
31. Ibid., p. 69.
32. Ibid., p. 251.
33. Ibid., p. 751.
34. Ibid., p. 31.
35. Ibid., p. 67.
36. Moosa, *The Origins of Modern Arabic Fiction*, p. 162.
37. Al-Bustani, "Asma," p. 211.
38. Al-Bustani, "Asma," pp. 427–28.
39. For a comparative view, see Ian Watt, *The Rise of the Novel: Studies in Defoe, Richardson and Fielding* (London: Chatto & Windus, 1974), pp. 135–173; William H. Magee, "Instruments of Growth: The Courtship and Marriage Plot in Jane Austen's Novels," *Journal of Narrative Technique* 17: 2 (1987), pp. 198–208; Elise B. Mitchie, "Rich Woman, Poor Woman: Toward the Anthropology of the Nineteenth-Century Marriage Plot," *PMLA* 124: 2 (2009), pp. 421–436 and Ruth B. Yeazell, *Fictions of Modesty: Women and Courtship in the English Novel* (Chicago: University of Chicago Press).
40. Al-Bustani, "Asma," p. 175.
41. Ibid., pp. 466–467.
42. Ibid., p. 66.
43. Dawud al-Naqqash, "'Ilaj al-Zawaj," *Lisan al-Hal* issue 1631 (1894): p. 4.
44. Al-Bahith al-'Asri, "Ra'y fil -Zawaj," *Lisan al-Hal* issue 1635 (1894): p. 1.
45. Ibn al-Hakim, "al-Zawaj," *Lisan al-Hal* issue 1635 (1894): p. 3.
46. Khatir Iliyas Samaha, "al-Zawaj," *Lisan al-Hal* issue 1632 (1894), pp. 3–4.
47. Mayy, "al-Zawaj, Ra'y Anisa fihi," *Lisan al-Hal* issue 1638 (1894), pp. 1–2.

48. Bayt al-Din, Lubanan, "al-Zawaj," *Lisan al-Hal* issue 1640 (1894), p. 2. Apparently the editor censored part of the letter to tone down its authoritarian style.
49. Ibn al-Hakim, "al-Zawaj," *Lisan al-Hal* issue 1652 (1894), pp. 2–3.
50. See also, "Jamal al-Mar'a wa-Ta'thiruhu fil-Rajul," *Lisan al-Hal* issue 1596, 1894 (1894), p. 3.
51. Li-Ahad al-Udaba' al-Fadil, "al-Zawaj," *Lisan al-Hal* issue 1635 (1894), p. 3.
52. Salwa, "Tahdhib al-Banat," *Lisan al-Hal* issue 1678 (1894), p. 3.
53. Ibid.
54. Salwa, "Ruh al-Zawaj al-Thani," *Lisan al-Hal* issue 1702 (1894), p. 3.
55. Ibid.
56. Ibn al-Hakim, "Wajibat al-Rajul," *Lisan al-Hal* issue 1614 (1894), p. 3.
57. Al-Bustani, *Asma*, pp. 283, 358.
58. See Ibid., pp. 103, 176, 213, 283, 358, 749.
59. Ibid., pp. 32–33, 103, 358, 825.
60. See Moosa, *The Origins of Modern Arabic Fiction*, pp. 185–218.
61. See Thomas Philipp, *Gugri Zaidan: His Life and Thought* (Beirut/Weisbaden: Orient-Institut der Deutschen Morgenlandischen Gesellschaft/Franz Steiner, 1979) and Lewis B. Ware "Jurji Zaidan: The Role of Popular History in the Formation of a New Arab World-View" (Ph.D. Dissertation: Princeton University, 1973).
62. See Donald J. Cioeta, "Ottoman Censorship in Lebanon and Syria, 1876–1908," *International Journal of Middle Eastern Studies* 10 (1979), pp. 167–186, and Fruma Zachs and Basilius Bawardi, "Ottomanism and Syrian Patriotism in Salim al-Bustani's Thought," in Itzchak Weismann and Fruma Zachs (eds.), *Ottoman Reforms and Muslim Regeneration: Studies in Honor of Butrus Abu-Manneh* (London and New York: I.B.Tauris, 2005), pp. 111–126.

Chapter 3   Repaving the Path of *Muru'a*: Manly Virtue and the Emergence of a Modern Masculinity in Greater Syria

1. Nu'man 'Abduh al-Qasatli, "Riwayat Murshid wa Fitna," *al-Jinan* 11 (1880), p. 154.
2. Al-Qasatli, "Riwayat Murshid wa Fitna," 12 (1881), p. 319.
3. For studies discussing Arab masculinities in periods, see Watenpaugh, *Being Modern in the Middle East*, pp. 89–91; Samira Aghacy, *Masculine Identity in the Fiction of the Arab East since 1967* (Syracuse, New York: Syracuse University Press, 2009); Lisa Pollard, "From Husbands and Housewives to Suckers and Whores: Marital-Political Anxieties in the 'House of Egypt', 1919–48," *Gender and History* 2:3 (2009), pp. 647–699, and Wilson C. Jacob, *Working Out Egypt: Effendi Masculinity and Subject Formation in Colonial Modernity, 1870–1940* (Durham and London: Duke University Press, 2011).

4. For discussions of masculinity in adjacent Muslim, but non-Arab cultures, see Afsaneh Najambadi, *Women with Mustaches and Men without Beards: Gender and Sexual Anxieties of Iranian Modernity* (Berkeley, Los Angeles, London: University of California Press, 2005); David B. Edwards, *Heroes of the Age: Moral Fault Lines on the Afghan Frontier* (Berkeley: University of California Press, 1996); Wail S. Hassan, "Gender (and) Imperialism: Structures of Masculinity in Tayeb Salih's Season of Migration to the North," *Men and Masculinities* 5:3 (2003), pp. 309–324.

5. Hoda Elsadda, "Imaging the 'New Man' Gender and Nation in Arab Literary Narratives in the Early Twentieth Century," *Journal of Middle East Women's Studies* 3:2 (2007), pp. 31–55; Linda Jones, "Islamic Masculinities," in Joseph M. Armengol and Angels Carabi (eds.), *Debating Masculinity* (Harriman: Men's Studies Press, 2009), pp. 93–112.

6. Deniz Kandiyoti, "The Paradoxes of Masculinity: Some Thoughts on Segregated Societies," in Andrea Cornwall and Nancy Lindisfarne (eds.), *Dislocating Masculinity: Comparative Ethnographies* (London and New-York: Routledge, 1994), 197, 198; Booth, "*Woman in Islam*: Men and the 'Women's Press,' in Turn-of-the-20th-Century Egypt," pp. 171–201.

7. Lenore Davidoff and Catherine Hall, *Family Fortunes: Men and Women of the English Middle Class 1780–1850* (London: Hutchison, 1987), p. 29.

8. Stanley H. Brandes, *Metaphors of Masculinity: Sex and Status in Andalusian Folklore* (Philadelphia: University of Pennsylvania Press, 1980).

9. R. W. Connell, *Masculinities* (Sydney: Allen & Unwin, 1995), pp. 77, 82; see also Demetrakis Z. Demetriou, "Connell's Concept of Hegemonic Masculinity: A Critique," *Theory and Society* 30: 3 (2001), pp. 337–361.

10. Frank S. Pittman, *Man Enough: Fathers, Sons and the Search for Masculinity* (New York: Berkley Publishing Group, a division of the Penguin Group, 1993), p. xv.

11. For a detailed discussion of the concept of *muru'a*, see Charles Pellat, "Hawla Mafhum al-Muru'a 'inda Qudama' al-'Arab," *al-Karmel* 4 (1983): pp. 1–17; Bashar Faris, *Mabahith 'Arabiyya* (Cairo: Matba'at al-Ma'arif, 1939), pp. 57–74; Jones, "Islamic Masculinities," pp. 93–112; Farès Bichr, "Muru'a," in P. J. Bearman, T. Bianquis, C. E. Bosworth, E. van Donzel and W. P. Heinrichs (eds.), *Encyclopedia of Islam*, 2nd ed., (Leiden: Brill, 2010). BrillOnline.4 May 2010. http://www.brillonline.nl/subscriber/entry?entry=islam_SIM-555; Muhibb al-Din Abu Fayad Muhammad Murtada al-Husayni, "Muru'a," in *Taj al-'Arus min Jawahir al-Qamus* (Kuwait: Dar al-Fikr lil-Tiba'a wal-Nashr wal-Tawzi', 1994), pp. 247–248; Sayyid 'Asim 'Ali, *al-Muru'ah* (Tanta: Dar al-Sahaba lil-Turath bi-Tanta, 1990); Mashhur Hasan Mahmud al-Salman, *al-Muru'a wa-Khawarimuha* (Cairo: Dar Ibn 'Afan lil-Nashr wal-Tawzi', 2000).

12. Al-Bustani, "Asma"; Al-Bustani, "Bint al-'Asr"; Al-Bustani, "Fatina"; Al-Bustani, "Salma"; Al-Bustani, "Samya."

13. Nu'man 'Abduh al-Qasatli, "al-Fatat Amina wa-Ummuha," *al-Jinan* 11 (1880), and Nu'man 'Abduh al-Qasatli "Riwayat Anis," *al-Jinan* 12–13 (1881–82).

14. Jurji Zaydan, "Jihad al-Muhibbin," in Husayn Mu'nis (ed.), *Ta'rikh al-Tamaddum al-Islami* (Cairo: Dar al-Hilal, n.d.), v. 5. While an in-depth

analysis of each novel lies beyond the scope of this chapter, all were examined in detail.

15. The journals' content varied: they published regional news, news and commentary on foreign events, official Ottoman announcements, editorials, op-ed pieces, letters to the editor, advertisements and reviews of new books, serialized original novels, as well as excerpts and translations of short stories and novels. The question of the reception of these novels lies beyond the scope of this study; for information regarding the circulation numbers of these journals, see Hafez, *The Genesis of Arabic Narrative Discourse*, p. 279, fn. 75.

16. See for example Roger M.A. Allen, *The Arabic Novel: An Historical and Critical Introduction* (Syracuse: Syracuse University Press, 1982); Najm, *al-Qissa fil-Adab al-'Arabi al-Hadith*; Al-Qiyadi, *Isham al-Katiba al-'Arabiyya fi 'Asr al-Nahda hatta 1914* (Malta: Sharikat Elga, 1999); al-Sa'afin, *Tatawwur al-Riwaya al-'Arabiyya al-Haditha fi Bilad al-Sham*; Hamdi Sakkut, *The Arabic Novel: Bibliography and Critical Introduction, 1865–1995*, 6 vols. (Cairo: The American University in Cairo Press, 2000); Selim, *The Novel and the Rural Imaginary in Egypt 1880–1985*; Sha'ban, *100 'Am min al-Riwaya al-Nisa'iyya al-'Arabiyya 1899–1999*; Zeidan, *Arab Women Novelists: The Formative Years and Beyond*.

17. Doris Sommer, *Foundational Fictions: The National Romances of Latin America* (Berkeley and Los Angeles: University of California Press, 1991); Najmabadi, *Women with Mustaches and Men without Beards: Gender and Sexual Anxieties of Iranian Modernity*. See also, James S. Allen, "History and the Novels: Mentalité in Modern Popular Fiction," *History and Theory* 22 (1983), pp. 233–52; Richard Handler, "Cultural Theory in History Today," *American Historical Review* 107: 5 (2002), pp. 1512–1520; Sarah Maza, "Stephen Greenblatt, New Historicism, and Cultural History, or, What We Talk About When We Talk About Interdisciplinarity," *Modern Intellectual History* 1:2 (2004), pp. 249–265; Hayden White, "The Question of Narrative in Contemporary Historical Theory," *History and Theory* 23: 1 (1984), pp. 1–33.

18. Moosa, *The Origins of Modern Arabic Fiction*, pp. 157–159, 191, 197–198.

19. Al-Bustani, "Asma," p. 751; al-Qasatli, "al-Fatat Amina wa-Ummuha," pp. 25, 29.

20. It is possible that the writers did not wish to alienate their male readers, and thus mothers rather than fathers were given the role of enforcing the older generation's value system. Given what scholars know about the differential evaluation of mothers and fathers and the roles mothers play in the transmission of gender norms from one generation of women to the next, this characterization may also be reflective of reality. See Francine M. Deutsch and Susan E. Saxon, "The Double Standard of Praise and Criticism of Mothers and Fathers," *Psychology of Women Quarterly* 22:4 (1998), pp. 665–683, and Phyllis Moen, Mary A. Erickson and Donna Dempster-McClain, "Their Mother's Daughters? The Intergenerational Transmission of Gender Attitudes in a World of Changing Roles," *Journal of Marriage and Family* 59:2 (1997), pp. 281–293.

21. Al-Qasatli, "al-Fatat Amina wa-Ummuha," pp. 60, 62. In some cases the mothers (such as Sa'da's mother in "Asma") are portrayed as jealous or resentful of their daughters, al-Bustani, "Asma," pp. 427–428.

22. Al-Qasatli, "al-Fatat Amina wa-Ummuha," p. 89.

23. Zachs, *The Making of a Syrian Identity*, pp. 160–161; Ayalon, *Reading Palestine: Printing and Literacy, 1900–1948*, pp. 39–42.

24. Li-Ahad al-Kataba, "al-Zawaj," *Lisan al-Hal* issue 1626 (21 June 1894), p. 3. Leila Hudson, "Investing by Women or Investing in Women? Merchandise, Money and the Formation of a Pre-National Bourgeoisie in Damascus," *Comparative Studies of South Asia, Africa, and the Middle East* 26:1 (2006), p. 116.

25. Fathallah Jawish, "al-Mar'a fil-Hay'a al-Ijtima'iyya," *Lisan al-Hal* issue 1601 (4 April 1894), p. 4; see also Amin Kna'an Talhuq, "al-Rajul wal-Mar'a," *Lisan al-Hal* issue 1358 (1891), p. 2; Anonymous, "al-Mar'a," *Lisan al-Hal* issue 1583 (1894), p. 2; Anonymous, "al-Mar'a fi Manziliha," *Lisan al-Hal* issue 1615 (1894), p. 4.

26. Dawud al-Naqqash, "'Ilaj al-Zawaj," *Lisan al-Hal* issue 1631 (27 June 1894), p. 4; Salim al-Kassab, "al-Mar'a," *Lisan al-Hal* issue 1653 (1894), p. 2.

27. In his 20s, al-Qasatli visited the Sinai Peninsula and Egypt where he became well-acquainted with the Bedouins and his admiration for them is clearly visible throughout this novel. For a more general consideration of the place of Bedouins in Arab socio-cultural imagination, see Dale E. Eickelman, "Being Bedouin: Nomads and Tribes in the Arab Social Imagination, in Joseph Ginat and Anatoly M. Khazanov (eds.). *Changing Nomads in Changing Worlds* (Brighton: Sussex Academic Press, 1998), pp. 38–49.

28. Fitna chases off bandits who attempt to steal her sheep and later chases and kills the wolves that attacked her herd. Although wounded she binds her wounds and continues the hunt, bringing home the dead wolf; al-Qasatli, *Riwayat Murshid wa Fitna*, 11, pp. 155, 157–158.

29. For more details on the novel see, Mustafa Shakir, *Muhadarat 'an al-Qissa fi Suriyya hatta al-Harb al-'Alamiyya al-Thaniya* (Cairo: Ma'had al-Dirasat al-'Arabiyya, 1957), pp. 104–107.

30. Al-Qasatli, *Riwayat Murshid wa Fitna*, 11, p. 155.

31. The urban-rural divide referred to here is unlike to one which would appear in twentieth-century Arab novels; it refers to a nomadic-rural (Bedouin) versus urban rather than an agricultural-rural (*fallahun*) versus urban which so dominates the later novels.

32. While the *Zamzam* (sacred spring) and the *Ka'ba* have great symbolic importance in Islam, it is well known that they had a cultural and economic role in pre-Islamic times, see Hava Lazarus-Yafeh, "The Religious Dialectics of the Hadjdj," in Gerald R. Hawting (ed), *The Development of Islamic Ritual* (Aldershot: Ashgate Publishing, 2004), pp. 263–291.

33. Al-Qasatli, *Riwayat Murshid wa Fitna*, 11, p. 154.

34. For the role of women in *jahiliyya* and early Islamic periods, see Leor Halevi, "Wailing for the Dead: The Role of Women in Early Islamic Funerals, " *Past &*

Present 183:1 (2004), pp. 3–39; Barbara Freyer-Stowasser, "The Study of Women in Early Islam, " in Freda Hussain (ed.) *Muslim Women* (New York: St. Martin's Press, 1984), pp. 11–43; Leila Ahmed, "Women and the Advent of Islam, " *Signs* 11:4 (1986), pp. 665–691; Terri DeYoung, "Love, Death, and the Ghost of Al-Khansa': The Modern Female Poetic Voice in Fadwa Tuqan's Elegies for Her Brother Ibrahim," in Kamal Abdel-Malek and Wael B. Hallaq (eds.), *Tradition, Modernity, and Postmodernity in Arabic Literature: Essays in Honor of Professor Issa J. Boullata* (Leiden: Brill, 2000), pp. 47–50; Al-Qasatli, *Riwayat Murshid wa Fitna*, 11, p. 154. For the role of poetry in the lives of modern Bedouin women, see Lila Abu-Lughud, *Veiled Sentiments: Honor and Poetry in a Bedouin Society* (Berkeley: University of California Press, 1988).

35. Al-Qasatli, *Riwayat Murshid wa Fitna*, pp. 11, 345–348; 445–446. During this period Fitna also joins her tribe in battle, leads the women onto the battlefield, and tends to the wounded.

36. Al-Qasatli, "al-Fatat Amina wa-Ummuha," p. 58.

37. Zaynab Fawwaz, *Husn al-Awaqib aw Ghada al-Zahira* (Cairo: Matabi' al-Hay'a al-Misriyya, 1899; reprinted 2004), ed. Hilma al-Namnam, pp. 69–70; Labiba Hashem, *Qalb Rajul* (Damascus: Dar al-Thaqafa wal-Nashr, 2002; first published Cairo, 1904), ed. Yumna al-'Id, p. 21. Fawwaz uses an alternative spelling of *muru'a, murawwa*.

38. Salim al-Bustani, "al-Zawj wal-Zawja," *al-Jinan* 6 (1877), pp. 382–384. Despite an extensive search we were unable to locate this article.

39. Nu'man 'Abduh al-Qasatli, "al-Nisa' wa-Hququna," *Lisan al-Hal* issue 458 (1882), pp. 2–3.

40. Yusuf Afandi Shalhat, "Bahth fi Huquq al-Mar'a," *al-Muqtataf*, 18 (1893), pp. 329–334; Wadi' al-Khuri, "Huquq al-Mar'a," *al-Muqtataf*, 7 (1882), pp. 17–22. Al-Khuri was part owner of *Hadiqat al-Akhbar*, the first Arabic newspaper (1858–*c*.1911), and a prolific writer and contributor to the journals.

41. Al-Qasatli, "Anis," 13 (1883), p. 383.

42. For a brief discussion of the Islamic incorporation of pre-Islamic values, see Muhammad Abu al-Hadi Abu Rida, "Norms and Values," in Abdelwahab Boouhdiba and Muhammad Ma'ruf Dawalibi (eds.), *The Different Aspects of Islamic Culture: The Individual and Society in Islam* (Paris: UNESCO Publications, 1998), pp. 19–60.

43. See for example Armstrong, *Desire and Domestic Fiction: A Political History of the Novel*; Michael McKeon, "Generic Transformation and Social Change: Rethinking the Rise of the Novel," *Cultural Critique* 1 (1985), pp. 159–181; John W. Van Cleve, *The Merchant in German Literature of the Enlightenment* (Chapel Hill: University of North Carolina Press, 1986).

44. Connell, *Masculinities*, pp. 77, 82; Sandra Silberstein, "Ideology as Process: Gender Ideology in Courtship Narratives," in Alexandra Dundas Todd and Sue Fisher (eds.), *Gender and Discourse: The Power of Talk* (Norwood: Ablex Publishing, 1988), p. 127.

45. The Urabi Revolt occurred in Egypt in 1881–1882, instigated by a group of disaffected Egyptian army officers, led by Col. Ahmed Urabi, against the Khedive Tawfiq. The British, concerned that Urabi would default on Egypt's debts and gain control of the Suez Canal, invaded Egypt. This "temporary" invasion lasted in effect until 1954. For more details, see Thomas Mayer, *The Changing Past: Egyptian Historiography of the Urabi Revolt, 1883–1983* (Gainsville: University of Florida Press, 1988).

46. Mona L. Russell, *Creating the New Egyptian Woman: Consumerism, Education, and National Identity, 1863–1922* (New York: Palgrave Macmillan, 2004), p. 88; Elizabeth Thompson, *Colonial Citizens: Republican Rights, Paternal Privilege and Gender in French Syria and Lebanon* (New York: Columbia University Press, 2000), p. 3. See also Lisa Pollard, *Nurturing the Nation: The Family Politics of Modernizing, Colonizing and Liberating Egypt, 1805–1923* (Berkeley and Los Angeles: University of California Press, 2005), p. 161. For additional details on the lives of Egyptian women in the period, see Beth Baron, *Egypt as a Woman: Nationalism, Gender, and Politics* (Berkeley and Los Angeles: University of California Press, 2005); Tucker, *Women in Nineteenth-Century Egypt*.

Chapter 4   "Like a Planet Without a Star": The Glocalization of Domestic Discourse

1. "The woman is the lifeblood of a society, its beauty and wealth. Without the woman a society will become like a planet without a star." Anonymous, "Manzilat al-Mar'a," *al-Muqtataf* 7 (1883), p. 584.

2. Salma al-Nawfal, "Zirr al-Qamis," *al-Fatat* 1:3 (1893), pp. 105–109; al-Nawfal claimed to have read the original version in a French newspaper.

3. Mary P. Ryan, *Cradle of the Middle Class: The Family in Oneida County, New York, 1790–1865* (Cambridge: Cambridge University Press, 1981), p. 4; see also Nancy Armstrong, "The Rise of the Domestic Woman," in Nancy Armstrong and Leonard Tennenhouse (eds.), *The Ideology of Conduct: Essays on Literature and the History of Sexuality* (New York: Methuen, 1987), pp. 96–141.

4. See also Jeanne Boydston, *Home and Work: The Industrialization of Housework in the Northeastern United States from the Colonial Period to the Civil War* (New Haven: Yale University Press, 1984); Margaret H. Darrow, "French Noblewomen and the New Domesticity, 1750–1850," *Feminist Studies* 5:1 (1979), pp. 41–65; Sibylle Meyer, "The Tiresome Work of Conspicuous Leisure: On the Domestic Duties of the Wives of Civil Servants in the German Empire (1871–1918)," in Marilyn J. Boxer and Jean H. Quataert (eds.), *Connecting Spheres: Women in the Western World, 1500 to the Present* (New York and Oxford: Oxford University Press, 1987), pp. 156–165; Nancy R. Reagin, *Sweeping the German Nation: Domesticity and National Identity Germany, 1870–*

1945 (Cambridge: Cambridge University Press, 2007); Bonnie G. Smith, *Ladies of the Middles Class: The Bourgeoisies of Northern France in the Nineteenth Century* (Princeton: Princeton University Press, 1981).

5. Jean Comaroff and John Comaroff, "Homemade Hegemony: Modernity, Domesticity, and Colonialism in South Africa," in Karen T. Hansen (ed.), *African Encounters with Domesticity* (New Brunswick, NJ: Rutgers University Press, 1992), pp. 37–74. See also Chie Ikeya, "The Scientific-and-Hygienic Housewife and Mother: Education, Consumption and the Discourse of Domesticity," *Journal of Burma Studies* 14 (2010), pp. 59–89.

6. Pollard, *Nurturing the Nation: The Family Politics of Modernizing, Colonizing and Liberating Egypt*, pp. 6–8; see also Baron, *Egypt as a Woman: Nationalism, Gender, and Politics*, p. 33; Russell, *Creating the New Egyptian Woman: Consumerism Education and National Identity, 1863–1922*, pp. 80–81, 84–87; Hanan Kholoussy, *For Better, For Worse: The Marriage Crisis That Made Modern Egypt* (Stanford: Stanford University Press, 2010), pp. 59–65; Cathlyn Mariscotti, *Gender and Class in the Egyptian Women's Movement, 1925–1939: Changing Perspectives* (Syracuse: Syracuse University Press, 2008), pp. 57–76; Elsadda, "Gendered Citizenship: Discourses on Domesticity in the Second Half of the Nineteenth Century," pp. 1–28; Omnia Shakry, "Schooled Mothers and Structured Play: Child Rearing in Turn-of-the-Century Egypt," in Lila Abu-Lughod (ed.), *Remaking Women: Feminism and Modernity in the Middle East* (Princeton: Princeton University Press, 1998), pp. 126–170.

7. Edward Said, "Traveling Theory," in *The World, the Text, and the Critic* (Cambridge, MA: Harvard University Press, 1983), p. 227.

8. Stuart Hall, "The Local and the Global: Globalization and Ethnicity," in Anthony D. King (ed.), *Culture, Globalization and the World System: Contemporary Conditions for the Representation of Identity* (London: Macmillan, 1991), pp. 19–40; Stuart Hall, "Old and New Identities, Old and New Ethnicities," in *Culture, Globalization and the World System*, pp. 41–68. For a more general discussion of globalization and glocalization, see Roland Robertson, *Globalization: Social Theory and Globe Culture* (London: Sage, 1992); Roland Robertson, "Glocalization: Time-Space and Homogeneity-Heterogeneity," in Mike Featherstone et al. (eds.) *Global Modernities* (London: Sage, 1995), pp. 25–44; Victor Roudometof, "Transnationalism, Cosmopolitanism and Glocalization," *Current Sociology* 53:1 (2005), pp. 113–135.

9. Marwan M. Kraidy, "Hybridity in Cultural Globalization," *Communication Theory* 12:3 (2002), p. 317; see also, Marwan M. Kraidy, "From Imperialism to Glocalization: A Theoretical Framework of the Information Age," in Bosah Ebo (ed.) *Cyberimperialism?: Global Relations in the New Electronic Frontier* (Westport, CT: Praeger, 2001), pp. 27–42.

10. Booth, "She Herself Was the Ultimate Rule," pp. 427–448, especially, 430–431; Elizabeth Thompson, "Public and Private in Middle Eastern Women's History," *Journal of Women's History* 15:1 (2003), pp. 52–69. See also Heather J. Sharkey, *American Evangelicals in Egypt: Missionary Encounters in an Age of Empire*

(Princeton: Princeton University Press, 2008), pp. 18–95; Nancy L. Stockdale, *Colonial Encounters among English and Palestinian Women, 1800–1948* (Gainesville: University of Florida Press, 2007).

11. Judith E. Walsh, *Domesticity in Colonial India: What Women Learned When Men Gave Them Advice* (Lanham: Rowman and Littlefield Pub., 2004), p. 18; see also Susan Zlotnick, "Domesticating Imperialism: Curry and Cookbooks in Victorian England," *Frontiers: A Journal of Women's Studies* 16:2/3 (1996), pp. 51–68.

12. While *al-Muqtataf* and *al-Fatat* placed items concerning domestic matters under columns entitled *tadbir al-manzil*; other journals such as *Thamarat al-Funun* did not.

13. Ibn Khaldun's *Muqaddima* is an excellent example of how from the medieval period onward this literature on *tadbir al-manzil* expanded into *tadbir al-madina* (organization of the city), which looked at the workings of a far larger economic unit. Louis Baeck, "The Economic Thought of Classical Islam," *Diogenes* 30 (1991), pp. 99–115; Hamid S. Hosseini, "Contributions of Medieval Muslim Scholars to the History of Economics and their Impact: A Refutation of the Schumpeterian Great Gap," in Warren J. Samuels, Jeff E. Biddle, and John B. Davis (eds.), *A Companion to the History of Economic Thought* (Malden: Blackwell, 2003), pp. 28–45.

14. W. Heffening, "Tadbir," *Encyclopedia of Islam*, Second Edition, eds. P. J. Bearman, T. Bianquis, C. E. Bosworth, E. van Donzel and W. P. Heinrichs (Leiden: Brill, 2010). BrillOnline, accessed June 1, 2011: http://www.brillonline.nl/subscriber/entry?entry=islam_COM-1139; Abdul Azim Islahi, "The Myth of Bryson and Economic Thought in Islam," *Islamic Economics* 21:1 (2008), pp. 73–79. Most modern scholars refer to the 1921 version of this text, Luyis Shikhu (ed. and intro.), "Kitab Tadbir al-Manzil," *al-Mashriq* 19:3 (1921), pp. 161–181; however, there were at least two earlier versions of this text circulating among the reading public. We were unable to ascertain whether these versions were translations of Bryson's text or adaptations, which included the ideas and references to more modern European and American texts on domestic management. See also Simon Swain, *Economy, Family, and Society from Rome to Islam: A Critical Edition*, English Translation, and Study of Bryson's Management of the Estate (Cambridge and New-York: Cambridge University Press, 2013), pp. 27–37.

15. Shikhu, "Kitab Tadbir al-Manzil," p. 172.

16. Anonymous, "Fil-Mar'a wa-Wajibatiha wa-Huquqiha – fi Tadbir al-Manzil," *al-Fatat* 1:5 (1 April 1893), pp. 212–215; Khalil Ghanim, *Kitab al-Iqtisad al-Siayasi aw Tadbir al-Manzil* (Alexandria: Matba'at Jaridat Misr, 1879). Examination of the Egyptian journal *Rawdat al-Madaris* (1870–1877) reveals an embryonic discussion on educational, health and medical issues; however, the economic component is missing. While women may have read the journal, it was clearly not published with them in mind. See Rifa'a Rafi' al-Tahtawi, *Rawdat al-Madaris al-Misriyya*, 8 vols. (Cairo: Dar al-Kutub wal-Watha'iq al-

Qawmiyya, 1998), ed. Jabir 'Asfur; see also Hoda A. Yousef, "Reassessing Egypt's Dual System of Education Under Isma'il: Growing 'Ilm and Shifting Ground in Egypt's First Educational Journal, Rawdat al-Madaris, 1870–1877," *International Journal of Middle East Studies* 40:1 (2008), pp. 109–130.

17. Jurjis Qusah, *Kitab Tadbir al-Manzil* (Egypt: Matba'at al-Adab, 1889); Anonymous, "Fi Tadbir al-Manzil-fil-Mar'a wa-Wajibatiha wa-Huquqiha," *al-Fatat* 1:5 (1 April 1893), p. 212; Anonymous, "Fi Tadbir al-Manzil-fil-Mar'a wa-Wajibatiha wa-Huquqiha, " *al-Fatat* 1:6 (1 May 1893), pp. 281–282.

18. Anonymous, "al-Ma' wal-Sabun la al-Hamra wal-Duhun," *al-Muqtataf* 6 (1881), pp. 201–203; Yakut Sarruf, "Maryam Nimr Makariyus Firaq al-Rifaq," *al-Muqtataf* 12 (1888), pp. 435–439.

19. Anonymous, "Fa'ida Adabiyya," *al-Fatat* 1:10 (15 February 1894), pp. 446–447. See also Doray Marie-France, "Cleanliness and Class in the Countess de Ségur's Novels," (trans. Margaret R. Higgonet), *Children's Literature* 17 (1989), pp. 64–80.

20. Yakut Sarruf, "Tarkib al-Insan," *al-Muqtataf* 5 (1880), pp. 110–115, 141–143, 165–169. Mary J. Studley, *What Our Girls Ought to Know* (New York: M. L. Holbrook & Co., 1878). The book was reprinted several times over the next few decades.

21. Anonymous, "Fa'ida Adabiyya," pp. 446–448. The column had been printed earlier in *Lisan al-Hal*. For later lists of reading material and the literary practices of middle-class women in the period in Greater Syria and Egypt, see Booth, *May Her Likes Be Multiplied*, pp. 113–115; Baron, "Readers and the Women's Press", pp. 217–240; Khater, *Inventing Home: Emigration, Gender, and the Middle Class in Lebanon*, pp. 136–138.

22. See also Carla Hesse, *The Other Enlightenment: How French Women Became Modern* (Princeton: Princeton University Press, 2001), p. 47; Wendy Greenberg, *Uncanonical Women: Feminine Voice in French Poetry, 1830–1871* (Amsterdam: Rodopi, 1999); Bonnie G. Smith, *The Gender of History: Men, Women, and Historical Practice* (Cambridge: Harvard University Press, 1998), p. 84.

23. Shams Shahada, "al-Haqq Awla an Yuqal," pp. 203–207.

24. Butrus al-Bustani, "Khitab fi Ta'lim al-Nisa'," pp. 45–53, see especially pp. 47, 50. Al-Bustani collated eighteen such addresses in *A'mal al-Jam'iyya al-Suriyya* (Beirut: Dar al-Huda, 1852). A summary of the lecture was reprinted in 1882 in *al-Jinan*. The refrain is from the American poet William Ross Wallace's (1819–1881) poem *The Hand That Rocks the Cradle* (1865); given the dates, it is possible that al-Bustani added the refrain years after the lecture.

25. Several of the *tadbir al-manzil* columns in *al-Muqtataf* were reprints of lectures previously presented by the members of the literary and cultural society *Bakurat Suriyya*. Lecture topics on domestic issues ranged from arranging the home and selecting furniture, to clothes, to beauty. Marilyn Booth states that the society was founded in 1880; however, Shereen Khairallah indicates 1879, and historian Jurj Kallas dates it to 1873. Booth, *May Her Likes Be Multiplied*, xv; Shereen Khairallah, *The Sisters of Men* (Beirut: The Institute for Women's

Studies in the Arab World, Lebanese American University, 1996), p. 165; Kallas, *al-Haraka al-Fikriyya al-Nasawiyya fi 'Asr al-Nanda*, p. 212.

26. Anonymous, "al-Ma' wal-Sabun la al-Hamra wal-Duhun," *al-Muqtataf* 6 (1881), pp. 201–203; Anonymous, "Hifz al-Sihha," *al-Muqtataf*, 8 (1883), pp. 22–23. See also Victoria Kelley, "'The Virtues of a Drop of Cleansing Water': Domestic Work and Cleanliness in the British Working Classes, 1880–1914," *Women's History Review* 18:5 (2009), pp. 715–735; Mona Russell, "Marketing the Modern Egyptian Girl: Whitewashing Soap and Clothes from the Late Nineteenth Century to 1936," *Journal of Middle East Women's Studies* 6:3 (2010), pp. 19–57.

27. E.G., "Izalat al-Buqa' wa-Nahwiha 'an al-Thiyab," *al-Muqtataf* 6 (1881), p. 11; Anonymous, "Ghasl al-Aqmisha al-Haririyya al-Mulawwana," *al-Muqtataf* 6 (1881), p. 204; Anonymous, "Ghasl Kufuf al-Jild al-Faransawiyya," *al-Muqtataf* 6 (1881), p. 224; Anonymous, "Tanzif al-Rukham," *al-Muqtataf* 6 (1881), p. 224.

28. Anonymous, "Bab Tadbir al-Manzil," *al-Fatat* 1:11 (1894), pp. 510–512; Ibrahim Afandi al-Hurani, "Milh al-Ta'am," *al-Muqtataf* 3 (1878), pp. 185–186; Anonymous, "Halawat al-Bandura," *al-Muqtataf* 6 (1881), p. 37; Anonymous, "Halawat al-Ijjas," *al-Muqtataf* 6 (1881), p. 37; Dr. Niqula Nimr, "al-Tat'im bil-Madda al-Judariyya," *al-Muqtataf* 8 (1883), pp. 164–166. For a comparative view of dietary changes in Ottoman Turkey, see Tülay Artan, "Aspects of the Ottoman Elite's Food Consumption: Looking for 'Staples,' 'Luxuries,' and 'Delicacies' in a Changing Century," in Donald Quataert (ed.), *Consumption Studies and the History of the Ottoman Empire, 1550–1922: An Introduction* (Albany: SUNY Press, 2000), pp. 107–200.

29. Yakut Sarruf, "Turaf Tarkib al-Insan," *al-Muqtataf* 5 (1880), pp. 110–115, 141–143, 165–169; Maryam Nimr Makariyus, "Ba'd Khurafat al-Ifranj," *al-Muqtataf* 5 (1880), pp. 169–171; Anonymous, "al-Nisa' wal-Tibb," *al-Muqtataf* 7 (1882), pp. 25–26. See also Rima D. Apple, "Constructing Mothers: Scientific Motherhood in the Nineteenth and Twentieth Centuries," *Social History of Medicine* 8:2 (1995), pp. 161–178.

30. For medieval views on childrearing and education, see Avner Giladi, "Islamic Educational Theories in the Middle Ages: Some Methodological Notes with Special Reference to al-Ghazali," *Bulletin (British Society for Middle East Studies)* 14:1 (1987), pp. 3–10; Avner Giladi, *Infants, Parents and Wet Nurses: Medieval Islamic Views of Breastfeeding and Social Implications* (Leiden: Brill, 1999).

31. Anonymous, "Shadhrat fi Tarbiyat al-Awlad," *al-Muqtataf* 6 (1881), p. 11; Anonymous, "Libas al-Sighar fil-Sayf," *al-Muqtataf* 6 (1881), p. 46; G. H., "Laysa al-Ta'lim Huwa al-Tarbiya," *al-Muqtataf* 7 (1882), pp. 173–174; Helena (Hilana) Bar Wadi, "al-Akhlaq wal-Awa'id," *al-Muqtataf* 7 (1882), pp. 367–369. The quotation is from Anonymous, "Shadhrat fil Tarbiyya wal-Ta'lim," *al-Muqtataf* 7 (1882), p. 425; Salim Kassab, "al-Mara'," *Lisan al-Hal* issue 1653 (1894), p. 2; Salim Kassab, "al-Mara'," *Lisan al-Hal* issue 1655 (1894), pp. 3–4.

32. Julia Tu'ma, "al-Sama' al-Ula," *al-Hasna'* 2:1 (1910), p. 9.

33. Jens Hanssen, "'Your Beirut is on My Desk': Ottomanizing Beirut under Sultan Abdülhamid II," in Peter Rowe and Hashim Sarkis (eds.), *Projecting Beirut: Episodes in the Construction and Reconstruction of a Modern City* (Munich: Prestel, 1998), pp. 41–67; Bruce Masters, "The Political Economy of Aleppo in the Age of Ottoman Reform," *Journal of the Economic and Social History of the Orient* 53 (2010), pp. 290–316.

34. Ralph Bodenstein, "Housing the Foreign: A European's Exotic Home in Late Nineteenth-Century Beirut," in Jens Hanssen, Thomas Philipp and Stefan Weber (eds.), *The Empire and the City: Arab Provincial Capitals in the Late Ottoman Empire* (Beirut: Ergon Verlag Würzburg, 2002), pp. 105–127; Stefan Weber, "Images of Imagined Worlds: Self-Image and Worldview in Late Ottoman Wall Paintings of Damascus," in *The Empire and the City*, pp. 145–171; Stefan Weber, "Reshaping Damascus: Social Change and Patterns of Architecture in Late Ottoman Times," in Thomas Philipp and Christoph Schumann (eds.), *From the Syrian Land to the States of Syria and Lebanon* (Beirut: Ergon Verlag Würzburg 2003), pp. 41–58; Heghnar Z. Watenpaugh, "The Harem as Biography: Domestic Architecture, Gender, and Nostalgia in Modern Syria," in Marilyn Booth (ed.), *Harem Histories: Envisioning Places and Living Spaces* (Durham and London: Duke University Press, 2010), pp. 211–236; Leila Hudson, "Late Ottoman Damascus: Investments in Public Space and the Emergence of Popular Sovereignty," *Critique: Critical Middle Eastern Studies* 15 (2006), pp. 152–169.

35. Sandy Isenstadt, and Kishwar Rizvi "Introduction: Modern Architecture and the Middle East: The Burden of Representation," in Sandy Isenstadt and Kishwar Rizvi (eds.), *Modernism and the Middle East: Architecture and Politics in the Twentieth Century* (Seattle: University of Washington Press, 2008), pp. 3–36; Haris Exertzoglou, "The Cultural Uses of Consumption: Negotiating Class, Gender, and Nation in the Ottoman Urban Centers during the 19th Century," *International Journal of Middle East Studies* 35 (2003), pp. 77–101.

36. Mary A. Fay, "From Warrior-Grandees to Domesticated Bourgeoisie: The Transformation of the Elite Egyptian Household into a Western-Style Nuclear Family," in Beshara Doumani (ed.), *Family History in the Middle East: Household, Property and Gender* (Albany: SUNY Press, 2003), pp. 77–98; Mona Russell, "Modernity, National Identity and Consumerism: Visions of the Egyptian Home, 1805–1922" in Relli Shechter (ed.), *Transitions in Domestic Consumption and Family Life in the Modern Middle East: Houses in Motion* (New York: Palgrave Macmillan, 2003), pp. 37–63.

37. Toufoul Abou-Hodeib, "Taste and Class in Late Ottoman Beirut," *International Journal of Middle East Studies* 43:3 (2011), pp. 475–492.

38. Shukri, a graduate of the American School for Girls, also presented the main argument of this article several years earlier as a lecture to the *Bakurat Suriyya*.

39. Rujina Shukri, "Farsh al-Buyut wa-Tartibuha," *al-Muqtataf* 9 (1885), p. 743.

40. Jirjis Hamam, "Ikhtiyar al-Manzil," *Lisan al-Hal* issue 1271 (1891), p. 3.

41. Akram F. Khater, "Building Class: Emigration, the Central Hall House, and the Construction of a Rural Middle Class in Lebanon, 1890–1914," in Michael F.

Davie (ed.), *La Maison Beyrouthine aux Trois Arcs: Une Architecture Bourgeoise du Levant* (Beirut: Académie Libanaise des Beaux-Arts; Tours: Centre de Recherches et d'Études sur l'Urbanization du Monde Arabe, 2003), pp. 371–393; Anne Mollenhauer, "Reading Late-Ottoman Architecture: Exterior Expression and Interior Organization of Central-Hall Houses between Beirut and Latakia," in *La Maison Beyrouthine aux Trois Arcs*, pp. 115–135.

42. Shukri, "Farsh al-Buyut wa-Tartibuha," p. 743.

43. Karen Haltunnen, *Confidence Men and Painted Women: A Study of Middle-Class Culture in America, 1830–1870* (New Haven and London: Yale University Press, 1982), p. 59; see also Mike Hepworth, "Privacy, Security and Respectability: The Ideal Victorian Home," in Tony Chapman and Jenny Hockey (eds.), *Ideal Homes? Social Change and Domestic Life* (London and New York: Routledge, 1999), pp. 17–29.

44. Shukri, "Farsh al-Buyut wa-Tartibuha," p. 744.

45. Maurice Cerasi, "Some Considerations on the Mediterranean Archetypes Active in the Constitution of the Three-Arched Lebanese House Type: Fashion and Groove of Memory," in *La Maison Beyrouthine aux Trois Arcs*, pp. 19–342.

46. Farida Hubayqa, "Adab al-Ma'ida," *al-Muqtataf* 9 (1884), p. 370; Dr. Niqula Nimr (1883), "al-Tat'im bil-Madda al-Judariyya," *al-Muqtataf* 8, pp. 164–166; Anonymous, "Zinat al-Ma'ida," *al-Muqtataf* 9 (1884), pp. 554–556. In the older *service à la francaise* all the dishes were placed on the table and the guests served themselves; in the newer *service à la russe* food was placed on the sideboard, and then the servants served the guests course by course. Natalie Kapetanios-Meir, "'A Fashionable Dinner is Arranged as Follows': Victorian Dining Taxonomies," *Victorian Literature and Culture* 33 (2005), pp. 133–148; see also Jeffrey A. Auerbach, "What They Read: Mid-Nineteenth Century English Women's Magazines and the Emergence of a Consumer Culture," *Victorian Periodicals Review* 30:3 (1997), pp. 121–140; Diana Di Zerega Wall, "Sacred Dinners and Secular Teas: Constructing Domesticity in Mid-19th-Century New York," *Historical Archaeology* 25:4 (1991), pp. 69–81.

47. Anonymous, "'Id al-Awlad," *al-Muqtataf* 18 (1894): p. 558. See also Alison J. Clarke, "Making Sameness: Mothering, Commerce and the Culture of Children's Birthday Parties," in Emma Casey and Lydia Martens (eds.), *Gender and Consumption: Domestic Cultures and the Commercialization of Everyday Life* (Aldershot: Ashgate Publishing, 2007), pp. 79–96. Anonymous, "[Advertisement for separate swimming hours for men and women at the beach]," *al-Janna* issue 1300 (1883), p. 4; see also Julia Clancy-Smith, "Where Elites Meet: Harem Visits, Sea Bathing, and Sociabilities in Precolonial Tunisia, c. 1800–1881," in *Harem Histories: Envisioning Places and Living Spaces*, pp. 177–210.

48. Elizabeth M. Holt, "Narrative and the Reading Public in Beirut," *Journal of Arabic Literature* 40 (2009), pp. 37–70.

49. Fayiqah Ghabril, "al-Sa'ada al-Baytiyya," *al-Hasna'* 2:2 (1910), p. 109; S. J. Kleinberg, "Gendered Space: Housing, Privacy and Domesticity in the Nineteenth-Century United States," in Janet Floyd (ed.) *Domestic Space: Reading*

the Nineteenth-Century Interior (Manchester: Manchester University Press, 1999), pp. 142–161.

50. Daphne Spain, *Gendered Spaces* (Chapel Hill and London: University of North Carolina Press, 1992), pp. 111–140; Moira Munro and Ruth Madigan, "Negotiating Space in the Family Home, " in Irene Cieraad (ed.), *At Home: An Anthropology of Domestic Space* (Syracuse: Syracuse University Press, 1999), pp. 107–117.

51. Shukri, "Farsh al-Buyut wa-Tartibuha," p. 745; see also Himam, "Ikhtiyar al-Manzil," p. 3.

52. Jessica Gerard, "Invisible Servants: The Country House and the Local Community," *Historical Research* 57:136 (1984), pp. 178–188; Lakshmi Srinivas, "Master-Servant Relationships in a Cross-Cultural Perspective," *Economic and Political Weekly* 30 (1995), pp. 269–278; Fouad C. Debbas, *Beirut, Our Memory: A Guided Tour Illustrated with Picture Postcards*, 2nd ed. (Beirut: César Debbas & Fils, 1994); Debbas, *Des photographes à Beyrouth, 1840–1918* (Paris: Marval, 2001); see also Dorothea Duda, *Innenarchitektur Syrischer Stadthäuser des 16. bis 18. Jahrhunderts: die Sammlung Henri Pharaon in Beirut* (Beirut: In Kommission bei F. Steiner, 1971). Friedrich Ragette claims that the Lebanese (and especially the Beiruti) cuisine differed significantly from the elaborate Arab cuisines of cities such as Aleppo and Cairo. It relied mainly on fresh fruit and vegetables and baked and grilled foods, for which a small oven and simple charcoal grill would suffice. Friedrich Ragette, *Architecture in Lebanon: The Lebanese House during the 18th and 19th Centuries* (Beirut: American University of Beirut, 1974), pp. 114–115. For additional photographs, see the Fouad Debbas Collection and the Arab Image Foundation. http://www. thefouaddebbascollection.com.

53. Abou-Hodeib, "Taste and Class in Late Ottoman Beirut."; Uri M. Kupferschmidt, "The Social History of the Sewing Machine in the Middle East," *Die Welt des Islams* 44:2 (2004), pp. 195–213; Relli Shechter, "Selling Luxury: The Rise of the Egyptian Cigarette and the Transformation of the Egyptian Tobacco Market, 1850–1914," *International Journal of Middle East Studies* 35 (2003), pp. 41–75; Mary L. Roberts, "Gender, Consumption and Commodity Culture," *American Historical Review* 103 (1998), pp. 817–844.

54. Deborah Cohen, *Household Gods: The British and their Possessions* (New Haven: Yale University Press, 2006), p. 86; Beverley Gordon, "Woman's Domestic Body: The Conceptual Conflation of Women and Interiors in the Industrial Age," *Winterthur Portfolio* 31 (1996), pp. 281–301.

55. A similar line of argument is hinted at in Fay, p. 2003.

56. Salim Al-Bustani, "al-Zawj wal-Zawja," *al-Jinan* 6 (1877), pp. 382–384.

57. Ghabril, "al-Sa'ada al-Baytiyya," p. 110.

58. Tu'ma, "al-Sama' al-Ula," p. 12.

59. 'Abd al-Basit Fathallah, "'Ilm al-Ijtima' al-Bashari Libas al-Sayf wa-Nasij al-Watan," *Thamarat al-Funun* issue 1287 (1900), p. 3.

60. Khalil al-Khuri, "Way...Idhan Lastu bi Ifranji, " *Hadiqat al-Akhbar* issue 106 (1860), p. 3; issue 108 (1860), pp. 2–3.

61. Al-Bustani, "Asma," p. 66.

62. Al-Bustani, "Asma," p. 69.

63. Al-Bustani, "Bint al-'Asr," pp. 66, 69.

64. For a comparative view of a similar sentiments expressed in the late Ottoman press, see Elizabeth Brown Fierson, "Mirrors Out, Mirrors In: Domestication and Rejection of the Foreign in Late-Ottoman Women's Magazines (1875–1908)," in D. Fairchild Ruggles (ed.), *Women, Patronage, and Self-Representation in Islamic Societies* (Albany: SUNY Press, 2000), pp. 177–204.

65. Al-Bustani, "Bint al-'Asr," p. 68. For an eyewitness account of the fashions and social practices of the middle class in Beirut, see A. Krimski, *Bayrut wa Jabal Lubnan 'ala Masharif al-Qarn al-'Ishrin Dirasa fil-Ta'rikh al –Ijtima'i min Khilal Mudhakkirat al-'Alim al-Rusi al-Kabir, Rasa'il min Lubnan, 1896–1898* Ed. Mas'ud Dahir (Beirut: Dar al-Mada lil-Tiba'a wal-Nashr wal-Tawzi', 1985), pp. 44–46, 239.

66. Most of the studies on fashion in the Ottoman Empire have focused on Turkey; see Charlotte Jirousek, "The Transition to Mass Fashion System Dress in the Later Ottoman Empire," in *Consumption Studies and the History of the Ottoman Empire*, pp. 201–242; Nora Şeni, "Fashion and Women's Clothing in the Satirical Press of Istanbul at the End of the 19th Century," in Sirin Tekeli (ed.), *Women in Modern Turkish Society: A Reader* (London: Zed Books, 1995), pp. 25–45; Nancy Micklewright, "Public and Private for Ottoman Women of the Nineteenth Century" in *Women, Patronage, and Self-Representation in Islamic Societies*, pp. 155–176.

67. Anonymous, "al-Mishadd," *al-Hilal* 5 (1896), pp. 134–137; Anonymous, "al-Fatat al-Sharqiyya fi Akhir al-Qarn al-Tasi' 'Ashr," *al-Hilal* 6 (1897), pp. 169–174; Farida Hubayqa, "al-Dhawq fil-Libas wal-Jamal," *al-Muqtaraf* 7 (1882), pp. 112–115. See also Anonymous, "I'tibar al-Nisa' li-Libas al-Rijal," *al-Muqtaraf* 8 (1883), pp. 20–21; Sayyida Bajit, "Azya' al-Nisa' – translated from the English newspaper, The Nineteenth Century," *al-Muqtaraf* 8 (1883), pp. 21–22. The article was a translation of a piece written by Eliza (Wilson) Bagehot (wife of Walter Bagehot) for the English journal the *Nineteenth Century*.

68. Anonymous, "Mabahith 'Ilmiyya Adabiyya Ta'rikhiyya – al-'Ilm wal -Mar'a," *Thamarat al-Funun* issue 1220 (1899). For a comparative view of similar discourse emerging in Europe, see Mariana Valverde, "The Love of Finery: Fashion and the Fallen Woman in Nineteenth-Century Social Discourse," *Victorian Studies* 32 (1989), pp. 168–88; Erika Rappaport, "A Husband and His Wife's Dresses': Consumer Credit and the Debtor Family in England, pp. 1864–1914," in Victoria de Grazia with Ellen Furlough (eds.), *The Sex of Things: Gender and Consumption in Historical Perspective* (Berkeley: University of California Press, 1996), pp. 163–187.

69. Bustros al-Bustani, "Khitab fil-Hay'a al-Ijtima'iyya wal-Muqabala bayna al-'Awa'id al-'Arabiyya wal-Ifranjiyya," in *A'mal al-Jam'iyya al-'Ilmiyya*

al-Suriyya, 1868–1869 (Beirut: Dar al-Huda, 1990), pp. 204–217, especially pp. 210–217.

70. Anonymous, "Malabis al-Nisa'," *Thamarat al-Funun* issue 936 (1893); Anonymous, "Malabis al-Nisa'," *Thamarat al-Funun* issue 1001 (1894). For examples of similar rhetoric used in other periods, see Elizabeth Currie, "Prescribing Fashion: Dress, Politics and Gender in 16th-Century Italian Conduct Literature," *Fashion Theory: The Journal of Dress, Body and Culture* 4:2 (2000), pp. 157–177; Linzy A. Brekke, "The 'Scourge of Fashion': Political Economy and the Politics of Consumption in the Early Republic," *Early American Studies* 3:1 (2005), pp. 111–139.

71. Ya'qub Sarruf, "al-Nazar fi Hadirina wa-Mustaqbalina," *al-Muqtataf* 8 (1884), pp. 193–199; Yaqut Sarruf, "al-Tamaddun al-Sari'," *al-Muqtataf* 9 (1885), pp. 284–288; Hannih Yanni, "Madarir al-Tamaddun al-Urubi wa-Manafi'uhu," *al-Muqtataf* 10 (1885), pp. 36–37; Shams Shahada, "Madarr al-Tamaddun al-Urubi wa-Manafi'uhu," *al-Muqtataf* 8 (1884), pp. 565–56; 'Abd al-Basit Fathallah, "'Ilm al-Ijtima' al-Bashari Libas al-Sayf wa-Nasij al-Watan," *Thamarat al-Funun* issue 1287 (1900), p. 3.

72. Hanna Kurani, "Inhad al-Ghayra al-Wataniyya li-Tarqiyat al-Bada'i' al-Sharqiyya," *al-Fatat* 1:5 (1893), p. 224, and *al-Fatat* 1:6 (1893), pp. 275–281. When lecturing abroad Kurani made a point of appearing dressed in "the Eastern fashion." During the 1890s the silk industry declined as mulberry trees were uprooted in favor of other more profitable crops, such as grapes, olives, and tobacco; see Kais Firro, "Silk and Agrarian Changes in Lebanon, 1860–1914," *International Journal of Middle East Studies* 22:2 (1990), pp. 151–190; Akram F. Khater, "'House' to 'Goddess of the House': Gender, Class, and Silk in 19th-Century Mount Lebanon," *International Journal of Middle East Studies* 28:3 (1996), pp. 325–348.

73. Svetlana Boym, *The Future of Nostalgia* (New York: Basic Books, 2001), p. xv; Felski, *The Gender of Modernity*, p. 18. For details on these economic and social changes and their impact on the rise of patriotic sentiments see Zachs, *The Making of a Syrian Identity*, pp. 39–85.

74. Anne McClintock, "Family Feuds: Gender, Nationalism and the Family," *Feminist Review* no. 44 (1993), p. 62.

75. Anonymous, "Tadbir al-Manzil," *Anis al-Jalis* 2:4 (30 April 1899), pp. 155–157. We follow the dates provided by Emily Faris Ibrahim; a different date is found under the entry for Averino, in Rawda Ashour, Ferial Jabouri Ghazoul, Hasna Reda-Mekdashi (eds.), *Arab Women Writers: A Critical Reference Guide, 1873–1999*, translated by Mandy McClure (Cairo: The American University Press, 2009), pp. 361–362.

76. In some ways this view of women's roles strongly resembles the stance of contemporary Islamic feminists and Islamist women who support democracy and equality as political ideals and at the same time depict the family as organized around gendered hierarchies, see Ellen McLarney, "The Private is Political: Women and Family in Intellectual Islam, *Feminist Theory* 11 (2010),

pp. 129–148, and Mervat F. Hatem, "The Nineteenth Century Discursive Roots of the Continuing Debate on the Social-Sexual Contract in Today's Egypt," *Hawwa* 2 (2006), pp. 1–28.

Chapter 5   The "Missing Link"? The Nahda Novelists and Intellectuals from Social Commentary to Political Critique and Activism

1. Thompson, *Colonial Citizens: Republican Rights*, p. 117.
2. Ibid., p. 119; see also pp. 117–126.
3. M. M. Badawi, *A Short History of Modern Arabic Literature* (Oxford: Clarendon Press, 1993), p. 97.
4. Elliott Colla, "How *Zaynab* Became the First Arabic Novel," *History Compass* 7:1 (2009), p. 214; Moosa, *The Origins of Modern Arabic Fiction*, p. 263; see also Selim, *The Novel and the Rural Imaginary in Egypt, 1880*.
5. Michael E. Gaspar, *The Power of Representation: Publics, Peasants, and Islam in Egypt* (Stanford: Stanford University Press, 2009), p. 5. In his discussion of *Zaynab*, Gaspar argues that this novel and others like it drew symbolic ties between different classes in a way that "implied a form of identity transcending regional and indeed incipient class differences," p. 192.
6. Nancy K. Miller, *The Heroine's Text: Readings in the French and English Novel, 1722–1782* (New York: Columbia University Press, 1980), p. 145.
7. Idlid (Adelaide) al-Bustani, "Hanri wa-Imilya," pp. 366–367, 406–407. Almost nothing is known about Idlid al-Bustani, although the fact that her work appeared in *al-Jinan* which was owned and edited by Butrus and Salim al-Bustani suggests that she may have been related to them.
8. Fathallah Jawish, "al-Mar'a fil-Hay'a Ijtima'iyya," *Lisan al-Hal*, issue 1601 (1894), p. 4; Anonymous, "Jamal al-Mar'a wa-Ta'thiruhu fil-Rajul," *Lisan al-Hal*, issue 1596 (1894), p. 3.
9. Salwa, "Tahdhib al-Banat," *Lisan al-Hal* issue 1678 (1894), p. 3; Salwa, "Ruh al-Zawaj," *Lisan al-Hal* issue 1702 (1894), p. 3; see also May, "Anonymous, al-Zawaj, Ra'y Anisa Fihi," *Lisan al-Hal* issue 1631 (1894), p. 3.
10. Jabel Amel is a plateau situated in southern Lebanon between the western mountain range of Lebanon and the Galilee.
11. Al-'Id, "Lebanon," in *Arab Women Writers: A Critical Reference Guide, 1873–1999*, p. 14; Hoda Elsaada, "Egypt," in *Arab Women Writers: A Critical Reference Guide, 1873–1999*, pp. 105–106; Nadia Nuwayhid al-Jurdi, *Nisa' min Biladi* (Beirut: al-Mu'assasa al-'Arabiyya lil-Dirasat wal-Nashr, 1986), pp. 199–204; Khairallah, *The Sisters of Men*, pp. 203–206. There is considerable divergence in the dates associated with these women writers; for example, Beth Baron believes

that *Ghada al-Zahira* was published earlier in 1893. Thus, we decided to follow those provided by the editors of *Arab Women Writers*.

12. Zaynab Fawwaz, *Husn al-'Awaqib aw Ghada al-Zahira* ed. Hilma al-Namnam. (Cairo: Matabi' al-Hay'a al-Misriyya, 1899; reprinted 2004), For information on the rivalry between 'Ali Bek al-As'ad (1821–1865) and his cousin Tamir Bek Husayn, see Muhammad Jabir al-Safa, *Ta'rikh Jabal 'Amil* (Beirut: Dar Matn al-Lugha, 1960), pp. 51–61, 158–62.

13. Marilyn Booth, "Fiction's Imaginative Archive and the Newspaper's Local Scandals: The Case of Nineteenth-Century Egypt," in Antoinette Burton (ed.), *Archive Stories: Facts, Fictions, and the Writing of History* (Durham: Duke University Press, 2005), p. 282; see also Marilyn Booth, "On Gender, History...and Fiction," in Israel Gershoni, Amy Singer and Y. Hakan Erdem (eds.). *Middle East Historiographies: Narrating the Twentieth Century* (Seattle: University of Washington Press, 2006), pp. 211–241.

14. Al-Qiyadi, *Isham al-Katiba al-'Arabiyya fi 'Asr al-Nahda Hatta 1914*, pp. 119–120; Akram F. Khater, "Becoming 'Syrian' in America: A Global Geography of Ethnicity and Nation," *Diaspora: A Journal of Transnational Studies* 14:2/3 (2005), pp. 299–331.

15. Labiba Hashim, *Qalb Rajul*, ed. Yumna al-'Id (Damascus: Dar al-Thaqafa wal-Nashr, 2002; first published Cairo, 1904). For information on the events of the 1860s in Mount Lebanon, see J. P. Sangnolo, "Constitutional Change in Mount Lebanon, pp. 1861–1864," *Middle Eastern Studies* 7:1 (1971), pp. 25–48; Leila T. Fawaz, *An Occasion for War: Civil Conflict in Lebanon and Damascus in 1860* (Berkeley and Los Angeles: University of California Press, 1994); Ussama Makdisi, *The Culture of Sectarianism: Community, History and Violence in Nineteenth-Century Ottoman Lebanon* (Berkeley and Los Angeles: University of California Press, 1994).

16. Zachs, *The Making of a Syrian Identity*, pp. 183–186.

17. Eric Hobsbawm, "Inventing Traditions," in Eric Hobsbawm and Terence Ranger (eds.) *The Invention of Tradition* (Cambridge: Cambridge University Press, 1984), pp. 1–15.

18. Ya'qub Sarruf, *Amir Lubnan* (Cairo: Matba'at al-Muqtataf, 1907); Moosa, *The Origins of Modern Arabic Fiction*, p. 246.

19. Najm, *al-Qissa fil-Adab al-'Arabi al-Hadith*, p. 227; Khairallah, *Sisters of Men*, pp. 209–10.

20. Farida 'Atiyya, *Bayna 'Arshayn* (Tripoli: Matba'at al-Najah, 1912); see also Najm, *al-Qissa fil-Adab al-'Arabi al-Hadith*, pp. 227–30.

21. For the impact of the Young Turks' coup d'état on the Arab provinces, and Greater Syria in particular, see Erik J. Zürcher, *Turkey: A Modern History* (London: I.B.Tauris, 1993), pp. 93–132; Hasan Kayali, *Arabs and Young Turks: Ottomanism, Arabism, and Islamism in the Ottoman Empire, 1908–1918* (Berkeley and Los Angeles: University of California Press, 1997), pp. 78–79; Rashid Khalidi, "Ottomanism and Arabism in Syria before 1914: A Reassessment," in

Rashid Khalidi et al. (eds.), *The Origins of Arab Nationalism* (New York: Columbia University Press, 1991), pp. 50–71.

22. Labiba Mikha'il Sawaya, *Hasna' Salonik* (Damascus: Orthodox Patriarch Press, 1909). Yusuf Najm claims that Sawaya relied heavily on several historical sources for her description of the Young Turks' rise to power. Najm, *al-Qissa fil-Adab al-'Arabi al-Hadith*, pp. 222, 225–26.

23. 'Atiyya, *Bayna 'Arshayn*, pp. 26–27.

24. Ibid., pp. 182–87.

25. Historians estimate that between 15,000 and 30,000 Armenians were killed in the course of the Adana massacre. For more information on these events, see M. Şükrü Hanioğlu, *Preparation for a Revolution: The Young Turks, 1902–1908* (Oxford: Oxford University Press, 2001); Vahakn N. Dadrian, *The History of the Armenian Genocide: Ethnic Conflict from the Balkans to Anatolia to the Caucasus* (Providence: Berghahn Press, 1997).

26. 'Atiyya, *Bayna 'Arshayn*, p. 97.

27. Khater, *Inventing Home: Emigration, Gender, and the Middle Class in Lebanon*, p. 156. Lebanese historian Emily Faris Ibrahim also disagrees with the "conservative vs. liberal" interpretation of the debate; see Imili Faris Ibrahim, *Adibat Lubnaniyyat* (Beirut: Dar al-Rayhani lil-Tiba'a wal-Nashr, 1964), pp. 49–51.

28. Jane Rendall, "Citizenship, Culture and Civilization: The Languages of British Suffragists, 1866–1874," in Caroline Daley and Melanie Nolan (eds.), *Suffrage and Beyond: International Feminist Perspectives* (New York: New York University Press, 1994), pp. 127–150; Virginia Sapiro, "When are Interests Interesting? The Problem of Political Representation of Women," *American Political Science Review* 75 (1981), p. 702.

29. Thompson, *Colonial Citizens: Republican Rights*, pp. 240–241.

30. Anonymous, "Death List of a Day: Mme. Hanna K. Korany," *New York Times* (August 2, 1898); Khairallah, *The Sisters of Men*, pp. 206–208.

31. Anonymous, "Club Women and Students," *New York Times* (March 4, 1894).

32. Hanna Kurani, "Ta'lim al-Banat," *Lisan al-Hal* issue 1283 (1890), p. 3, and *Lisan al-Hal* issue 1284 (1890), p. 2–3.

33. Hanna Kurani, "Majd al-Mar'a," *Lisan al-Hal* issue 1279 (1890), p. 3. An English version of this article entitled "Hanna Kurani, The Glory of Womanhood," can be found in Mary Kavanaugh Oldham (ed.), *The Congress of Women: Held in the Woman's Building, World's Columbian Exposition, Chicago, U.S. A., 1893* (Chicago: Monarch Books, 1894), pp. 359–360.

34. Anonymous, "Notes about Women," *New York Times* (November 4, 1894); Anonymous, "A Fair Visitor from Syria," *New York Times* (February 20, 1894).

35. Tucker, *Women in Nineteenth-Century Egypt*, p. 87; Khater, *Inventing Home: Emigration, Gender, and the Middle Class in Lebanon*, pp. 33–34.

36. Gayle Gullett, "'Our Great Opportunity': Organized Women Advance Women's Work at the World's Columbian Exposition of 1893," *Illinois Historical Journal* 87 (1994), p. 259; see also Anne-Marie Kinahan, "Transcendent Citizenship: Suffrage, the National Council of Women of

Canada, and the Politics of Organized Womanhood," *Journal of Canadian Studies/Revue d'Études Canadiennes* 42:3 (2008), pp. 5–27.

37. Paula Baker, "The Domestication of Politics: Women and American Political Society, 1780–1920," *American Historical Review* 89 (1984), pp. 620–647; see also Eileen Boris, "The Power of Motherhood: Black and White Activist Women Redefine the Political," *Yale Journal of Law and Feminism* 25 (1989/90), pp. 25–50.

38. Anonymous, "To Get Work for Women," *New York Times* (December 30, 1894).

39. Hanna Kurani [Untitled – "A Letter from Hanna Kurani]," *al-Fatat* 1:2 (1 January 1893), pp. 78–79; Hanna Kurani, "Murasalat al-Jinat – A Letter from Hanna Kurani," *al-Fatat* 1:9 (11 August 1893), p. 353; Maryam Hadad, "al-'Ilm wal-Mal," *al-Fatat* 1:6 (27 March 1893), pp. 256–260. Anisa Shartuni, "Fasl al-Khitab fil-Rajul wal-Mar'a," *al-Muqtataf* 34 (1909), pp. 289–294. As this piece was published posthumously it is unclear when Shartuni wrote it.

40. Zaynab Fawwaz, "Fair and Equal Treatment," in *Opening the Gates: A Century of Arab Feminist Writing*, pp. 223–226. Fawwaz was responding to Kurani's views in general. This piece was written as a specific rebuttal to Kurani's article "al-Mar'a wal-Siyasa," published in the journal *Lubnan*. Zaynab Fawwaz, *al-Rasa'il al-Zaynabiyya* (Cairo: Matabi' al-Hay'a al-Misriyya al 'Amma lil-Katib, 2007) ed. Ahmad Muhammad Salim, pp. 54–61, 70–84; Al-Qiyadi, *Isham al-Katiba al-'Arabiyya fi 'Asr al-Nahda Hatta 1914*, pp. 242–249; 'Umar Rida Kahala, *A'lam al-Nisa' fi 'Alamayy al-'Arab wal-Islam*, vol. 2 (Damascus: al-Matba'a al-Hashimiyya, 1958), pp. 82–91.

41. Salma al-Sa'igh, *Suwar wa Dhikrayat* (Beirut: Dar al-Hadara, 1964), p. 86; Booth, *May Her Likes Be Multiplied*, p. 143; Jurji Niqula Baz, *Imili Sursuq: Bimunasabat Sittin 'Am Muhsina* (Beirut: al-Matba'a al-Adabiyya, 1937), pp. 5–7; Thompson, *Colonial Citizens: Republican Rights*, p. 93. For information on the Sursuq family, see Zachs, *The Making of a Syrian Identity*, pp. 238–39.

42. Julya Tu'ma, "al-Mar'a al-Fadila man Yajiduha," *al-Hasna'* 1:3 (1909), pp. 203–210; Julya Tu'ma, "al-Malak al-Awwal," *al-Hasna'* 2:7 (1911), pp. 254–257, 2:8 (1911), pp. 292–295.

43. Al-'Id, "Lebanon," in *Arab Women Writers: A Critical Reference Guide, 1873–1999*, p. 15; al-Sa'igh, *Suwar wa Dhikrayat*, p. 150; Mishal Jiha, *Julya Tu'ma al-Dimashqiyya* (Beirut: Riyad al-Rayyis Lil-Tawzi' wal-Nashr, 2003), pp. 25–26.

44. 'Aisa Futuh, "Nahdat al-Mar'a al-'Arabiyya al-Suriyya hatta Muntasif al-Qarn al-'Ishrin," *al- Ma'rifa* 32:364 (1994), pp. 63–66; Iman al-Qadi and Subhi Hadidi, "Syria," in *Arab Women Writers: A Critical Reference Guide, 1873–1999*, p. 60; Jurji Niqula Baz, *Mari Ajami Tadhakkur li-Yubiliha al-Fiddi* (Beirut: Matba'at Sadir, 1926). We encountered a few unreferenced secondary sources which claim that 'Ajami's involvement in the cause of the political prisoners began with the arrest of her fiancé, who was later executed. We were unable to substantiate this claim.

45. Jurji Niqula Baz, *Nazik al-'Abid* (Beirut: Matba'at al-Salam, 1927), p. 5; Elizabeth Williams, "Nazik al-'Abid and the Nur al-Fayha Society:

Independent Modernity, Colonial Treat and the Space of Women," in Muhammad A. Bamyeh (ed.) *Intellectuals and Civil Society in the Middle East* (New York: I.B.Tauris, 2012), pp. 29–56.

46. James L. Gelvin, *Divided Loyalties: Nationalism and Mass Politics in Syria at the Close of Empire* (Berkeley: University of California Press, 1998), p. 215. For more information on the postwar activities of many of the women discussed here, see Charlotte Weber, "Between Nationalism and Feminism: The Eastern Women's Congresses of 1930 and 1932," *Journal of Middle East Women's Studies* 4 (2008), pp. 83–106.

47. Thompson, *Colonial Citizens: Republican Rights*, p. 120.

48. Malek Abisaab, "'Unruly' Factory Women in Lebanon: Contesting French Colonialism and the National State, 1940–1946," *Journal of Women's History* 16:3 (2004), pp. 55–82. One of the women who did manage to remain active after 1920 was activist and journalist 'Adila Bayhum al-Jaza'iri (1900–1975), a relative of Nazik Khatim al-'Abid Bayhum; Sami M. Moubayed, *Silk and Steel: Men and Women Who Shaped Syria, 1900–2000* (Seattle: Cune Press, 2004), pp. 430–432.

Chapter 6   Beyond the Marriage Plot: Marriage, Sexuality and the Rise of "Outlaw Emotions" in Turn-of-the-century Novels

1. Jubran Khalil Jubran, "Warda al-Hani," in *al-Arwah al-Mutamarrida* (Beirut: n.p., 1970), p. 34. An English translation is available: Gibran Khalil Gibran, *Spirits Rebellious*, translated by H. M. Nahmad (London: Heinemann, 1971; first published 1908), p. 22.

2. Alison M. Jaggar, "Love and Knowledge: Emotion in Feminist Epistemology," in Alison M. Jaggar and Susan R. Bordo (eds.), *Gender/ Body/ Knowledge: Feminist Reconsiderations of Being and Knowing* (New Brunswick: Rutgers University Press, 1989), pp. 164; 160–161.

3. Yumna al-'Id, "Lebanon," in *Arab Women Writers: A Critical Reference Guide, 1873–1999*, p. 21.

4. On the al-Bustanis, see: Jessup, *The Women of the Arabs*, pp. 114–139; Edward W. Hooker (ed.), *Memoir of Mrs. Sarah Smith Late of the American Mission in Syria* (New York: American Tract Society, 1845), pp. 371–373; Booth, "'She Herself Was the Ultimate Rule': Arabic Biographies of Missionary Teachers and their Pupils," pp. 427–448; Anonymous, (Untitled Obituary of Rahil al-Bustani), *al-Fatat* 1:11 (1894), pp. 519–520; Baz, *al-Nisa'iyyat: Kitab Adabi Akhlaqi Ijtima'i*, p. 65; Al-Qiyadi, *Isham al-Katiba al-'Arabiyya fi 'Asr al-Nahda hatta 1914*, p. 184; Najm, *al-Qissa fil-Adab al-'Arabi al-Hadith*, p. 85; Moosa, *The Origins of Modern Arabic Fiction*, p. 222; Zeidan, *Arab Women Novelists*, p. 13.

5. Alice al-Bustani, *Riwayat al-Sa'iba* (Beirut: al-Matba'a al-Adabiyya, 1891), p. 34. Denise A. Spellberg, *Politics, Gender and the Islamic Past: The Legacy of 'A'isha bint Abi Bakr* (New York: Columbia University Press, 1994); see also Leila Ahmed, "Women and the Advent of Islam," *Signs* 11:4 (1986), pp. 665– 691 and Delfina Serrano, "Muslim Feminists' Discourse on *Zina*: New Paradigms in Sight?" in Roswitha Badry, Maria Roher and Karin Steiner (eds.), *Liebe, Sexualität, Ehe und Partnerschaft – Paradigmen im Wandel* (Freiburg: Fördergemeinschaft Wissenschaftlicher Publikationen von Frauen, 2009), pp. 106–125.

6. For more on cousin marriages, see Raphael Patai, "Cousin-Right in Middle Eastern Marriage," *Southwestern Journal of Anthropology* 11:4 (1955), pp. 371– 390.

7. For the "price" of flaunting such conventions in the modern period, see Suad Joseph, "Brother-Sister Relationships: Connectivity, Love and Power in the Reproduction of Patriarchy in Lebanon," in Suad Joseph (ed.), *Intimate Selving in Arab Families: Gender, Self and Identity* (Syracuse: Syracuse University Press, 1999), pp. 113–140. See also, Judith E. Tucker, "Marriage and the Family in Nablus, 1720–1856: Toward a History of Arab Marriage," *Journal of Family History* 13:1 (1988), pp. 165–179.

8. At the outset of this project before we began re-reading these novels (and numerous others), in which the heroine often finds herself facing a loveless marriage or is imprisoned, threatened, and starved, or told of her beloved's untimely death in order to secure her compliance to her guardians' wishes, we believed that the authors were indulging themselves in heartbreaking romantic plots and wondered about the readers' reception of these plots.

9. Engin D. Akarli, "Daughters and Fathers: A Young Druze Woman's Experience (1894–1897)," in Baki Tezcan and Karl K. Barabir (eds.), *Identity and Identity Formation in the Ottoman World: A Volume of Essays in Honor of Norman Itzkovitz* (Madison: University of Wisconsin Press, 2007), pp. 167–184; Jens Hanssen, "Sexuality, Health and Colonialism in Postwar 1860 Beirut," in Samir Khalaf and John Gagnon (eds.), *Sexuality in the Arab World* (London: Saqi, 2006), 63–84. See also, Hudson, "Investing by Women or Investing in Women?," p. 116.

10. Akarli, "Daughters and Fathers: A Young Druze Woman's Experience (1894– 1897)," p. 182.

11. Ibid; Kayali, *Arabs and Young Turks: Ottomanism, Arabism and Islamism in the Ottoman Empire, 1908–1918*, p. 42.

12. Niqula Haddad, *al-Ishtirakiyya* (Damascus: Dar al-Mada lil-Thaqafa wal-Nashr, 2002; first published in 1920). Haddad was also the first to translate Einstein's theory of relativity into Arabic. Widad Sakakini, "Niqula Haddad fi Hayatihi wa-Thaqafatihi-Suwar Lubnaniyyya wa-Suriyya min Difaf al-Nil," *al-Adib* 10: 7 (1951), pp. 40–43; Donald M. Reid, "The Syrian Christians and Early Socialism in the Arab World," *International Journal of Middle East Studies* 5:2 (1974), pp. 177–193; Caesar E. Farah, "Nationalist Concerns for Syria: The

Case of Farah Anyun, Mayy Ziadah, and al-Kawakibi," in Adel Beshara (ed.), *The Origins of Syrian Nationhood: Histories, Pioneers and Identity* (London and New York: Routledge, 2011), pp. 215–216; Najm, *al-Qissa fil-Adab al-'Arabi al-Hadith*, pp. 101–109. For Rose Antun, see Khairallah, *The Sisters of Men*, p. 181; Booth, *May Her Likes Be Multiplied*, pp. 46–47.

13. Donald Reid claims that the Haddad novel *Asirat al-Hubb* was condemned in the press as titillating and indecent, and Badir suggests that originally (perhaps fearing such accusations) Haddad had presented this novel as a translation and only acknowledged authorship at Jurji Zaydan's urging, see Reid, "The Syrian Christians," p. 186; 'Abd al-Muhsin Badir, *Tatawwur al-Riwaya al-'Arabiyya al-Haditha fi Misr 1870–1938* (Cairo: Dar al-Ma'arif, 1963).

14. Niqula Haddad, *Kulluhu Nasib* (Cairo: Matba'at al-Tawfiq, 1903).

15. M. Jeanne Peterson, "The Victorian Governess: Status Incongruence in Family and Society," *Victorian Studies* 14:1 (1970), pp. 7–26; Martha Vicinus, "'Helpless and Unfriended': Nineteenth-Century Domestic Melodrama," *New Literary History* 13:1 (1981), pp. 127–143. The modern governess in Arab fiction should be distinguished from the traditional figure of the nanny, see Farzaneh Milani, "The Mediatory Guile of the Nanny in Persian Romance," *Iranian Studies* 32:2 (1999), pp. 181–201.

16. Niqula Haddad, *Hawwa al-Jadida aw Yvonne Monar* (Cairo: Matba'at al-Shams, 1929; originally published 1906), p. 29.

17. Ibid.

18. Ibid., p. 86.

19. Ibid., p. 91.

20. Ibid., pp. 3–4.

21. Ibid., p. 116

22. Marina Warner, *Alone of Her Sex: The Myth and the Cult of the Virgin Mary* (New York: Knopf, 1976), pp. 50–67.

23. Gail Cunningham, *The New Woman and the Victorian Novel* (London: Macnillan Press, 1978); Sally Ledger, *The New Woman: Fiction and Feminism at the Fin de Siècle* (Manchester: Manchester University Press, 1997); Elizabeth K. Menon, *Evil by Design: The Creation and Marketing of the Femme Fatale* (Urbana and Chicago: University of Illinois, 2006).

24. Elizabeth K. Menon, "*Les filles d'Eve* in Word and Image," in Rui Carvalho Homem and Maria de Fátima Lambert (eds.), *Writing and Seeing: Essays on Word and Image* (Amsterdam: Edition Rodopi, 2006), pp. 157–174. Menon took the view that contrary to Karen Offen's characterization, *l'Ève nouvelle* is not a "mystic-romantic" novel; see Karen Offen, "Depopulation, Nationalism and Feminism in Fin-de-Siècle France," *American Historical Review* 89:3 (1984), pp. 648–676.

25. For more on Jules Bois (1868–1943), see Menon, in *Writing and Seeing*, p. 165.

26. Anonymous, "al-Mar'a al-Jiniyya," *al-Mabahith* issue 11 (1909), p. 511–514. For more information on Caesar Lombroso and the impact of his work, see Paul Rock, "Caesar Lombroso as a Signal Criminologist," *Criminology and Criminal Justice* 7:2 (2007), pp. 117–133.

27. Anonymous, "al-Intiqad, al-Zahawi Yara fil Mar'a Ghayr Ra'y al-Qur'an," *al-Haqa'iq*, 1:3 (1910), pp. 89–103; Farid Bik Wajdi, "Mas'alat al-Mar'a al-Misriyya," *al-Haqa'iq* 1:20 (1910), p. 216.

28. Marilyn Booth, "From the Horses' Rump and the Whorehouse Keyhole: Ventriloquized Memoirs as Political Voice in 1920s Egypt," *Maghreb Review* 32:2–3 (2007), pp. 233–61; Marilyn Booth, "Between Harem and Houseboat: 'Falleness,' Gendered Spaces, and the Female National Subject in 1920s Egypt," in *Harem Histories: Envisioning Places and Living Spaces*, pp. 342–373; Marilyn Booth, "Un/safe/ly at Home: Narratives of Sexual Coercion in 1920s Egypt," *Gender and History* 16:3 (2004), pp. 744–768.

29. Amanda Anderson, *Tainted Souls and Painted Faces: The Rhetoric of Falleness in Victorian Britain* (Ithaca: Cornell University Press, 1993); Nina Auerbach, "The Rise of the Fallen Woman," *Nineteenth-Century Fiction* 35:1 (1980), pp. 29–5; Ellen Rooney, "Criticism and the Subject of Sexual Violence," *Modern Language Notes* 98:5 (1983), pp. 1269–1278; George Watt, *The Fallen Woman in the Nineteenth-Century English Novel* (Beckenham, Kent: Taylor & Francis, 1984).

30. Jane I. Smith and Yvonne Y. Haddad, "Eve – The Islamic Image of Woman," *Women's Studies International Forum* 5:2 (1982), pp. 135–144; Denise. A. Spellberg, "Writing the Unwritten Life of the Islamic Eve: Menstruation and the Demonization of Motherhood," *International Journal of Middle East Studies* 28:3 (1986), pp. 305–324.

31. Haddad, *Hawwa al-Jadida aw Yvonne Monar*, p. 80.

32. Ibid., pp. 115, 108, 111, 114.

33. Ibid., pp. 103–104. For more on Rashid Rida, see Tauber, "Rashid Rida as Pan-Arabist: Before World War I," pp. 102–112, and Tauber, "Three Approaches, One Idea: Religion and State in the Thought of 'Abd al-Rahman al-Kawkabi, Najib 'Azuri and Rashid Rida," pp. 190–198.

34. Kate Flint, *The Woman Reader, 1837–1914* (Oxford: Clarendon, 1993), pp. 253–255.

35. Jubran Khalil Jubran, *al-Ajniha al-Mutakassira* (Jerusalem: Dar Tammuz lil-Nashr, 1982), p. 9.

36. Robin Waterfield, *Prophet: The Life and Times of Khalil Gibran* (New York: St. Martin's Press, 1998); Robin Ostle, "The Literature of the Mahjar," in Albert Hourani and Nadim Shehadi (eds.), *The Lebanese in the World: A Century of Emigration* (London: I.B.Tauris, 1992), pp. 211–213; Adel Beshara, "A Rebel Syrian: Gibran Khalil Gibran," in *The Origins of Syrian Nationhood: Histories, Pioneers and Identity*, pp. 143–162.

37. Jubran, *al-Ajniha al-Mutakassira*, p. 80.

38. Thompson, *Colonial Citizens: Republican Rights*, pp. 86–87; Jens Hanssen, "Public Morality and Marginality in Fin-de-Siècle Beirut," in Eugene Rogan (ed.), *Outside In: On the Margins of the Modern Middle East* (London: I.B.Tauris, 2002), p. 196. For prostitution in Ottoman Greater Syria, see Elyse Smerdjian, *'Off the Straight Path': Illicit Sex, Law and Community in Ottoman Aleppo* (Syracuse: Syracuse University Press, 2008), pp. 99–129; Elyse Smerdjian, "Sinful

Professions Illegal Occupations of Women in Ottoman Aleppo," *Hawwa* 1:1 (2003), pp. 60–85. For a comparative view from other cities in the Ottoman Empire see Khaled Fahmy, "Prostitution in Egypt in the Nineteenth-Century," in *Outside In: On the Margins of the Modern Middle East*, pp. 77–103. See also, Karin Van Nieuwkerk, *A Trade Like Any Other: Female Singers and Dancers in Egypt* (Austin: University of Texas Press, 1995); A. Holly Shissler, "Womanhood is Not for Sale: Saiba Zekeriya Sertal against Prostitution and for Women's Employment," *Journal of Middle East Women's Studies* 4:3 (2008), pp. 12–30; Samir Khalaf, "Correlates of Prostitution: Some Proper Errors and Misconceptions," *Journal of Sex Research* 4:2 (1968), pp. 147–162.

39. At the beginning of the nineteenth century the population of Beirut was estimated at 6,000 and at its close it was about 120,000. Zachs, *The Making of a Syrian Identity*, 43; Leila T. Fawaz, *Merchants and Migrants in Nineteenth Century Beirut* (Cambridge, MA: Harvard University Press, 1983), p. 1.

40. Al-Bustani, "Khitab fil-Hay'a al-Ijtima'iyya wal-Muqabala bayna al-'Awa'id al-'Arabiyya wal-Ifranjiyya," in *A'mal al-Jam'iyya al-'Ilmiyya al-Suriyya, 1868–1869*, 207; Hanssen, "Public Morality and Marginality," pp. 183–211.

41. In 1881 writer and educator Ahemd Midhat (1844–1913) published a novel about prostitution, *Henüz Onyedi Yaşinda (Still Only Seventeen)*; he also contracted a second marriage in 1884 with a Greek prostitute in order to rehabilitate her. See Marilyn Booth "Between Harem and Houseboat: 'Falleness,' Gendered Spaces, and the Female National Subject in 1920s Egypt," in *Harem Histories: Envisioning Places and Living Spaces*, pp. 325–326. See also Carter V. Findley, "An Ottoman Occidentalist in Europe: Ahmed Midhat Meets Madame Gülnar, 1889," *American Historical Review* 103:1 (1998), p. 21, fn. 34. The interest in prostitution (as a social and literary topic) echoed similar interests in Europe, see Charles Bernheimer, *Figures of Ill Repute: Representing Prostitution in Nineteenth-Century France* (Durham: Duke University Press, 1997); Deborah Epstein Nord, *Walking the Victorian Streets: Representation and the City* (Ithaca: Cornell University Press, 1995).

42. Jubran Khalil Jubran, "Martha al-Baniya," in *Ara'is al-Muruj* (Beirut: n.p., 1970; first published 1906), p. 32. For the English version, see Gibran Khali Gibran, "Martha," in *Nymphs of the Valley*, translated by H. M. Nahmad (London: Heinemann, 1972).

43. Gibran, "Warda al-Hani," in *al-Arwah al-Mutamarrida*, pp. 18–19.

44. Ibid., pp. 25–26.

45. Ibid., p. 34.

46. Gibran Khali Gibran, "Madja'" ("The Marriage Bed")," in *al-Arwah al-Mutamarrida* (Beirut: n.p., 1970), p. 62.

47. Gibran, *al-Ajniha al-Mutakassira*, p. 44.

48. Ibid., p. 47.

49. Ibid., p. 58.

50. Ibid., p. 70.

51. Ibid., p. 86.

52. Gibran, "Letter to Mary Haskell, 9 February 1912," and "Letter to Mary Haskell, 6 May, 1912," in Virginia Hilu (ed.), *Beloved Prophet: The Love Letters of Khalil Gibran and Mary Haskell and her Private Journal* (London: Quartet Books, 1972), pp. 65, 79.

53. Mary Haskell, "Journal, 3 September 1913," in *Beloved Prophet*, pp. 151–152.

54. Moosa, *The Origins of Modern Arabic Fiction*, p. 250.

55. Hanssen, "Sexuality, Health and Colonialism," in *Sexuality in the Arab World*, p. 69.

56. Thompson, *Colonial Citizens: Republican Rights*, p. 3.

57. Ibid., p. 4.

58. Hafez, *The Genesis of Arabic Narrative Discourse*, p. 73.

Epilogue: Did Women Have a *Nahda*?

1. Sharabi, *Neopatriarchy: A Theory of Distorted Change in Arab Society*, pp. 4, 6.

2. Stephen Sheehi, "Failure, Modernity, and the Works of Hisham Sharabi: Towards a Post-Colonial Critique of Arab Subjectivity," *Critique: Critical Middle Eastern Studies* 6:10 (1997), p. 47.

3. Hisham Sharabi, *Arab Intellectuals and the West: The Formative Years, 1875–1914* (Baltimore: Johns Hopkins University Press, 1970), pp. 10, 20.

4. Sheehi, "Failure, Modernity, and the Works of Hisham Sharabi," p. 49.

5. Chandra Talpade Mohanty, "Under Western Eyes: Feminist Scholarship and Colonial Discourses," in Ann Russo, and Lourdes Torres (eds.), Chandra Talpade Mohanty, *Third World Women and the Politics of Feminism* (Bloomington: Indiana University Press, 1991), p. 56; Kumari Jayawardena, *Feminism and Nationalism in the Third World* (London: Zed Books, 1986), p. 2; Uma Narayan, "Essence of Culture and a Sense of History: A Feminist Critique of Cultural Essentialism," *Hypatia* 13:2 (1998), pp. 86–106; Alison Jaggar, "Globalizing Feminist Ethics," *Hypatia* 13:2 (1998), pp. 7–31.

6. Narayan, "Essence of Culture and a Sense of History: A Feminist Critique of Cultural Essentialism," pp. 92, 93.

7. Jaggar, "Globalizing Feminist Ethics," pp. 12–13.

8. Ibid., p. 14.

BIBLIOGRAPHY

Primary Sources

Arabic

Abu Khatir, Amin. "Huquq al-Nisa'," *al-Muqtataf* 10 (1886), pp. 621–623.

Abu Rizq, Wadi'. "Huquq al-Nisa'," *al-Muqtataf* 20 (1896), pp. 130–132.

'Ali, Amir. "Al-Nisa' fil-Islam," *al-Muqtataf* 23 (1899), pp. 427–433; 489–497.

Aliye, Fatma. "Nisa' al-Muslimin," *Thamarat al-Funun* issue 916 (1893).

Anonymous. "[Advertisement for separate swimming hours for men and women at the beach]," *al-Janna* issue 1300 (1883), p. 4.

———— "Bab Tadbir al-Manzil," *al-Fatat* 1: 11 (1894), pp. 510–512.

———— "Fa'ida Adabiyya," *al-Fatat* 1: 10 (15 February 1894), pp. 446–448.

———— "Al-Fatat al-Sharqiyya fi Akhir al-Qarn al-Tasi' 'Ashr," *al-Hilal* 6 (1897), pp. 169–174.

———— [Untitled]. *Al-Fatat* 1 (Mar. 1894), p. 521.

———— "Fil-Mar'a wa-Wajibatiha wa-Huquqiha – fi Tadbir al-Manzil," *al-Fatat* 1: 5 (1 April 1893), pp. 212–215.

———— "Fi Tadbir al-Manzil-fil- Mar'a wa-Wajibatiha wa-Huquqiha," *al-Fatat* 1: 6 (1 May 1893), pp. 281–282.

———— "Fransis Fathallah Marrash [Obituary]," *al-Hilal* 5 (1897), pp. 742–744.

———— "Jamal al-Mar'a wa-Ta'thiruhu fil-Rajul," *Lisan al-Hal* issue 1596 (14 March 1894), p. 3.

———— "Hadaya wa-Tatriz," *al-Muqtataf* 16 (1892), p. 708.

———— "Halawat al-Bandura," *al-Muqtataf* 6 (1881), p. 37.

———— "Halawat al-Ijjas," *al-Muqtataf* 6 (1881), p. 37.

———— "Hifz al-Sihha," *al-Muqtataf* 8 (1883), pp. 22–23.

———— "Hal lil-Nisa' an Yatlubna Kull Huquq al-Rijal," *al-Hilal* 2 (1894), pp. 491–493.

———— "Hal lil-Nisa' an Yatlubna Kull Huquq al-Rijal," *al-Hilal* 2 (1894), pp. 567–569.

———— "Huquq al-Nisa'," *al-Muqtataf* 20 (1896), pp. 198–199.

———— "'Id al-Awlad," *al-Muqtataf* 18 (1894), p. 558.

———— "Ikhtira' Tilighraf Jadid, *Hadiqat al-Akhbar* issue 30 (July 1858), p. 4.

———— "Al-Intiqad, al-Zahawi Yara fil Mar'a Ghayr Ra'y al-Qur'an," *al-Haqa'iq* 1: 3 (21 April 1910), pp. 89–103.

———— "I'tibar al-Nisa' li-Libas al-Rijal," *al-Muqtataf* 8 (1883), pp. 20–21.

———— "Ghasl al-Aqmisha al-Haririyya al-Mulawwana," *al-Muqtataf* 6 (1881), p. 204.

———— "Ghasl Kufuf al-Jild al-Faransawiyya," *al-Muqtataf* 6 (1881), p. 224.

———— "Libas al-Sighar fil-Sayf," *al-Muqtataf* 6 (1881), p. 46.

———— "Al-Ma' wal-Sabun la al-Hamra wal-Duhun," *al-Muqtataf* 6 (1881), pp. 201–203.

———— "Mabahith 'Ilmiyya Adabiyya Ta'rikhiyya – al-'Ilm wal-Mar'a," *Thamarat al-Funun* issue 1220 (1899).

———— "Malabis al-Nisa'," *Thamarat al-Funun* issue 936 (1893).

———— "Malabis al-Nisa'," *Thamarat al-Funun* issue 1001 (1894).

———— "Manzilat al-Mar'a," *al-Muqtataf* 7 (1883), pp. 583–584.

———— "Al-Mar'a," *Lisan al-Hal* issue 1583 (26 November 1894), p. 2.

———— "Al-Mar'a fi Manziliha," *Lisan al-Hal* issue 1615 (23 April 1894), p. 4.

———— "Al-Mar'a al-Jiniyya," *al-Mabahith* issue 11 (15 May 1909), pp. 511–514.

———— "Al-Mishadd," *al-Hilal* 5 (1896), pp. 134–137.

———— "Maqdirat al-Mar'a," *al-Muqtataf* 21 (1897), pp. 59–60.

———— "Al-Nisa' wal-Tibb," *al-Muqtataf* 7 (1882), pp. 25–26.

———— "Shadhrat fi Tarbiyat al-Awlad," *al-Muqtataf* 6 (1881), p. 11.

———— "Shadhrat fil Tarbiya wal-Ta'lim," *al-Muqtataf* 7 (1882), pp. 425–426.

———— "Shibli Shumayyil, Tarjamatuhu," *al-Muqtataf* 50 (1917), pp. 105–112.

———— "Tadbir al-Manzil," *Anis al-Jalis* 2: 4 (30 April 1899), pp. 155–157.

———— "Tanzif al-Rukham," *al-Muqtataf* 6 (1881), p. 224.

———— "Al-Zawaj wa-Mu'asharat al-'Iyal fi Uruba," *Thamarat al-Funun* issue 930 (1893).

———— "Al-Zawaj," *Lisan al-Hal* issue 1640 (7 July 1894), p. 2.

———— Al-Zawaj, Ra'y Anisa Fihi," *Lisan al-Hal* issue 1631 (27 June 1894), p. 3.

———— [Untitled Obituary of Rahil al-Bustani], *al-Fatat* 1:11 (1 March 1894), pp. 519–520.

———— "Zinat al-Ma'ida," *al-Muqtataf* 9 (1884), pp. 554–556.

Antaki, Maram. "Al-Haqq Ahaqq an Yutba'," *al-Fatat* 1:12 (Mar. 1894), pp. 560–567.

Antunyus, Najib. "Huquq al-Nisa'," *al-Muqtataf* 11 (1886), pp. 232–237.

Al-Azhari, Istir. "Hal lil-Nisa' an Yatlubna Kull Huquq al-Rijal," *al-Hilal* 2 (1894), pp. 438–440.

———— [Untitled] *al-Hilal* 2 (1894), pp. 561–563.

Al-Bahith al-'Asri, "Ra'y fil-Zawaj," *Lisan al-Hal* issue 1635 (2 July 1894), p. 1.

Bahiyya. "Hal lil-Nisa' an Yatlubna Kull Huquq al-Rijal," *al-Hilal* 2 (1894), pp. 590–593.

Bajit, Sayyida. "Azya' al-Nisa'," – translated from the English newspaper, *The Nineteenth Century*," *al-Muqtataf* 8 (1883), pp. 21–22.

Baz, Jurji Niqula. *Imili Sursuq: Bimunasabat Sittin 'Am Muhsina*. Beirut: al-Matba'a al-Adabiyya, 1937.

——— *Al-Nisa'iyyat: Kitab Adabi Akhlaqi Ijtima'i.* Beirut: Al-Matb'a al-'Abasiyya, 1919.

——— *Mari Ajami Tadhakkur li-Yubiliha al-Fiddi.* Beirut: Matba'at Sadir, 1926.

——— *Nazik al-'Abid.* Beirut: Matba'at al-Salam, 1927.

Al-Bustani, Butrus. *A'mal al-Jam'iyya al-Suriyya.* Beirut: Dar al-Huda', 1852.

——— "Khitab fi Ta'lim al-Nisa'," in Yusuf Qizma al-Khuri (ed.). *Al-Jam'iyya al-Suriyya lil-'Ulum wal-Funun 1847–1852.* Beirut: Dar al-Huda', 1990, pp. 45–53.

——— "Khitab fil-Hay'a al-Ijtima'iyya wal-Muqabala bayna al-'Awa'id al-'Arabiyya wal-Ifranjiyya," in Yusuf Qizma Khuri (ed.). *A'mal al-Jam'iyya al-'Ilmiyya al-Suriyya, 1868–1869.* Beirut: Dar al-Huda', 1990, pp. 204–217.

——— "Khutba fi Adab al-'Arab," in Yusuf Qizma Khuri (ed.). *Al-Jam'iyya al- Suriyya lil-'Ulum wal-Funun 1847–1852.* Beirut: Dar al-Huda', 1990, pp. 101–117.

——— *Muhit al-Muhit.* 2 vols. Beirut, n.p., 1870.

Al-Bustani, Salim. "Al-Zawj wal-Zawja," *al-Jinan* 6 (1877), pp. 382–384.

Damit, Jabir. "Hal lil-Nisa' an Yatlubna Kull Huquq al-Rijal," *al-Hilal* 2 (1894), pp. 526–532.

E.G., "Izalat al-Buqa' wa-Nahwiha 'an al-Thiyab," *al-Muqtataf* 6 (1881), p. 11.

Fathallah, 'Abd al-Basit. "Mas'alat al-Nisa'," *Thamarat al-Funun* issues 1258, 1259, 1260, 1280, 1282, 1293, 1296, 1301, 1306, 1307, 1323 (1899).

——— "'Ilm al-Ijtima' al-Bashari Libas al-Sayf wa-Nasij al-Watan," *Thamarat al-Funun* issue 1287 (1900), p. 3.

G. H. "Laysa al-Ta'lim Huwa al-Tarbiyya," *al-Muqtataf* 7 (1882), pp. 173–174.

Ghabril, Fayiqah. "Al-Sa'ada al-Baytiyya," *al-Hasna'* 2:2 (August 1910), pp. 109–111.

Ghanim, Khalil. *Kitab al-Iqtisad al-Siayasi aw Tadbir al-Manzil.* Alexandria: Matba'at Jaridat Misr, 1879.

Al-Ghazzi, Kamil. *Kitab Nahr al-Dhahab fi Ta'rikh Halab.* 3 vols, 2nd ed. Eds. Shawqi Sha'th and Mahmud Fakhuri. Aleppo: Dar al-Qalam al-'Arabi, 1991–93.

Hadad, Maryam. "Al-'Ilm wal-Mal," *al-Fatat* 1: 6 (27 March 1893), pp. 256–260.

Hajjar, Rahil. "Difa' al-Nisa' 'an al-Nisa'," *al-Muqtataf* 11 (1887), pp. 686–687.

Hamam, Jirjis. "Ikhtiyar al-Manzil," *Lisan al-Hal* issue 1271 (25 January 1891), p. 3.

Hubayqa, Farida. "Adab al-Ma'ida," *al-Muqtataf* 9 (1884), pp. 370–372.

Al-Hurani, Ibrahim Afandi. "Milh al-Ta'am," *al-Muqtataf* 3 (1878), pp. 185–186.

Ibn al-Hakim. "Wajibat al-Rajul," *Lisan al-Hal* issue 1614 (21 April 1894), p. 3.

——— "al-Zawaj," *Lisan al-Hal* issue 1639 (6 July 1894), p. 3.

Jawish, Fathallah. "Al-Mar'a fil-Hay'a al-Ijtima'iyya," *Lisan al-Hal* issue 1601 (4 April 1894), p. 4.

Kassab, Salim. "Ta'thir al-Walida," *al-Jinan* 16 (1885), pp. 138–142; 182–184.

——— "Al-Mar'a," *Lisan al-Hal* issue 1653 (23 July 1894), p. 2.

——— "Al-Mar'a," *Lisan al-Hal* issue 1655 (25 July 1894), pp. 3–4.

Al-Khalidi, 'Anbara Salam. *Jawla fil-Dhikrayat bayna Lubnan wa-Filastin.* Beirut: Dar al-Nahar lil-Nashr, 1978.

Khalid, Maryam. "Iqtirah Hasna' ba'd Wajibat al-Mar'a," *al-Fatat* 1:7 (June 1893), pp. 295–300.

Al-Khuri, Amin. "Hal lil-Nisa' an Yatlubna Kull Huquq al-Rijal," *al-Hilal* 2 (1893), pp. 366–369.

——— "Hal lil-Nisa' an Yatlubna Kull Huquq al-Rijal," *al-Hilal* 2 (1894), pp. 463–470; 532–535; 563–567; 622–629.

Al-Khuri, Jurjus Iliyas. "Hal lil-Nisa' an Yatlubna Kull Huquq al-Rijal," *al-Hilal* 2 (1894), pp. 435–438.

Al-Khuri, Khalil. "Al-Kitab al-Faransawi al-Musamma bil-Nisa'," *Hadiqat al-Akhbar* issue 77 (July 1859), p. 4.

——— "Talab al-Samah," *Hadiqat al-Akhbar* issue 31 (Aug. 1858), p. 3.

Al-Khuri, Wadi'. "Huquq al-Mar'a," *al-Muqtataf* 7 (1882), pp. 17–22.

——— "Huquq al-Nisa'," *al-Muqtataf* 11 (1886), pp. 170–175.

——— "Al-Nisa'," *al-Jinan* 16 (1885), pp. 178–181; 210–214.

Krimski, A. *Bayrut wa Jabal Lubnan 'ala Masharif al-Qarn al-'Ishrin Dirasa fil-Ta'rikh al –Ijtima'i min Khilal Mudhakkirat al-'Alim al-Rusi al-Kabir Rasa'il min Lubnan, 1896–1898.* Ed. Mas'ud Dahir. Beirut: Dar al-Mada lil-Tiba'a wal-Nashr wal-Tawzi', 1985.

Kurani, Hanna. "Inhad al-Ghayra al-Wataniyya li-Tarqiyat al-Bada'i' al-Sharqiyya," *al-Fatat* 1: 5 (1893), p. 224.

——— "Inhad al-Ghayra al-Wataniyya li-Tarqiyat al-Bada'i' al-Sharqiyya," *al-Fatat* 1: 6 (1893), pp. 275–281.

——— "Murasalat al-Jihat – A Letter from Hanna Kurani," *al-Fatat* 1:9 (11 August 1893), p. 353.

——— [Untitled – "A Letter from]," *al-Fatat* 1: 2 (1 January 1893), pp. 78–79.

——— "Majd al-Mar'a," *Lisan al-Hal* issue 1279 (27 October, 1890), p. 3.

——— "Ta'lim al-Banat," *Lisan al-Hal* issue 1283 (10 November, 1890), p. 3.

——— "Ta'lim al-Banat," *Lisan al-Hal* issue 1284 (13 November, 1890), pp. 2–3.

Labiba Hanifa. "Letter to the editor," *al-Fatat* 1(15 January 1893), p. 153.

Li-Ahad al-Kataba. "Al-Zawaj," *Lisan al-Hal* issue 1626 (21 June 1894), p. 3.

Li-Ahad al-Udaba' al-Fadil. "Al-Zawaj," *Lisan al-Hal* issue 1635 (2 July 1894), p. 3.

Luyis Shikhu (ed. and intro.), "Kitab Tadbir al-Manzil," *al-Mashriq* 19: 3 (1921), pp. 161–181.

M. A. Y., "Difa' al-Nisa' 'an al-Nisa'," *al-Muqtataf* 11 (1887), pp. 685–686.

Makariyus, Maryam. "Difa' al-Nisa' 'an al-Nisa'," *al-Muqtataf* 11 (1887), pp. 688–689.

——— "Al-Khansa'," *al-Muqtataf* 9 (1885), pp. 622–626.

——— "Ba'd Khurafat al-Ifranj," *al-Muqtataf* 5 (1880), pp. 169–171.

Marrash, Fransis. "Fi Ta'lim al-Mar'a," *al-Jinan* 3 (1872), p. 769.

——— *Ghabat al-Haqq.* Beirut: Dar al-Hamra', 1990.

——— "Al-Mar'a bayna al-Khushuna wal-Tamaddun," *al-Jinan* 3 (1872), pp. 586–588.

Marrash, Maryana. "Shamat al-Jinan," *al-Jinan* 1 (1870), pp. 467–468.

Masarra,Wastin. "Al-Tarbiya," *al-Jinan* 2 (1871), pp. 54–56.

Matar, Maryam. "Difa' al-Nisa' 'an al-Nisa'," *al-Muqtataf* 11 (1887), pp. 745–747.

Mayy. "Al-Zawaj, Ra'y Anisa fihi," *Lisan al-Hal* issue 1638 (5 July 1894), pp. 1–2.

Al-Nahhas, Maryam. *Mithal li-Kitab Ma'rid al-Hasna' fi Tarajim Mashahir al-Nisa'.* Alexandria: Mataba'at Jaridat Misr, 1879.

Al-Naqqash, Dawud. "Ahlan bi Sahib al-Ra'y al-Jadid," *Lisan al-Hal* issue 1655 (25 July 1894), p. 3.

——— "'Ilaj al-Zawaj," *Lisan al-Hal* issue 1631 (27 June 1894), p. 4.

Al-Nawfal, Salma. "Zirr al-Qamis," *al-Fatat* 1: 3 (1893), pp. 105–109.

Nimr, Niqula. "Al-Tat'im bil-Madda al-Judariyya," *al-Muqtataf* 8 (1883), pp. 164–166.

Al-Qasatli, Nu'man 'Abduh. "Al-Nisa' wa-Huququna," *Lisan al-Hal* issue 458 (April 1882), pp. 2–3.

Qusah, Jurjis. *Kitab Tadbir al-Manzil.* Egypt: Matba'at al-Adab, 1889.

Saba', Anisa. "Thiyudura Haddad," *al-Muqtataf* 14 (1889), pp. 254–265.

Sa'd, Khalil. "Al-Mar'a wal-Rajul wa-hal Yatasawayan," *al-Muqtataf* 11 (1887), pp. 749–750.

Sadaqah, Jibra'il. "Fi Huquq al-Nisa'," *al-Jinan* 1 (1870), pp. 401–402.

Al-Sa'igh, Salma. *Suwar wa Dhikrayat.* Beirut: Dar al-Hadara, 1964.

Salwa. "Ruh al-Zawaj al-Thani," *Lisan al-Hal* issue 1702 (18 September 1894), p. 3.

—— "Tahdhib al-Banat," *Lisan al-Hal* issue 1678 (21 August 1894), p. 3.

Samaha, Khatir Iliyas. "al-Zawaj," *Lisan al-Hal* issue 1632 (28 July 1894), pp. 3–4.

Sarruf, Ya'qub. *Amir Lubnan.* Cairo: Matba'at al-Muqtataf, 1907.

—— "Al-Nazar fi Hadirina wa-Mustaqbalina," *al-Muqtataf* 8 (1884), pp. 193–199.

Sarruf, Yaqut. "Adrar al-Tamaddun al-Sari'," *al-Muqtataf* 9 (1885), pp. 284–288.

—— "Maryam Nimr Makariyus Firaq al-Rifaq," *al-Muqtataf* 12 (1888), pp. 435–439.

—— "Mu'tamar al-Nisa' al-'Amm," *al-Muqtataf* 23 (1899), pp. 564–568.

—— "Al-Sayyida Nasra Ilyas," *al-Muqtataf* 13 (1888), pp. 549–550.

—— "Tarkib al-Insan," *al-Muqtataf* 5 (1880), pp. 110–115, 141–143, 165–169.

Shahada, Shams. "Al-Haqq Awla an Yuqal," *al-Muqtataf* 8 (1883), pp. 203–207.

—— "Madarr al-Tamaddun al-Urubi wa-Manafi'uhu," *al-Muqtataf* 8 (1884), pp. 565–56.

Shalhat, Yusuf Afandi. "Bahth fi Huquq al-Mar'a," *al-Muqtataf* 18 (1893), pp. 329–334.

Shakur, Farida. "Fil-Nisa'," *al-Jinan* 5 (1874), p. 279.

Shartuni, Anisa. "Fasl al-Khitab fil-Rajul wal-Mar'a," *al-Muqtataf* 34 (1909), pp. 289–294.

Shukri, Rujina. "Farsh al-Buyut wa-Tartibuha," *al-Muqtataf* 9 (1885), pp. 743–745.

Shumayyil, Shibli. *Kitab Falsafat al-Nushu' wal-Irtiqa' Majmu'at al-Duktur Shibli Shumayyil.* 2 vols. Cairo: Matba'at al-Muqtataf, 1910.

—— "Al-Mar'a wal-Rajul wa-hal Yatasawayan," *al-Muqtataf* 11 (1887), pp. 355–360; 401–405.

—— "Al-Mar'a wal-Rajul wa-hal Yatasawayan – Radd," *al-Muqtataf* 12 (1887), pp. 50–59.

Al-Tahtawi, Rifa'a Rafi'. *Rawdat al-Madaris al-Misriiyya,* 8 vols. Cairo: Dar al-Kutub wal-Watha'iq al-Qawmiyya, 1998. Ed. Jabir 'Asfur.

Talhuq, Amin Kna'an. "Al-Rajul wal-Mar'a," *Lisan al-Hal* issue 1358 (19 June 1891), p. 2.

Tu'ma, Julya. "Al-Mar'a al-Fadila man Yajiduha," *al-Hasna'* 1:3 (1909), pp. 203–210.

—— "Al-Malak al-Awwal," *al-Hasna'* 2: 7 (1911), pp. 254–257, 2: 8 (1911), pp. 292–295.

—— "Al-Sama' al-Ula," *al-Hasna'* 2:1 (1910), pp. 9–14.

Wadi, Helena (Hilana) Bar. "Al-Akhlaq wal-Awa'id," *al-Muqtataf* 7 (1882), pp. 367–369.

Wajdi, Farid Bik. "Mas'alat al-Mar'a al-Misriyya," *al-Haqa'iq* 1: 20 (20 December 1910), p. 216.

Yanni, Hannih. "Madarr al-Tamaddun al-Urubi wa-Manafi'uhu," *al-Muqtataf* 10 (1885), pp. 36–37.

Zaki. M. "Hal lil-Nisa' an Yatlubna Kull Huquq al-Rijal," *al-Hilal* 2 (1894), pp. 304–306.

Ziyada, Mayy. "Warda al-Yaziji," *al-Muqtataf* 65 (1924), pp. 1–7; 137–141; 257–262.

Novels and Short Stories in Arabic

'Atiyya, Farida. *Bayna 'Arshayn*. Tripoli: Matba'at al-Najah, 1912.

Al-Bustani, Adelaide (Idlid). "Hanri wa-Imilya," *al-Jinan* 1 (1870), pp. 366–367, 406–407.

Al-Bustani, Alice. *Riwayat al-Sa'iba*. Beirut: al-Matba'a al-Adabiyya, 1891.

Al-Bustani, Salim. "Asma," *al-Jinan* 4 (1873).

—— "Bint al-'Asr," *al-Jinan* 6 (1875).

—— "Budur," *al-Jinan* 3 (1872).

—— "Fatina," *al-Jinan* 8 (1877).

—— "Al-Huyam fi Futuh al-Sham," *al-Jinan* 5 (1874).

—— "Salma," *al-Jinan* 9 and 10 (1878–79).

—— "Samya," *al-Jinan* 13 (1882).

—— "Zanubya, " *al-Jinan* 1 (1870).

Fawwaz, Zaynab. *Husn al-'Awaqib aw Ghada al-Zahira*. Ed. Hilma al-Namnam. Cairo: Matabi' al-Hay'a al-Misriyya, 1899; reprinted 2004.

Haddad, Niqula. *Hawwa al-Jadida aw Yvonne Monar*. Cairo: Matba'at al-Shams, 1929; originally published 1906.

—— Kulluhu Nasib. Cairo: Matba'at al-Tawfiq, 1903.

Hashem, Labiba. *Qalb Rajul*. Ed. Yumna al-'Id. Damascus: Dar al-Thaqafa wal-Nashr, 2002; first published Cairo, 1904.

Jubran Khalil, Jubran. *Al-Ajniha al-Mutakassira*. Jerusalem: Dar Tammuz lil-Nashr, 1982.

—— "Madja'" ("The Marriage Bed"), in *al-Arwah al-Mutamarrida*. Beirut: n.p., 1970, pp. 52–65.

—— "Martha al-Baniya," in *'Ara'is al-Muruj*. Beirut: n.p., 1970; first published 1906, pp. 21–36.

—— "Warda al-Hani," in *al-Arwah al-Mutamarrida*. Beirut: n.p., 1970, pp. 15–36.

Al-Khuri, Khalil. "Way…Idhan Lastu bi Ifranji," *Hadiqat al-Akhbar*, 1859–1861.

Al-Qasatli, Nu'man 'Abduh. "Al-Fatat Amina wa-Ummuha," *al-Jinan* 11 (1880).

—— "Riwayat Anis," *al-Jinan* 12–13 (1881–82).

—— "Riwayat Murshid wa-Fitna," *al-Jinan* 11 (1880).

Sawaya, Labiba Mikha'il. *Hasna' Salonik*. Damascus: Orthodox Patriarch Press, 1909.

Zaydan, Jurji. "Jihad al-Muhibbin," in Husayn Mu'nis (ed.). *Ta'rikh al-Tamaddum al-Islami*. 5 vols. Cairo: Dar al-Hilal, n.d.

European Languages

Anonymous, "A Fair Visitor from Syria," *New York Times* (February 20 1894).

———— "Club Women and Students," *New York Times* (March 4 1894).

———— "Death List of a Day: Mme. Hanna K. Korany," *New York Times* (August 2 1898).

———— "Notes about Women," *New York Times* (November 4 1894).

———— "To Get Work for Women," *New York Times* (December 30 1894).

Fawwaz, Zaynab. "Fair and Equal Treatment," in Margot Badran and Miriam Cooke (eds.). *Opening the Gates: A Century of Arab Feminist Writing*. Bloomington: Indiana University Press, 1990, pp. 221–226.

Gibran Khalil Gibran, "Martha," in *Nymphs of the Valley*. Translated by H.M. Nahmad. London: Heinemann, 1972, pp. 1–17.

Gibran Khalil Gibran, *Spirits Rebellious*, Translated by H.M. Nahmad. London: Heinemann, 1971. First published 1908, pp. 1–24.

Hilu, Virginia (ed.). *Beloved Prophet: The Love Letters of Khalil Gibran and Mary Haskell and her Private Journal*. London: Quartet Books, 1972.

Hooker, Edward W. (ed.). *Memoir of Mrs. Sarah Smith Late of the American Mission in Syria*. New York: American Tract Society, 1845.

Jessup, Henry H. *The Women of the Arabs*. New York: Dodd & Mead, Pub. 1873, reprinted 1982.

Kurani, Hanna. "The Glory of Womanhood," in Mary Kavanaugh Oldham (ed.). *The Congress of Women: Held in the Woman's Building, World's Columbian Exposition, Chicago, U.S.A., 1893*. Chicago: Monarch Books, 1894, pp. 359–360.

Kyat, Assad Y. *Voice from Lebanon with the Life and Travels*. London: Madden & Co., 1847.

Studley, Mary J. *What Our Girls Ought to Know*. New York: M.L. Holbrook & Co., 1878.

Al-Taimuriya, Aisha Ismat "Introduction to The Results of Circumstances in Words and Deeds, 1887/8," in Margot Badran and Mariam Cooke (eds.). *Opening the Gates: A Century of Arab Feminist Writing*. Translated by Marilyn Booth, Bloominton and Indianapolis: Indiana Unversity Press, 1990, 126–133.

Secondary Sources

Arabic

Abu Fayad, Muhibb al-Din. "Muru'a," in *Taj al-'Arus min Jawahir al-Qamus*. Kuwait: Dar al-Fikr lil-Tiba'a wal-Nashr wal-Tawzi', 1994.

'Ali, Sayyid 'Asim. *Al-Muru'ah*. Tanta: Dar al-Sahaba lil-Turath bi-Tanta, 1990.

Badir, 'Abd al-Muhsin. *Tatawwur al-Riwaya al-'Arabiyya al-Haditha fi Misr 1870–1938*. Cairo: Dar al-Ma'arif, 1963.

Faris, Bashar. *Mabahith 'Arabiyya*. Cairo: Matba'at al-Ma'arif, 1939.

Futuh, Aisa. "Nahdat al-Mar'a al-'Arabiyya al-Suriyya hatta Muntasif al-Qarn al-'Ishrin," *al-Ma'rifa* 32: 364 (1994), pp. 63–83.

Haddad, Niqula. *Al-Ishtirakiyya*. Damascus: Dar al-Mada lil-Thaqafa wal-Nashr, 2002; first published in 1920.

Ibrahim, Imili Faris. *Adibat Lubnaniyyat*. Beirut: Dar al-Rayhani lil-Tiba'a wal-Nashr, 1964.

Jiha, Mishal. *Julya Tu'ma al-Dimashqiyya*. Beirut: Riyad al-Rayyis Lil-Tawzi' wal-Nashr, 2003.

Al-Jurdi, Nadia Nuwayhid. *Nisa' min Biladi*. Beirut: al- Mu'assasa al-'Arabiyya lil-Dirasat wal-Nashr, 1986.

Kahala, 'Umar Rida. *A'lam al-Nisa' fi 'Alamayy al-'Arab wal-Islam*. 5 vols. Damascus: al-Matba'a al-Hashimiyya, 1958.

Kallas, Jurj. *Al-Haraka al-Fikriyya al-Nasawiyya fi 'Asr al-Nahda, pp. 1849–1923*. Beirut: Dar al-Jil, 1996.

——— *Ta'rikh al-Sihafa al-Nasawiyya, Nash'atuha wa-Tatawwuruha 1892–1932*. Beirut: Dar al-Jil, 1996.

Najm, Muhammad Yusuf. *Al-Qissa fil-Adab al-'Arabi al-Hadith*. 3rd ed. Beirut: Dar al-Thaqafa, 1961.

Pellat, Charles. "Hawla Mafhum al-Muru'a 'inda Qudama' al-'Arab," *al-Karmel* no.4 (1983), pp. 1–17.

Al-Qiyadi, Sharifa. *Isham al-Katiba al-'Arabiyya fi 'Asr al-Nahda hatta 1914*. Malta: Sharikat Elga, 1999.

Al-Sa'afin, Ibrahim. *Tatawwur al-Riwaya al-'Arabiyya al-Haditha fi Bilad al-Sham* Baghdad: Dar al-Rashid lil-Nashr, 1980.

Al-Safa, Muhammad Jabir. *Ta'rikh Jabal 'Amil*. Beirut: Dar Matn al-Lugha, 1960.

Sha'ban, Buthayna. *100 'Am min al-Riwaya al-Nisa'iyya al-'Arabiyya 1899–1999*. Beirut: Dar al-Adab lil-Nashr wal-Tawzi', 1999.

Shakir, Mustafa. *Muhadarat 'an al-Qissa fi Suriyya hatta al-Harb al-'Alamiyya al-Thaniya*. Cairo: Ma'had al-Dirasat al-'Arabiyya, 1957.

Sakakini, Widad. "Niqula Haddad fi Hayatihi wa-Thaqafatihi-Suwar Lubnaniyya wa-Suriyya min Difaf al-Nil," *al-Adib* 10:7 (1951), pp. 40–43.

Al-Sakkut, Hamdi. *Al-Riwaya al-'Arabiyya: Bibliyugrafiya wa-Madkhal Naqdi, 1865–1995*. 6 vols. Cairo: The American University in Cairo Press, 2000.

Al-Salman, Mashhur Hasan Mahmud. *Al-Muru'a wa-Khawarimuha*. Cairo: Dar Ibn 'Afan lil-Nashr wal-Tawzi', 2000.

Yaghi, 'Abd al-Rahman. *Fil-Juhud al-Riwa'iyya Ma Bayna Salim Bustani wa Najib Mahfuz*, 2nd ed. Beirut: Dar al-Farabi, 1981.

Ziyada, Khalid. *Al-Sura al-Taqlidiyya lil-Mujtama' al-Madani: Qira'a Manhajiyya fi Sijillat Mahkamat Tarablus al-Shar'iyya fil-Qarn al-Sabi' 'Ashar wa-Bidayat al-Qarn al-Thamin 'Ashar*. Tripoli: Manshurat Ma'had al-'Ulum al-Ijtima'iyya, 1983.

Western Languages

Abdulrazzak, Patel. *The Arab Nahda: The Making of the Intellectual and Humanist Movement*. London: Edinburgh University Press, 2013.

Abisaab, Malek. "'Unruly' Factory Women in Lebanon: Contesting French Colonialism and the National State, 1940–1946," *Journal of Women's History* 16:3 (2004), pp. 55–82.

Abou-Hodeib, Toufoul. "Taste and Class in Late Ottoman Beirut," *International Journal of Middle East Studies* 43: 3 (2011), pp. 475–492.

Abu-Lughud, Lila. *Veiled Sentiments: Honor and Poetry in a Bedouin Society.* Berkeley: University of California Press, 1988.

Abu-Manneh, Butrus. *Studies on Islam and the Ottoman Empire in the 19th Century, 1826–1876.* Istanbul: Isis Press, 2001.

Abu Rida, Muhammad Abu al-Hadi "Norms and Values," in Abdelwahab Boouhdiba and Muhammad Ma'ruf Dawalibi (eds.). *The Different Aspects of Islamic Culture: The Individual and Society in Islam.* Paris: UNESCO Publications, 1998, pp. 19–60.

Aghacy, Samira. "Contemporary Lebanese Fiction: Modernization without Modernity," *International Journal of Middle Eastern Studies* 38 (2006), pp. 561–580.

——— *Masculine Identity in the Fiction of the Arab East since 1967.* Syracuse: Syracuse University Press, 2009.

Ahmed, Leila. "Women and the Advent of Islam," *Signs* 11:4 (1986), pp. 665–691.

——— *Women and Gender in Islam.* New Haven: Yale University Press, 1992.

Akarli, Engin D. "Daughters and Fathers: A Young Druze Woman's Experience (1894–1897)," in Baki Tezcan and Karl K. Barabir (eds.). *Identity and Identity Formation in the Ottoman World: A Volume of Essays in Honor of Norman Itzkovitz.* Madison: University of Wisconsin Press, 2007, pp. 167–184.

Alaya, Flavia. "Victorian Science and the 'Genius' of Woman," *Journal of the History of Ideas* 38 (1977), pp. 261–280.

Alcalay, Ammiel. *After Jews and Arabs: Remaking Levantine Culture.* Minneapolis: University of Minnesota Press, 1993.

Allen, James S. "History and the Novels: Mentalité in Modern Popular Fiction," *History and Theory* 22 (1983), pp. 233–52.

Allen, Roger. *The Arabic Novel: An Historical and Critical Introduction.* Syracuse: Syracuse University Press, 1982.

Anderson, Amanda. *Tainted Souls and Painted Faces: The Rhetoric of Falleness in Victorian Britain.* Ithaca: Cornell University Press, 1993.

Appadurai, Arjun. "Disjuncture and Difference in the Global Cultural Economy," *Theory, Culture and Society* 7 (1990), pp. 295–310.

Apple, Rima D. "Constructing Mothers: Scientific Motherhood in the Nineteenth and Twentieth Centuries," *Social History of Medicine* 8:2 (1995), pp. 161–178.

Armstrong, Nancy. *Desire and Domestic Fiction: A Political History of the Novel.* New York: Oxford University Press, 1987.

——— "The Rise of the Domestic Woman," in Nancy Armstrong and Leonard Tennenhouse (eds.). *The Ideology of Conduct: Essays on Literature and the History of Sexuality.* New York: Methuen, 1987, pp. 96–141.

Artan, Tülay. "Aspects of the Ottoman Elite's Food Consumption: Looking for 'Staples,' 'Luxuries,' and 'Delicacies' in a Changing Century," in Donald Quataert (ed.). *Consumption Studies and the History of the Ottoman Empire, 1550–1922: An Introduction.* Albany: SUNY Press, 2000, pp. 107–200.

Auerbach, Jeffrey A. "What They Read: Mid-Nineteenth Century English Women's Magazines and the Emergence of a Consumer Culture," *Victorian Periodicals Review* 30:3 (1997), pp. 121–140.

Auerbach, Nina. "The Rise of the Fallen Woman," *Nineteenth-Century Fiction* 35: 1 (1980), pp. 29–52.

Ayalon, Ami. "Modern Texts and Their Readers in Late Ottoman Palestine," *Middle Eastern Studies* 38 (2002), pp. 17–40.

——— "Private Publishing in the Nahda," *International Journal of Middle East Studies* 40 (2008), pp. 561–577.

——— *The Press in the Arab Middle East: A History.* New York and Oxford: Oxford University Press, 1995.

——— *Reading Palestine: Printing and Literacy, 1900–1948.* Austin: University of Texas, 2004.

Badawi, M.M. "Introduction," in M.M. Badawi (ed.). *The Cambridge History of Arabic Literature: The Modern Arabic Literature.* Cambridge: Cambridge University Press, 1992, pp. 1–23.

——— *A Short History of Modern Arabic Literature.* Oxford: Clarendon Press, 1993.

Badran, Margot. *Feminists, Islam, and Nation: Gender and the Making of Modern Egypt.* Princeton: Princeton University Press, 1995.

——— "The Feminist Vision in the Writings of Three Turn-of-the-Century Egyptian Women," *Bulletin of the British Society for Middle Eastern Studies* 15:1/2 (1988), pp. 11–20.

Baeck, Louis. "The Economic Thought of Classical Islam," *Diogenes* 30 (1991), pp. 99–115.

Baer, Marc. "Islamic Conversion Narratives of Women: Social Changes and Gendered Religious Hierarchy in Early Modern Ottoman Istanbul," *Gender and History* 16: 2 (2004), pp. 425–458.

Baker, Paula. "The Domestication of Politics: Women and American Political Society, 1780–1920," *American Historical Review* 89 (1984), pp. 620–647.

Baron, Beth. "Readers and the Women's Press in Egypt," *Poetics Today* 15:2 (1994), pp. 217–240.

——— *The Women's Awakening in Egypt: Culture, Society and the Press.* New Haven and London: Yale University Press, 1994.

——— *Egypt as a Woman: Nationalism, Gender, and Politics.* Berkeley and Los Angeles: University of California Press, 2005.

Bawardi, Basilius. "*Hadiqat al-Akhbar* Newspaper and Its Pioneering Role in the Arabic Narrative Fiction," *Die Welt der Islam* 48 (2008), pp. 170–195.

Bawardi, Basilius and Zachs, Fruma. "Between Adab al-Rihlat and 'Geo-Literature': The Constructive Narrative Fiction of Salim al-Bustani," *Middle Eastern Literatures* 10 (2007), pp. 203–217.

Beetham, Margaret. "Towards a Theory of the Periodical as a Publishing Genre," in Laurel Brake, Aled Jones and Lionel Madden (eds.). *Investigating Victorian Journalism.* London: Macmillan, 1990, pp. 19–32.

Bernheimer, Charles. *Figures of Ill Repute: Representing Prostitution in Nineteenth-Century France.* Durham: Duke University Press, 1997.

Beshara, Adel. "A Rebel Syrian: Gibran Khalil Gibran," in Adel Beshara (ed.). *The Origins of Syrian Nationhood: Histories, Pioneers and Identity.* London and New York: Routledge, 2011, pp. 143–162.

Bichr, Farès. "Muru'a," in P.J. Bearman, T. Bianquis, C.E. Bosworth, E. van Donzel and W.P. Heinrichs (eds.). *Encyclopedia of Islam,* 2nd ed. Leiden: Brill, 2010. Brill Online. Accessed May 4, 2010. http://www.brillonline.nl/subscriber/entry?entry=islam_SIM-555

Bier, Laura. "Modernity and the Other Woman: Gender and National Identity in the Egyptian Women's Press, 1952–1967," *Gender and History* 16 (2004), pp. 99–112.

Bodenstein, Ralph. "Housing the Foreign: A European's Exotic Home in Late Nineteenth-Century Beirut," in Jens Hanssen, Thomas Philipp and Stefan Weber (eds.). *The Empire and the City: Arab Provincial Capitals in the Late Ottoman Empire.* Beirut: Ergon Verlag Würzburg, 2002, pp. 105–127.

Boone, Joseph A. *Tradition and Counter Tradition: Love and the Form of Fiction.* Chicago and London: University of Chicago Press, 1987.

Booth, Marilyn. "Between Harem and Houseboat: 'Falleness,' Gendered Spaces, and the Female National Subject in 1920s Egypt," in Marilyn Booth (ed.), *Harem Histories: Envisioning Places and Living Spaces.* Durham and London: Duke University Press, 2010, pp. 342–373.

———— "Fiction's Imaginative Archive and the Newspaper's Local Scandals: The Case of Nineteenth-Century Egypt," in Antoinette Burton (ed.). *Archive Stories: Facts, Fictions, and the Writing of History.* Durham: Duke University Press, 2005, pp. 274–296.

———— "From the Horses' Rump and the Whorehouse Keyhole: Ventriloquized Memoirs as Political Voice in 1920s Egypt," *Maghreb Review* 32:2–3 (2007), pp. 233–61.

———— *May Her Likes Be Multiplied: Biography and Gender Politics in Egypt* Berkeley: University of California Press, 2001.

———— "On Gender, History. . .and Fiction," in Israel Gershoni, Amy Singer and Y. Hakan Erdem (eds.). *Middle East Historiographies: Narrating the Twentieth Century.* Seattle: University of Washington Press, 2006, pp. 211–241.

———— "'She Herself Was the Ultimate Rule': Arabic Biographies of Missionary Teachers and their Pupils," *Islam and Muslin-Christian Relations* 13 (2002), pp. 427–448.

———— "Un/safe/ly at Home: Narratives of Sexual Coercion in 1920s Egypt," *Gender and History* 16: 3 (2004), pp. 744–768.

———— "Women in Islam: Men and the 'Women's Press' in the Turn-of-the-20th-Century Press," *International Journal of Middle East Studies* 33 (2001), pp. 171–201.

Boris, Eileen. "The Power of Motherhood: Black and White Activist Women Redefine the Political," *Yale Journal of Law and Feminism* 25 (1989/90), p. 25–50.

Boydston, Jeanne. *Home and Work: The Industrialization of Housework in the Northeastern United States from the Colonial Period to the Civil War.* New Haven: Yale University Press, 1984.

Boym, Svetlana. *The Future of Nostalgia.* New York: Basic Books, 2001.

Brake, Laurel. "Writing, Cultural Production, and the Periodical Press in the Nineteenth Century," in J.B. Bullen (ed.). *Writing and Victorianism.* London and New York: Longman, 1997, pp. 54–72.

Brake, Laurel and Humphreys, Anne. "Critical Theory and Periodical Research," *Victorian Periodicals Review* 22: 3 (1989), pp. 94–95.

Brandes, Stanley H. *Metaphors of Masculinity: Sex and Status in Andalusian Folklore* Philadelphia: University of Pennsylvania Press, 1980.

Brekke, Linzy A. "The 'Scourge of Fashion': Political Economy and the Politics of Consumption in the Early Republic," *Early American Studies* 3:1 (2005), pp. 111–139.

Cachia, Pierre. "Translations and Adaptation, 1834–1914," in M.M. Badawi (ed.). *The Cambridge History of Arabic Literature: The Modern Arabic Literature*, Cambridge: Cambridge University Press, 1992, pp. 22–35.

Çakur, Serpil. "Fatma Aliye," in Francisca de Haan, Krasimira Daskalova, and Anna Loutfi (eds.). *Biographical Dictionary of Women's Movements and Feminisms: Central, Eastern, and Southeastern Europe, 19th and 20th Centuries*, Budapest: Central European University Press, 2006, pp. 21–24.

Cannon, Byron D. "Nineteenth-Century Arabic Writings on Women and Society: The Interim Role of the Masonic Press in Cairo (*al-Lata'if*, 1885–1895)," *International Journal of Middle East Studies* 17 (1985), pp. 462–484.

Cerasi, Maurice. "Some Considerations on the Mediterranean Archetypes Active in the Constitution of the Three-Arched Lebanese House Type: Fashion and Groove of Memory," in Michael F. Davie (ed.). *La Maison Beyrouthine aux Trois Arcs: Une Architecture Bourgeoise du Levant.* Beirut: Académie Libanaise des Beaux-Arts; Tours: Centre de Recherches et d'Études sur l'Urbanization du Monde Arabe, 2003, pp. 19–342.

Cioeta, Donald J. "Ottoman Censorship in Lebanon and Syria, 1876–1908," *International Journal of Middle Eastern Studies* 10 (1979), pp. 167–186.

Clancy-Smith, Julia. "Where Elites Meet: Harem Visits, Sea Bathing, and Sociabilities in Precolonial Tunisia, c. 1800–1881," in Marilyn Booth (ed.). *Harem Histories: Envisioning Places and Living Spaces.* Durham and London: Duke University Press, 2010, pp. 177–210.

Clarke, Alison J. "Making Sameness: Mothering, Commerce and the Culture of Children's Birthday Parties," in Emma Casey and Lydia Martens (eds.). *Gender and Consumption: Domestic Cultures and the Commercialization of Everyday Life.* Aldershot: Ashgate Publishing, 2007, pp. 79–96.

Cohen, Deborah. *Household Gods: The British and their Possessions.* New Haven: Yale University Press, 2006.

Cole, Juan R. "Feminism, Class, and Islam in Turn-of-the-Century Egypt," *International Journal of Middle East Studies* 13 (1981), pp. 387–407.

Colla, Elliott. "How *Zaynab* Became the First Arabic Novel," *History Compass* 7:1 (2009), pp. 214–225.

Comaroff, Jean and John Comaroff, "Homemade Hegemony: Modernity, Domesticity, and Colonialism in South Africa," in Karen T. Hansen (ed.). *African Encounters with Domesticity.* New Brunswick: Rutgers University Press, 1992, pp. 37–74.

Commins, David D. *Islamic Reform: Politics and Social Change in Late Ottoman Syria.* New York: Oxford University Press, 1990.

Connell, Raewyn. W. *Masculinities.* Sydney: Allen & Unwin, 1995.

Cunningham, Gail. *The New Woman and the Victorian Novel.* London: Macnillan Press, 1978.

Currie, Elizabeth. "Prescribing Fashion: Dress, Politics and Gender in 16th-Century Italian Conduct Literature," *Fashion Theory: The Journal of Dress, Body and Culture* 4:2 (2000), pp. 157–177.

Dadrian, Vahakn N. *The History of the Armenian Genocide: Ethnic Conflict from the Balkans to Anatolia to the Caucasus*. Providence: Berghahn Press, 1997.

Darnton, Robert. *The Great Cat Massacre and Other Episodes in French Cultural History*. New York: Basic Books, 1984.

Darrow, Margaret H. "French Noblewomen and the New Domesticity, 1750–1850," *Feminist Studies* 5: 1 (1979), pp. 41–65.

Davidoff, Lenore and Catherine Hall. *Family Fortunes: Men and Women of the English Middle Class 1780–1850*. London: Hutchison, 1987.

Davidson, Roderic H. *Reform in the Ottoman Empire, 1856–1876*. Princeton: Princeton University Press, 1963.

Davis, Natalie Z. *Fiction in the Archives: Pardon tales and their Tellers in Sixteenth-Century France* Cambridge: Polity Press, 1988.

Debbas, Fouad C. *Beirut, Our Memory: A Guided Tour Illustrated with Picture Postcards*. 2nd ed. Beirut: César Debbas & Fils, 1994.

—— *Des photographes à Beyrouth, 1840–1918*. Paris: Marval, 2001.

—— The Fouad Debbas Collection. http://www.thefouaddebbascollection.com

Demetriou, Demetrakis Z. "Connell's Concept of Hegemonic Masculinity: A Critique," *Theory and Society* 30: 3 (2001), pp. 337–361.

Deutsch Francine M. and Saxon, Susan E. "The Double Standard of Praise and Criticism of Mothers and Fathers," *Psychology of Women Quarterly* 22:4 (1998), pp. 665–683.

DeYoung, Terri. "Love, Death, and the Ghost of Al-Khansa': The Modern Female Poetic Voice in Fadwa Tuqan's Elegies for Her Brother Ibrahim," in Kamal Abdel-Malek and Wael B. Hallaq (eds.). *Tradition, Modernity, and Postmodernity in Arabic Literature: Essays in Honor of Professor Issa J. Boullata*. Leiden: Brill, 2000, pp. 47–50.

Duda, Dorothea. *Innerarchitektur Syrischer Stadthauser des 16. bis 18. Jahrhunderts: die Sammlung Henri Pharaon in Beirut*. Beirut: In Kommission bei F. Steiner, 1971.

Edwards, David B. *Heroes of the Age: Moral Fault Lines on the Afghan Frontier*. Berkeley: University of California Press, 1996.

Eickelman, Dale E. "Being Bedouin: Nomads and Tribes in the Arab Social Imagination," in Joseph Ginat and Anatoly M. Khazanov (eds.). *Changing Nomads in Changing Worlds*. Brighton: Sussex Academic Press, 1998, pp. 38–49.

Eisenstadt, Shmuel. N. "Multiple Modernities," *Daedalus* 129:1 (2000), pp. 1–29.

El-Ariss, Tarek. *Trails of Arab Modernity: Literary Affects and the New Political Identity*. New York: Fordham University Press, 2013.

El-Enany, Rasheed. *Arab Representations of the Occident: East-West Encounters in Arabic Fiction*. London and New York: Routledge, 2006.

Elsadda, Hoda. "Egypt," in Rawda Ashur, Ferial Jabouri Ghazoul, Hasna Reda-Mekdashi (eds.). *Arab Women Writers: A Critical Reference Guide, 1873–1999*, translated by Mandy McClure. Cairo: The American University Press, 2009, pp. 98–161.

—— "Gendered Citizenship: Discourses on Domesticity in the Second Half of the Nineteenth Century," *Hawwa: Journal of Women of the Middle East and the Islamic World* 4 (2006), pp. 1–28.

—— "Imaging the 'New Man' Gender and Nation in Arab Literary Narratives in the Early Twentieth Century," *Journal of Middle East Women's Studies* 3:2 (2007), pp. 31–55.

Elshakry, Marwa. "The Gospel of Science and American Evangelicalism in Late Ottoman Beirut," *Past and Present* 196 (2007), pp. 173–214.

Enis, Ayşe Z. *Everyday Lives of Ottoman Muslim Women: Hanimlara Mahsûs Gazete (Newspaper for Ladies) (1895–1908)*. Istanbul: Libra Kitapcilik ve Yayincilik, 2013.

Escovitz, Joseph S. "'He Was the Muhammad 'Abduh of Syria': A Study of Tahir al-Jaza'iri and his Influence," *International Journal of Middle East Studies* 18:3 (1986), pp. 293–310.

Exertzoglou, Haris. "The Cultural Uses of Consumption: Negotiating Class, Gender, and Nation in the Ottoman Urban Centers during the 19th Century," *International Journal of Middle East Studies* 35 (2003), pp. 77–101.

Farag, Nadia. "The Lewis Affair and the Fortunes of al-Muqtataf," *Middle Eastern Studies* 8 (1972), pp. 73–83.

Farah, Caesar E. "Nationalist Concerns for Syria: The Case of Farah Antun, Mayy Ziadah, and al-Kawakibi," in Adel Beshara (ed.). *The Origins of Syrian Nationhood: Histories, Pioneers and Identity*. London and New York: Routledge, 2011, pp. 210–222.

Fawwaz, Leila T. *An Occasion for War: Civil Conflict in Lebanon and Damascus in 1860*. Berkeley and Los Angeles: University of California Press, 1994.

––––––– *Merchants and Migrants in Nineteenth-Century Beirut*. Cambridge, MA: Harvard University Press, 1983.

Fay, Mary A. "From Warrior-Grandees to Domesticated Bourgeoisie: The Transformation of the Elite Egyptian Household into a Western-Style Nuclear Family," in Beshara Doumani (ed.). *Family History in the Middle East: Household, Property and Gender*. Albany: SUNY Press, 2003, pp. 77–98.

Fee, Elizabeth. "The Sexual Politics of Victorian Social Anthropology," *Feminist Studies* 1:3/4 (1973), pp. 22–39.

Felski, Rita. *The Gender of Modernity*. Cambridge, MA.: Harvard University Press, 1995.

Fierson, Elizabeth Brown. "Mirrors Out, Mirrors In: Domestication and Rejection of the Foreign in Late-Ottoman Women's Magazines (1875–1908)," in D. Fairchild Ruggles (ed.). *Women, Patronage, and Self-Representation in Islamic Societies* Albany: SUNY Press, 2000, pp. 177–204.

Findley, Carter V. "An Ottoman Occidentalist in Europe: Ahmed Midhat Meets Madame Gülnar, 1889," *American Historical Review* 103: 1 (1998), pp. 15–49.

Firro, Kais. "Silk and Agrarian Changes in Lebanon, 1860–1914," *International Journal of Middle East Studies* 22:2 (1990), pp. 151–190.

Forward, Martin. *The Failure of Islamic Modernism? Syed Ameer Ali's Interpretation of Islam*. Bern: Peter Lang, 1999.

Freyer-Stowasser, Barbara. "The Study of Women in Early Islam," in Freda Hussain (ed.). *Muslim Women*. New York: St. Martin's Press, 1984, pp. 11–43.

Gaspar, Michael E. *The Power of Representation: Publics, Peasants, and Islam in Egypt*. Stanford: Stanford University Press, 2009.

Gelvin, James L. *Divided Loyalties: Nationalism and Mass Politics in Syria at the Close of Empire*. Berkeley: University of California Press, 1998.

Gerard, Jessica. "Invisible Servants: The Country House and the Local Community." *Historical Research* 57: 136 (1984), pp. 178–188.

Giladi, Avner. *Infants, Parents and Wet Nurses: Medieval Islamic Views of Breastfeeding and Social Implications*. Leiden: Brill, 1999.

———— "Islamic Educational Theories in the Middle Ages: Some Methodological Notes with Special Reference to Al-Ghazali," *Bulletin (British Society for Middle East Studies)* 14:1 (1987), pp. 3–10.

Glass, Dagmar. *Der Muqtataf und Seine Öffentlichkeit: Aufklärung, Räsonnement und Meinungsstreit in der Frühen Arabisschen Zeitschriftenkommunikation*. 2 vols. Würtzburg, Germany: Ergon Verlag, 2004.

Göçek, Fatma M. "Ethnic Segmentation, Western Education, and Political Outcomes: Nineteenth-Century Ottoman Society," *Poetics Today* 14:3 (1993), pp. 507–538.

———— *Rise of the Bourgeoisie, Demise of Empire: Ottoman Westernization and Social Change*. Oxford and New York: Oxford University Press, 1996.

Gordon, Beverley. "Woman's Domestic Body: The Conceptual Conflation of Women and Interiors in the Industrial Age," *Winterthur Portfolio* 31 (1996), pp. 281–301.

Greenberg, Wendy. *Uncannonical Women: Feminine Voice in French Poetry, 1830–1871*. Amsterdam: Rodopi, 1999.

Gullett, Gayle. "'Our Great Opportunity': Organized Women Advance Women's Work at the World's Columbian Exposition of 1893," *Illinois Historical Journal* 87 (1994), pp. 259–276.

Haddad, Mahmoud. "Ottoman Economic Nationalism in the Press of Beirut and Tripoli (Syria) at the End of the Nineteenth Century," in Gisela Procházka Eisl and Martin Strohmeier (eds.). *The Economy as an Issue in the Middle Eastern Press*. Vienna and Berlin: LIT Verlag GmbH, 2008, pp. 75–84.

Hafez, Sabry. *The Genesis of Arabic Narrative Discourse: A Study in the Sociology of Modern Arabic Literature*. London: Saqi Books, 1993.

Hanioğlu, M. Şükrü. *Preparation for a Revolution: The Young Turks, 1902–1908* Oxford: Oxford University Press, 2001.

Halevi, Leor. "Wailing for the Dead: The Role of Women in Early Islamic Funerals," *Past & Present* 183:1 (2004), pp. 3–39.

Halevi, Sharon and Zachs, Fruma. "Asma (1873): The Early Arabic Novel as a Social Compass," *Studies in the Novel* 39 (2007), pp. 416–430.

Hall, Stuart. "The Local and the Global: Globalization and Ethnicity," in Anthony D. King (ed.). *Culture, Globalization and the World System: Contemporary Conditions for the Representation of Identity*. London: Macmillan, 1991.

———— "Old and New Identities, Old and New Ethnicities," in Anthony D. King (ed.). *Culture, Globalization and the World System: Contemporary Conditions for the Representation of Identity*. London: Macmillan, 1991, pp. 41–68.

Haltunnen, Karen. *Confidence Men and Painted Women: A Study of Middle-Class Culture in America, 1830–1870*. New Haven and London: Yale University Press, 1982.

Handler, Richard. "Cultural Theory in History Today," *American Historical Review* 107:5 (2002), pp. 1512–1520.

Hanssen, Jens. "Public Morality and Marginality in Fin-de-Siècle Beirut," in Eugene Rogan (ed.). *Outside In: On the Margins of the Modern Middle East* (London: I.B.Tauris, 2002, pp. 183–211.

———— "Sexuality, Health and Colonialism in Postwar 1860 Beirut," in Samir Khalaf and John Gagnon (eds.). *Sexuality in the Arab World*. London: Saqi, 2006, pp. 63–84.

————— "'Your Beirut is on My Desk': Ottomanizing Beirut under Sultan Abdülhamid II," in Peter Rowe and Hashim Sarkis (eds.). *Projecting Beirut: Episodes in the Construction and Reconstruction of a Modern City*. Munich: Prestel, 1998, pp. 41–67.

Hassan, Wail S. "Gender (and) Imperialism: Structures of Masculinity in Tayeb Salih's Season of Migration to the North," *Men and Masculinities* 5:3 (2003), pp. 309–324.

Hatem, Mervat F. *Literature, Gender, and Nation-Building in Nineteenth-Century Egypt: The Life and Works of 'A'isha Taymur*. New York: Palgrave Macmillan, 2011.

————— "The Nineteenth Century Discursive Roots of the Continuing Debate on the Social-Sexual Contract in Today's Egypt," *Hawwa* 2 (2004), pp. 70–78.

Heffening, W. "Tadbir," *Encyclopedia of Islam*, Second Edition. Eds. P.J. Bearman, T. Bianquis, C.E. Bosworth, E. van Donzel and W.P. Heinrichs. Leiden: Brill, 2010. BrillOnline. Accessed June 1, 2011. http://www.brillonline.nl/subscriber/entry?entry=islam_COM-1139

Hepworth, Mike. "Privacy, Security and Respectability: The Ideal Victorian Home," in Tony Chapman and Jenny Hockey (eds.). *Ideal Homes? Social Change and Domestic Life*. London and New York: Routledge, 1999, pp. 17–29.

Hesse, Carla. *The Other Enlightenment: How French Women Became Modern*. Princeton: Princeton University Press, 2001.

Hobsbawm, Eric. "Inventing Traditions," in Eric Hobsbawm and Terence Ranger (eds.). *The Invention of Tradition*. Cambridge: Cambridge University Press, 1984, pp. 1–15.

Holt, Elizabeth M. "Narrative and the Reading Public in 1870s Beirut," *Journal of Arabic Literature* 40 (2009), pp. 37–70.

Hosseini, Hamid S. "Contributions of Medieval Muslim Scholars to the History of Economics and their Impact: A Refutation of the Schumpeterian Great Gap," in Warren J. Samuels, Jeff E. Biddle, and John B. Davis (eds.). *A Companion to the History of Economic Thought*. Malden: Blackwell, 2003, pp. 28–45.

Hourani, Albert. *Arabic Thought in the Liberal Age, 1798–1939*. London: Oxford University Press, 1962; 1970 ed.

Hudson, Leila. "Investing by Women or Investing in Women? Merchandise, Money and the Formation of a Pre-National Bourgeoisie in Damascus," *Comparative Studies of South Asia, Africa, and the Middle East* 26: 1 (2006), pp. 105–120.

————— "Late Ottoman Damascus: Investments in Public Space and the Emergence of Popular Sovereignty," *Critique: Critical Middle Eastern Studies* 15 (2006), pp. 152–169.

Hunt, Lynn. *The Family Romance of the French Revolution*. Berkeley and Los Angeles: University of California Press, 1992.

Hunter, Paul J. *Before Novels: The Cultural Contexts of Eighteenth-Century English Fiction*. New York and London: W.W. Norton, 1990.

Al-'Id, Yumna. "Lebanon," in Rawda Ashour, Ferial Jabouri Ghazoul, Hasna Reda-Mekdashi (eds.). *Arab Women Writers: A Critical Reference Guide, 1873–1999*. Translated by Mandy McClure. Cairo: The American University Press, 2009, pp. 13–59.

Ikeya, Chie. "The Scientific-and-Hygienic Housewife and Mother: Education, Consumption and the Discourse of Domesticity," *Journal of Burma Studies* 14 (2010), pp. 59–89.

Isenstadt, Sandy and Kishwar Rizvi. "Introduction: Modern Architecture and the Middle East: The Burden of Representation," in Sandy Isenstadt and Kishwar Rizvi (eds.). *Modernism and the Middle East: Architecture and Politics in the Twentieth Century*. Seattle: University of Washington Press, 2008, pp. 3–36

Islahi, Abdul Azim. "The Myth of Bryson and Economic Thought in Islam," *Islamic Economics* 21:1 (2008), pp. 73–79.

Jacob, Wilson C. *Working Out Egypt: Effendi Masculinity and Subject Formation in Colonial Modernity, 1870–1940*. Durham and London: Duke University Press, 2011.

Jaggar, Alison M. "Globalizing Feminist Ethics," *Hypatia* 13:2 (1998), pp. 7–31.

——— "Love and Knowledge: Emotion in Feminist Epistemology," in Alison M. Jaggar and Susan R. Bordo (eds.). *Gender/ Body/ Knowledge: Feminist Reconsiderations of Being and Knowing*. New Brunswick: Rutgers University Press, 1989, pp. 145–171.

Jauss, Hans R. "Literary History as a Challenge to Literary Theory." *New Literary History* 2 (1970), pp. 3–37.

Jayawardena, Kumari. *Feminism and Nationalism in the Third World*. London: Zed Books, 1986.

Jirousek, Charlotte. "The Transition to Mass Fashion System Dress in the Later Ottoman Empire," in Donald Quataert (ed.). *Consumption Studies and the History of the Ottoman Empire, 1550–1922: An Introduction*. Albany: SUNY Press, 2000, pp. 201–242.

Jones, Linda. "Islamic Masculinities," in Joseph M. Armengol and Angels Carabi (eds.). *Debating Masculinity*. Harriman: Men's Studies Press, 2009, pp. 93–112.

Joseph, Suad. "Brother-Sister Relationships: Connectivity, Love and Power in the Reproduction of Patriarchy in Lebanon," in Suad Joseph (ed.). *Intimate Selving in Arab Families: Gender, Self and Identity*. Syracuse: Syracuse University Press, 1999, pp. 113–140.

Kandiyoti, Deniz. "Paradoxes of Masculinity: Some Thoughts on Segregated Societies," in Andrea Cornwall and Nancy Lindisfarne (eds.). *Dislocating Masculinity: Comparative Ethnographies*. London and New-York: Routledge, 1994, pp. 197–213.

Kapetanios-Meir, Natalie. "'A Fashionable Dinner Is Arranged as Follows': Victorian Dinning Taxonomies," *Victorian Literature and Culture* 33 (2005), pp. 133–148.

Kayali, Hasan *Arabs and Young Turks: Ottomanism, Arabism, and Islamism in the Ottoman Empire, 1908–1918*. Berkeley and Los Angeles: University of California Press, 1997.

Kedouri, Elie. *Afgahni and 'Abduh: An Essay on Religion Unbelief and Political Activism in Modern Islam*. London: Frank Cass, 1966.

Kelley, Victoria. "'The Virtues of a Drop of Cleansing Water': Domestic Work and Cleanliness in the British Working Classes, 1880–1914," *Women's History Review* 18:5 (2009), pp. 715–735.

Kelly, Joan. "Early Feminist Theory and the 'Querelle des Femmes', 1400–1789," *Signs* 8 (1982), pp. 4–28.

Kerber, Linda K. "The Republican Mother: Women and the Enlightenment – An American Perspective," *American Quarterly*, 28 (1976), pp. 187–205.

Kerr, Malcolm. *Islamic Reform: The Political and Legal Theories of Muhammad 'Abduh and Rashid Rida*. Berkeley: University of California Press, 1966.

Kesselman, Amy. "The 'Freedom Suit': Feminism and Dress Reform in the United States, 1848–1875," *Gender and Society* 5 (1991), pp. 494–510.

Khalaf, Samir. "Correlates of Prostitution: Some Proper Errors and Misconceptions," *Journal of Sex Research* 4: 2 (1968), pp. 147–162.

Khaled, Fahmy. "Prostitution in Egypt in the Nineteenth-Century," in Eugene Rogan (ed.). *Outside In: On the Margins of the Modern Middle East.* London: I.B. Tauris, 2002, pp. 77–103.

Khalidi, Rashid. "Ottomanism and Arabism in Syria before 1914: A Reassessment," in Rashid Khalidi et al. (eds.). *The Origins of Arab Nationalism.* New York: Columbia University Press, 1991), pp. 50–71.

Khairallah, Shereen. *The Sisters of Men: Lebanese Women in History* Beirut: American University of Beirut, 1996.

Khalidi, Boutheina. "Epistolarity in the Nahda Climate: The Role of Mayy Ziyadah's Letter Writing," *Journal of Arabic Literature* 40 (2009), pp. 1–36.

Khalidi, Rashid. "Ottomanism and Arabism in Syria Before 1914: A Reassessment," in Rashid Khalidi (ed.). *The Origins of Arab Nationalism.* New York: Columbia University Press, 1991, pp. 50–70.

Khater, Akram F. "Becoming 'Syrian' in America: A Global Geography of Ethnicity and Nation," *Diaspora: A Journal of Transnational Studies*, 14:2/3 (2005), pp. 299–331.

——— "Building Class: Emigration, the Central Hall House, and the Construction of a Rural Middle Class in Lebanon, 1890–1914," in Michael F. Davie (ed.). *La Maison Beyrouthine aux Trois Arcs: Une Architecture Bourgeoise du Levant.* Beirut: Académie Libanaise des Beaux-Arts; Tours: Centre de Recherches et d'Études sur l'Urbanization du Monde Arabe, 2003, pp. 371–393.

——— "'House' to 'Goddess of the House': Gender, Class, and Silk in 19th-Century Mount Lebanon," *International Journal of Middle East Studies* 28:3 (1996), pp. 325–348.

——— *Inventing Home: Emigration, Gender, and the Middle Class in Lebanon, 1870–1920.* Berkeley: University of California Press, 2001.

Kholoussy, Hanan. *For Better, For Worse: The Marriage Crisis That Made Modern Egypt.* Stanford: Stanford University Press, 2010.

Khuri-Makdisi, Ilham. *The Eastern Mediterranean and the Making of Global Radicalism, 1860–1914.* Berkeley and Los Angeles, University of California Press, 2010.

Khoury, Philip S. "Continuity and Change in Syrian Political Life: The Nineteenth and Twentieth Centuries," *American Historical Review* 96:5 (1991), pp. 1374–1395.

Kinahan, Anne-Marie. "Transcendent Citizenship: Suffrage, the National Council of Women of Canada, and the Politics of Organized Womanhood," *Journal of Canadian Studies/Revue d'Études Canadiennes* 42:3 (2008), pp. 5–27.

Kleinberg, S.J. "Gendered Space: Housing, Privacy and Domesticity in the Nineteenth-Century United States," in Janet Floyd (ed.). *Domestic Space: Reading the Nineteenth-Century Interior.* Manchester: Manchester University Press, 1999, pp. 142–161.

Kupferschmidt, Uri M. "The Social History of the Sewing Machine in the Middle East," *Die Welt des Islams* 44:2 (2004), pp. 195–213.

LaCapra, Dominick. *Rethinking Intellectual History: Texts, Contexts, Language.* Ithaca: Cornell University Press, 1983.

Lazarus-Yafeh, Hava. "The Religious Dialectics of the Hadjdj," in Gerald R. Hawting (ed.). *The Development of Islamic Ritual.* Aldershot: Ashgate Publishing, 2004, pp. 263–291.

Ledger, Sally. *The New Woman: Fiction and Feminism at the Fin de Siècle.* Manchester: Manchester University Press, 1997.

Levy, Lisa L. "Jewish Writers in the Arab East: Literature, History, and the Politics of Enlightenment, 1863–1914." Ph.D. dissertation, University of California–Berkeley, 2007.

Magee, William H. "Instruments of Growth: The Courtship and Marriage Plot in Jane Austen's Novels," *Journal of Narrative Technique* 17:2 (1987), pp. 198–208.

Makdisi Cortas, Wadad. *A World I Loved: The Story of an Arab Woman.* New York: Nation Book, 2009.

Makdisi, Ussama. *The Culture of Sectarianism: Community, History and Violence in Nineteenth-Century Ottoman Lebanon.* Berkeley and Los Angeles: University of California Press, 1994.

——— "Ottoman Orientalism," *American Historical Review* 107:3 (2002), pp. 768–796.

Maoz, Moshe. "Syrian Urban Politics in the Tanzimat Period between 1840 and 1861," *Bulletin of the School of Oriental and African Studies* 29:2 (1966), pp. 277–301.

Marie-France Doray. "Cleanliness and Class in the Countess de Ségur's Novels," (trans. Margaret R. Higgonet), *Children's Literature* 17 (1989), pp. 64–80.

Mariscotti, Cathlyn. *Gender and Class in the Egyptian Women's Movement, 1925–1939: Changing Perspectives.* Syracuse: Syracuse University Press, 2008.

Marwan M. Kraidy, "From Imperialism to Glocalization: A Theoretical Framework of the Information Age," in Bosah Ebo (ed.). *Cyberimperialism?: Global Relations in the New Electronic Frontier.* Westport: Praeger, 2001, pp. 27–42.

——— "Hybridity in Cultural Globalization," *Communication Theory* 12:3 (2002), pp. 316–339.

Massad, Joseph A. *Desiring Arabs.* Chicago: University of Chicago Press, 2007.

Masters, Bruce. "Aleppo: The Ottoman Empire's Caravan City," in Edhem Eldem, Daniel Goffman, and Bruce Masters (eds.). *The Ottoman City between East and West: Aleppo, Izmir, and Istanbul.* Cambridge: Cambridge University Press, 1999, pp. 17–78.

——— "The Political Economy of Aleppo in an Age of Ottoman Reform," *Journal of the Economic and Social History of the Orient* 53 (2010), pp. 290–316.

Mayer, Thomas. *The Changing Past: Egyptian Historiography of the Urabi Revolt, 1883–1983.* Gainsville: University of Florida Press, 1988.

Maza, Sarah. "Stephen Greenblatt, New Historicism, and Cultural History, or, What We Talk About When We Talk About Interdisciplinarity," *Modern Intellectual History* 1:2 (2004), pp. 249–265.

McClintock, Anne. "Family Feuds: Gender, Nationalism and the Family," *Feminist Review* no. 44 (1993), pp. 61–80.

McKeon, Michael. "Generic Transformation and Social Change: Rethinking the Rise of the Novel," *Cultural Critique* 1 (1985), pp. 159–181.

McLarney, Ellen. "The Private Is Political: Women and Family in Intellectual Islam, *Feminist Theory* 11 (2010), pp. 129–148.

Menon, Elizabeth K. *Evil by Design: The Creation and Marketing of the Femme Fatale.* Urbana and Chicago: University of Illinois, 2006.

—— "*Les Filles d'Eve* in Word and Image," in Rui Carvalho Homem and Maria de Fátima Lambert (eds.). *Writing and Seeing: Essays on Word and Image.* Amsterdam: Edition Rodopi, 2006, pp. 157–174.

Meriwether, Margaret. "Urban Notables and Rural Resources in Aleppo, 1770–1830," *International Journal of Turkish Studies* 4 (1987), pp. 55–73.

—— "Women and Economic Change in Nineteenth Century Syria: The Case of Aleppo," in Judith E. Tucker (ed.). *Arab Women: Old Boundaries, New Frontiers.* Bloomington: Indiana University Press, 1993, pp. 65–83.

Meyer, Sibylle. "The Tiresome Work of Conspicuous Leisure: On the Domestic Duties of the Wives of Civil Servants in the German Empire (1871–1918)," in Marilyn J. Boxer and Jean H. Quataert (eds), *Connecting Spheres: Women in the Western World, 1500 to the Present.* New York and Oxford: Oxford University Press, 1987.

Micklewright, Nancy. "Public and Private for Ottoman Women of the Nineteenth Century," in D. Fairchild Ruggles (ed.), *Women, Patronage, and Self-Representation in Islamic Societies.* Albany: SUNY Press, 2000, pp. 155–176.

Milani, Farzaneh. "The Mediatory Guile of the Nanny in Persian Romance," *Iranian Studies* 32:2 (1999), pp. 181–201.

Miller, Nancy K. *The Heroine's Text: Readings in the French and English Novel, 1722–1782.* New York: Columbia University Press, 1980.

Mitchell, Timothy. "The Stage of Modernity," in Timothy Mitchell (ed.). *Questions of Modernity.* Minneapolis: University of Minnesota Press, 2000, pp. 1–34.

Mitchie, Elise B. "Rich Woman, Poor Woman: Toward the Anthropology of the Nineteenth-Century Marriage Plot," *PMLA* 124: 2 (2009), pp. 421–436.

Moen, Phyllis, Erickson Mary A. and Dempster-McClain, Donna. "Their Mother's Daughters? The Intergenerational Transmission of Gender Attitudes in a World of Changing Roles," *Journal of Marriage and Family* 59:2 (1997), pp. 281–293.

Mohanty, Chandra Talpade. "Under Western Eyes: Feminist Scholarship and Colonial Discourses," in Chandra Talpade Mohanty, Ann Russo, and Lourdes Torres (eds). *Third World Women and the Politics of Feminism.* Bloomington: Indiana University Press, 1991, pp. 51–80.

Mollenhauer, Anne. "Reading Late-Ottoman Architecture: Exterior Expression and Interior Organization of Central-Hall Houses between Beirut and Latakia," in Michael F. Davie (ed.). *La Maison Beyrouthine aux Trois Arcs: Une Architecture Bourgeoise du Levant.* Beirut: Académie Libanaise des Beaux-Arts; Tours: Centre de Recherches et d'Études sur l'Urbanization du Monde Arabe, 2003, pp. 115–135.

Moosa, Matti. *The Origins of Modern Arabic Fiction*, 2nd ed. Boulder and London: Lynne Rienner Publishers, 1997.

Moubayed, Sami M. *Silk and Steel: Men and Women Who Shaped Syria, 1900–2000* Seattle: Cune Press, 2004.

Mullan, John. "Sentimental Novels." in John Richetti (ed.). *The Cambridge Companion to the Eighteenth-Century Novel.* Cambridge: Cambridge University Press, 1996, pp. 236–254.

Munro, Moira and Ruth Madigan. "Negotiating Space in the Family Home, " in Irene Cieraad (ed.). *At Home: An Anthropology of Domestic Space*. Syracuse: Syracuse University Press, 1999, pp. 107–117.

Naff, Alixa. "The Arabic-Language Press," in Sally M. Miller (ed.). *The Ethnic Press in the United States: A Historical Analysis and Handbook*. New York: Greenwood Press, 1987, pp. 1–14.

Najmabadi, Afsaneh. "Beyond the Americas: Are Gender and Sexuality Useful Categories of Historical Analysis?" *Journal of Women's History* 18:1 (2006), pp. 11–21.

——— *Women with Mustaches and Men without Beards: Gender and Sexual Anxieties of Iranian Modernity*. Berkeley and Los Angeles: University of California Press, 2005.

Narayan, Uma. "Essence of Culture and a Sense of History: A Feminist Critique of Cultural Essentialism," *Hypatia* 13:2 (1998), pp. 86–106.

Nieuwkerk, Karin van. *A Trade Like Any Other: Female Singers and Dancers in Egypt*. Austin: University of Texas Press, 1995.

Nord, Deborah Epstein. *Walking the Victorian Streets: Representation and the City*. Ithaca: Cornell University Press, 1995.

Offen, Karen. "Depopulation, Nationalism and Feminism in Fin-de-Siècle France," *American Historical Review* 89:3 (1984), pp. 648–676.

——— "Ernst Legouvé and the Doctrine of 'Equality in Difference' for Women: A Case Study of Male Feminism in Nineteenth-Century French Thought," *Journal of Modern History* 58 (1985), pp. 452–484.

Ostle, Robin. "The Literature of the Mahjar," in Albert Hourani and Nadim Shehadi (eds.). *The Lebanese in the World: A Century of Emigration*. London: I.B.Tauris, 1992, pp. 209–226.

——— "The Printing Press and the Renaissance of Modern Arabic Literature," *Culture and History* 16: 1 (1997), pp. 145–157.

Patai, Raphael. "Cousin-Right in Middle Eastern Marriage," *Southwestern Journal of Anthropology* 11:4 (1955), pp. 371–390.

Peterson, M. Jeanne. "The Victorian Governess: Status Incongruence in Family and Society," *Victorian Studies* 14:1 (1970), pp. 7–26.

Philipp, Thomas. *Gugri Zaidan: His Life and Thought*. Beirut/Weisbaden: Orient-Institut der Deutschen Morgenlandischen Gesellschaft/ Franz Steiner, 1979.

——— *The Syrians in Egypt*. Stuttgart: F. Steiner, 1985.

Pieterse, Jan N. "Globalization as Hybridization," in Mike Featherstone, Scott Lash and Roland Robertson (eds.). *Global Modernities*. London: Sage Publications, 1995, pp. 45–68.

Pittman, Frank S. *Man Enough: Fathers, Sons and the Search for Masculinity*. New York: Berkley Publishing Group, A division of Penguin Group, 1993.

Pollard, Lisa. "From Husbands and Housewives to Suckers and Whores: Marital-Political Anxieties in the 'House of Egypt', 1919–48," *Gender and History* 2:3 (2009), pp. 647–699.

——— *Nurturing the Nation: The Family Politics of Modernizing, Colonizing and Liberating Egypt, 1805–1923*. Berkeley and Los Angeles: University of California Press, 2005.

Pykett, Lynn. "Reading the Periodical Press: Text and Context," *Victorian Periodicals Review* 22:3 (1989), pp. 100–108.

Al-Qadi, Iman and Subhi Hadidi. "Syria," in Rawda Ashur, Ferial Jabouri Ghazoul, Hasna Reda-Mekdashi (eds.). *Arab Women Writers: A Critical Reference Guide, 1873–1999*, translated by Mandy McClure. Cairo: The American University Press, pp. 60–97.

Ragette, Friedrich. *Architecture in Lebanon: The Lebanese House during the 18th and 19th Centuries.* Beirut: American University of Beirut, 1974.

Rappaport, Erika. "'A Husband and His Wife's Dresses': Consumer Credit and the Debtor Family in England, 1864–1914," in Victoria de Grazia with Ellen Furlough (eds.). *The Sex of Things: Gender and Consumption in Historical Perspective.* Berkeley: University of California Press, 1996, pp. 163–187.

Reagin, Nancy R. *Sweeping the German Nation: Domesticity and National Identity Germany, 1870–1945.* Cambridge: Cambridge University Press, 2007.

Reid, Donald M. "The Syrian Christians and Early Socialism in the Arab World," *International Journal of Middle East Studies* 5:2 (1974), pp. 177–193.

Reilly, James A. "Damascus Merchants and Trade in the Transition to Capitalism," *Canadian Journal of History* 27 (1992), pp. 1–27.

——— "Inter-Confessional Relations in Nineteenth-Century Syria: Damascus, Homs and Hama Compared," *Islam and Christian-Muslim Relations* 7: 2 (1996), pp. 213–224.

Rendall, Jane. "Citizenship, Culture and Civilization: The Languages of British Suffragists, 1866–1874," in Caroline Daley and Melanie Nolan (eds.). *Suffrage and Beyond: International Feminist Perspectives.* New York: New York University Press, 1994, pp. 127–150.

Roberts, Mary L. "Gender, Consumption and Commodity Culture," *American Historical Review* 103 (1998), pp. 817–844.

Robertson, Roland. *Globalization: Social Theory and Globe Culture.* London: Sage, 1992.

——— "Glocalization: Time-Space and Homogeneity-Heterogeneity," in Mike Featherstone et al. (eds.). *Global Modernities.* London: Sage, 1995, pp. 25–44.

Rock, Paul. "Caesar Lombroso as a Signal Criminologist," *Criminology and Criminal Justice* 7:2 (2007), pp. 117–133.

Rooney, Ellen. "Criticism and the Subject of Sexual Violence," *Modern Language Notes* 98:5 (1983), pp. 1269–1278.

Roudometof, Victor. "Transnationalism, Cosmopolitanism and Glocalization," *Current Sociology* 53:1 (2005), pp. 113–135.

Russell, Mona L. *Creating the New Egyptian Woman: Consumerism, Education, and National Identity, 1863–1922.* New York: Palgrave Macmillan, 2004.

——— "Marketing the Modern Egyptian Girl: Whitewashing Soap and Clothes from the Late Nineteenth Century to 1936," *Journal of Middle East Women's Studies* 6:3 (2010), pp. 19–57.

——— "Modernity, National Identity and Consumerism: Visions of the Egyptian Home, 1805–1922" in Relli Shechter (ed.). *Transitions in Domestic Consumption and Family Life in the Modern Middle East: Houses in Motion.* New York: Palgrave Macmillan, 2003, pp. 37–63.

Ryan, Mary P. *Cradle of the Middle Class: The Family in Oneida County, New York, 1790–1865.* Cambridge: Cambridge University Press, 1981.

Said, Edward. "Traveling Theory," in *The World, the Text, and the Critic.* Cambridge, MA: Harvard University Press, 1983, pp. 226–247.

Sakkut, Hamdi. *The Arabic Novel: Bibliography and Critical Introduction, 1865–1995*. 6 vols. Cairo: The American University in Cairo Press, 2000.

Sangnolo, J.P. "Constitutional Change in Mount Lebanon: 1861–1864," *Middle Eastern Studies* 7:1 (1971), pp. 25–48.

Sapiro, Virginia. "When Are Interests Interesting? The Problem of Political Representation of Women," *American Political Science Review* 75 (1981), pp. 701–21.

Schilcher, Linda S. *Families in Politics: Damascene Families and Estates of the 18th and 19th Centuries* Stuttgart: Franz Steiner Verlag Wiesbaden GMBH, 1985.

Selim, Samah. "The Nahda, Popular Fiction and the Politics of Translations," *The MIT Electronic Journal of Middle East Studies* 4 (2004), pp. 75–89.

——— *The Novel and the Rural Imaginary in Egypt 1880–1995*. New-Routledge Curzon, 2004.

Şeni, Nora. "Fashion and Women's Clothing in the Satirical Press of Istanbul at the End of the 19th Century," in Sirin Tekeli (ed.). *Women in Modern Turkish Society: A Reader*. London: Zed Books, 1995, pp. 25–45.

Serrano, Delfina. "Muslim Feminists' Discourse on *Zina*: New Paradigms in Sight?" in Roswitha Badry, Maria Roher and Karin Steiner (eds.). *Liebe, Sexualität, Ehe und Partnerschaft – Paradigmen im Wandel*. Freiburg: Fördergemeinschaft wissenschaftlicher Publikationen von Frauen, 2009, pp. 106–125.

Shakry, Omnia. "Schooled Mothers and Structured Play: Child Rearing in Turn-of-the-Century Egypt," in Lila Abu-Lughod (ed.). *Remaking Women: Feminism and Modernity in the Middle East*. Princeton: Princeton University Press, 1998, pp. 126–170.

Sharabi, Hisham. *Arab Intellectuals and the West: The Formative Years, 1875–1914*. Baltimore: Johns Hopkins University Press, 1970.

——— *Neopatriarchy: A Theory of Distorted Change in Arab Society*. New York and Oxford: Oxford University Press, 1988, pp. 125–49.

Sharkey, Heather J. *American Evangelicals in Egypt: Missionary Encounters in an Age of Empire*. Princeton: Princeton University Press, 2008.

Shechter, Relli. "Selling Luxury: The Rise of the Egyptian Cigarette and the Transformation of the Egyptian Tobacco Market, 1850–1914," *International Journal of Middle East Studies* 35 (2003), pp. 41–75.

Sheehi, Stephen. "Failure, Modernity, and the Works of Hisham Sharabi: Towards a Post-Colonial Critique of Arab Subjectivity," *Critique: Critical Middle Eastern Studies* 6:10 (1997), pp. 39–54.

——— *Foundations of Modern Arab Identity*. Gainesville: University Press of Florida, 2004.

Shissler, A. Holly. "Womanhood is Not for Sale: Saiba Zekeriya Sertal Against Prostitution and for Women's Employment," *Journal of Middle East Women's Studies* 4:3 (2008), pp. 12–30.

Silberstein, Sandra. "Ideology as Process: Gender Ideology in Courtship Narratives," in Alexandra Dundas Todd and Sue Fisher (eds.). *Gender and Discourse: The Power of Talk*. Norwood: Ablex Publishing, 1988, pp. 125–49.

Smerdjian, Elyse. *'Off the Straight Path': Illicit Sex, Law and Community in Ottoman Aleppo*. Syracuse: Syracuse University Press, 2008.

——— "Sinful Professions Illegal Occupations of Women in Ottoman Aleppo," *Hawwa* 1:1 (2003), pp. 60–85.

Smith, Bonnie G. *Ladies of the Middles Class: The Bourgeoisies of Northern France in the Nineteenth Century*. Princeton: Princeton University Press, 1981.

———— *The Gender of History: Men, Women, and Historical Practice* (Cambridge: Harvard University Press, 1998.

Smith Jane I. and Yvonne Y. Haddad, "Eve – The Islamic Image of Woman," *Women's Studies International Forum* 5:2 (1982), pp. 135–144.

Smith-Rosenberg, Carroll and Rosenberg, Charles. "The Female Animal: Medical and Biological Views of Women and their Role in Nineteenth-Century America," *Journal of American History* 60 (1973), pp. 332–356.

Snir, Reuven. *Modern Arabic Literature: A Functional Dynamic Model*. Toronto: York Press, 2001.

Sommer, Doris. *Foundational Fictions: The National Romances of Latin America*. Berkeley and Los Angeles: University of California Press, 1991.

Spain, Daphne. *Gendered Spaces*. Chapel Hill and London: University of North Carolina Press, 1992.

Spellberg, Denise A. *Politics, Gender and the Islamic Past: The Legacy of 'A'isha bint Abi Bakr*. New York: Columbia University Press, 1994.

———— "Writing the Unwritten Life of the Islamic Eve: Menstruation and the Demonization of Motherhood," *International Journal of Middle East Studies* 28: 3 (1986), pp. 305–324.

Srinivas, Lakshmi. "Master-Servant Relationships in a Cross-Cultural Perspective." *Economic and Political Weekly* 30 (1995), pp. 269–278.

Stockdale, Nancy L. *Colonial Encounters among English and Palestinian Women, 1800–1948*. Gainesville: University of Florida Press, 2007.

Swain, Simon. *Economy, Family, and Society from Rome to Islam: A Critical Edition, English Translation, and Study of Bryson's Management of the Estate*. Cambridge and New York: Cambridge University Press, 2013.

Tauber, Eliezer. "Rashid Rida as Pan-Arabist: Before World War I," *The Muslim World* 79: 2 (1989), pp. 102–112.

———— "Three Approaches, One Idea: Religion and State in the Thought of 'Abd al-Rahman al-Kawkabi, Najib 'Azuri and Rashid Rida," *British Journal of Middle Eastern Studies* 21: 2 (1994), pp. 190–198.

Thompson, Elizabeth. *Colonial Citizens: Republican Rights, Paternal Privilege and Gender in French Syria and Lebanon*. New York: Columbia University Press, 2000.

———— "Public and Private in Middle Eastern Women's History," *Journal of Women's History* 15:1 (2003), pp. 52–69.

Toledano, Ehud. "Lishkoach et Heavar Haosmani shel Mitsrayim, (in Hebrew)" *Jama'a* 1 (1997), pp. 67–87.

Tompkins, Jane. *Sensational Designs: The Cultural Work of American Fiction 1760–1860*. New York: Oxford University Press, 1985.

Tucker, Judith E. "Marriage and the Family in Nablus, 1720–1856: Toward a History of Arab Marriage," *Journal of Family History* 13:1 (1988), pp. 165–179.

———— *Women in Nineteenth Century Egypt*. Cambridge: Cambridge University Press, 1985.

Valverde, Mariana. "The Love of Finery: Fashion and the Fallen Woman in Nineteenth-Century Social Discourse," *Victorian Studies* 32 (1989), pp. 168–88.

Van Cleve, John W. *The Merchant in German Literature of the Enlightenment*. Chapel Hill: University of North Carolina Press, 1986.

Vicinus, Martha. "'Helpless and Unfriended': Nineteenth-Century Domestic Melodrama," *New Literary History* 13:1 (1981), pp. 127–143.

Wall, Diana Di Zerega. "Sacred Dinners and Secular Teas: Constructing Domesticity in Mid-19th- Century New York," *Historical Archaeology* 25:4 (1991), pp. 69–81.

Walsh, Judith E. *Domesticity in Colonial India: What Women Learned When Men Gave Them Advice.* Lanham: Rowman and Littlefield Pub., 2004.

Ware, Lewis B. "Jurji Zaidan: The Role of Popular History in the Formation of a New Arab World-View." Ph.D. Dissertation: Princeton University, 1973.

Warner, Marina. *Alone of Her Sex: The Myth and the Cult of the Virgin Mary.* New York: Knopf, 1976.

Watenpaugh, Heghnar Z. "The Harem as Biography: Domestic Architecture, Gender, and Nostalgia in Modern Syria," in Marilyn Booth (ed.). *Harem Histories: Envisioning Places and Living Spaces.* Durham and London: Duke University Press, 2010, pp. 211–236.

Watenpaugh, Keith D. "Being Middle Class and Being Arab: Sectarian Dilemmas and Middle Class Modernity in the Arab Middle East, 1908–1936," in A. Ricardo Lopez and Barbara Weinstein (eds.). *The Making of the Middle Class: Toward a Transnational History.* Durham: Duke University Press, 2012, pp. 267–287.

——— *Being Modern in the Middle East: Revolution, Nationalism, Colonialism and the Arab Middle Class.* Princeton: Princeton University Press, 2006.

Waterfield, Robin. *Prophet: The Life and Times of Khalil Gibran.* New York: St. Martin's Press, 1998.

Watt, George. *The Fallen Woman in the Nineteenth-Century English Novel.* Beckenham, Kent: Taylor & Francis, 1984.

Watt, Ian. *The Rise of the Novel: Studies in Defoe, Richardson and Fielding.* London: Chatto & Windus, 1974.

Weber, Charlotte. "Between Nationalism and Feminism: The Eastern Women's Congresses of 1930 and 1932," *Journal of Middle East Women's Studies* 4 (2008), pp. 83–106.

Weber, Stefan. "Images of Imagined Worlds: Self-Image and Worldview in Late Ottoman Wall Paintings of Damascus," in Jens Hanssen, Thomas Philipp and Stefan Weber (eds.). *The Empire and the City: Arab Provincial Capitals in the Late Ottoman Empire.* Beirut: Ergon Verlag Würzburg, 2002, pp. 145–171.

——— "Reshaping Damascus: Social Change and Patterns of Architecture in Late Ottoman Times," in Thomas Philipp and Christoph Schumann (eds.). *From the Syrian Land to the States of Syria and Lebanon.* Beirut: Ergon Verlag Würzburg, 2003, pp. 41–58.

Wejnert, Barbara J. "Integrating Models of Diffusion of Innovations: A Conceptual Framework," *Annual Reviews in Sociology* 28 (2002), pp. 297–326.

White, Hayden. "The Question of Narrative in Contemporary Historical Theory," *History and Theory* 23:1 (1984), pp. 1–33.

Williams, Elizabeth. "Nazik al-'Abid and the Nur al-Fayha Society: Independent Modernity, Colonial Treat and the Space of Women," in Muhammad A. Bamyeh (ed.) *Intellectuals and Civil Society in the Middle East.* New York: I.B.Tauris, 2012, pp. 29–56.

Yeazell, Ruth B. *Fictions of Modesty: Women and Courtship in the English Novel.* Chicago: University of Chicago Press.

Yousef, Hoda A. "Reassessing Egypt's Dual System of Education Under Isma'il: Growing 'Ilm and Shifting Ground in Egypt's First Educational Journal, Rawdat al-Madaris, 1870–1877," *International Journal of Middle East Studies* 40:1 (2008), pp. 109–130.

Zachs, Fruma. "Building a Cultural Identity: The Case of Khalil al-Khuri," in Thomas Philipp and Christoph Schumann (eds.). *From the Syrian Land to the States of Syria and Lebanon.* Beirut: Beiruter Texte und Studien, 2004, pp. 27–39.

——— *The Making of a Syrian Identity: Intellectuals and Merchants in Nineteenth-Century Beirut.* Leiden and Boston: E.J. Brill, 2005.

Zachs, Fruma and Bawardi, Basilius. "Ottomanism and Syrian Patriotism in Salim al-Bustani's Thought," in Itzchak Weismann and Fruma Zachs (eds.). *Ottoman Reforms and Muslim Regeneration: Studies in Honor of Butrus Abu-Manneh.* London and New York: I.B.Tauris, 2005, pp. 111–126.

Zachs, Fruma and Halevi, Sharon. "From Difa' al-Nisa' to Mas'alat al-Nisa' in Greater Syria: Readers and Writers Debate Women and their Rights, 1858–1900," *International Journal of Middle East Studies* 41 (2009), pp. 615–634.

Ze'evi, Dror. "Changes in the Legal-Sexual Discourses: Sex Crimes in the Ottoman Empire," *Continuity and Change* 16: 2 (2001), pp. 219–242.

——— *Producing Desire: Changing Sexual Discourse in the Ottoman Middle East, 1500–1900.* Berkeley and Los Angeles: University of California Press, 2006.

Zeidan, Joseph T. *Arab Women Novelists: The Formative Years.* Albany: SUNY Press, 2005.

Ziegler, Anjte. "Arab Literary Salons at the Turn of the 20th Century," in Beatrice Gruendler and Verena Klemm (eds.). *Understanding Near Eastern Literatures: A Spectrum of Interdisciplinary Approaches.* Weisbaden: Reichart Verlag, 2000, pp. 241–253.

Zlotnick, Susan. "Domesticating Imperialism: Curry and Cookbooks in Victorian England," *Frontiers: A Journal of Women's Studies* 16:2/3 (1996), pp. 51–68.

Zürcher, Erik J. *Turkey: A Modern History.* London: I.B.Tauris, 1993.

INDEX